REGIMES OF DESIRE

MICHIGAN MONOGRAPH SERIES IN JAPANESE STUDIES

NUMBER 93

CENTER FOR JAPANESE STUDIES
UNIVERSITY OF MICHIGAN

# REGIMES OF DESIRE

*Young Gay Men, Media, and Masculinity in Tokyo*

Thomas Baudinette

UNIVERSITY OF MICHIGAN PRESS

*Ann Arbor*

For questions or permissions, please contact um.press.perms@umich.edu

Published in the United States of America by the
University of Michigan Press
Printed and bound by CPI Group (UK) Ltd, Croydon, CR0 4YY

First published November 2021

A CIP catalog record for this book is available from the British Library.

*Library of Congress Cataloging-in-Publication data has been applied for.*

ISBN 978-0-472-13264-5 (hardcover: alk. paper)
ISBN 978-0-472-03861-9 (paper: alk. paper)
ISBN 978-0-472-12918-8 (e-book)

Library of Congress Control Number: 2021945425

# Contents

Digital materials related to this title can be found on the Fulcrum platform via the following citable URL: https://doi.org/10.3998/mpub.11510904

# Acknowledgments

Traveling halfway across the globe to a foreign country to ask people probing questions about their sexual lives is a particularly nerve-racking experience, especially when you are a young man still trying to find your own way in the world. Consequently, I begin these acknowledgments by thanking the young men I have met over the past seven years in Tokyo—the people who graciously shared their lives, hopes, and fears with me as I conducted the research that has led to this book. I have been consistently overwhelmed by the generosity of spirit and depth of reflection that I have encountered among the men who gather in Shinjuku Ni-chōme, and it is to these men that I dedicate the following pages. I owe a special debt of gratitude to Junho, Yōichi, Haruma, and Shōtarō—the four key interlocutors whose lived experiences deeply informed my thinking over the years I worked on this project. Quite literally, without your help, this book would not exist.

This book had its genesis as a doctoral research project at Monash University, and I wish to thank my advisors, Carolyn Stevens and Sarah Pasfield-Neofitou, for their guidance as I took my first steps as a scholar. Both Carolyn's and Sarah's keen insights into contemporary Japan and their wealth of experience in a range of critical methodologies were essential to the development of my own competence and confidence. I was provided with a warm and stimulating environment at Monash and wish to thank Beatrice Trefalt, Naomi Kurata, Hiroko Hashimoto, Shimako Iwasaki, Helen Marriott, and Robyn Spence-Brown for nurturing my curiosity regarding all things Japanese. My fellow postgraduate student colleagues at both Monash and the University of Melbourne were a constant source of moral and intellectual support. I thank Rikki Corry, Asako Saito, Simon Gough, Mishka Kent, Allie Severin, Lola Sundin, Gwyn McClelland, Basil Cahusac de Caux, Kwannie Krairit, and Prue Holstein for the many hours of passionate conversation in our student offices. While at Monash, I was also privileged to share an office with Ross Mouer—a giant in our field whose undergraduate classes opened my eyes to new ways of thinking about Japan—with whom I spent many a lunch hour discussing the state of Japanese studies and the position of my work within it. I also wish to acknowledge funding provided by the Graduate School of Social Sciences at Monash University, which made both my ethnography and attendance at various international and domestic conferences possible.

Since completing my doctoral studies, I have found a new home in the Department of Media, Communications, Creative Arts, Language and Literature at Macquarie University. My colleagues here—including fellow Monash graduate Wes Robertson, to whom I give particular thanks for his continued friendship—have been instrumental in providing support as I conducted further research on Japan's gay media and completed this book. I especially thank Mio Bryce, Chavalin Svetanant, Kayo Nakazawa, Susanne Binder, Consuelo Martinez Reyes, Mei-Fen Kuo, Sijia Guo, Lan Zhang, Ulrike Garde, Jane Hanley, Stephanie Russo, Theresa Senft, and Hsu-Ming Teo for their continued encouragement as I balanced my teaching and research commitments. I feel it important to also thank Kathryn Phillips, Nobuaki Akagi, and Alison Luke, the wonderful TAs in our Department who have supported my teaching and thus provided me time to work on this book project. Further, I extend my gratitude to the students in my classes on contemporary Japanese society for sharing their own thoughts on my arguments as we workshopped them in our seminars. Last, but certainly not least, I thank our wonderful Department Administrators Eva Gabrielson, Shéyana La Brooy, Jennifer Heward, and Tina Kong.

Other current and former colleagues at Macquarie I must also thank include Katrina Hutchison, Malcolm Choat, Catharine Lumby, Clare Monagle, Robert Reynolds, Leigh Boucher, Rachel Yuen-Collingridge, Holly Doel-Mackaway, Amy Barrow, Sara Fuller, Alys Moody, Hui Ling Xu, and Kevin Carrico. The team in the Macquarie University Faculty of Arts Research Office has also provided me invaluable assistance over the years and has provisioned me with various forms of funding—including a Faculty Research Travel Grant, a Research Publication Subsidy, and support via the Macquarie Emerging Scholars Scheme—that have facilitated the completion of this project. My special thanks go to Jan Zwar and Emma Gleadhill for their advice and mentoring.

I have developed a large network of colleagues around the globe who have assisted my research and academic career in various ways. There are too many names to list you all, but please know that I thank you heartily for all your help and guidance. First and foremost, however, I must express my deep gratitude to the late Mark McLelland and Romit Dasgupta, two of the most generous senior colleagues within the field of Japanese gender and sexuality studies. We lost you both much too soon, and I will be forever grateful for the advice you provided over the years I have worked on this book. In particular, I wish to thank Mark for his active mentorship and for providing me with opportunities to share the results of my work with various national and international media outlets. I also owe special debts of gratitude to the following colleagues and friends: Vera Mackie, James Welker, Jo Elfving-Hwang, Claire Maree, Peter A. Jackson, Ishida Hitoshi, Hori Akiko, Fujimoto Yukari, Maekawa Naoya, Ota Fusami, Jacqueline Berndt, Watanabe Yukinori, Nagaike Kazumi, Jason Karlin, Patrick Galbraith, Alexandra Hambleton, Koichi Iwabuchi, Katrien Jacobs, Shibata Kaoru, Lee Taniguchi, Takahama Junko, Uekusa Masae, Inaba Miho, Takeda Kota, Yoda Maho, and my Japanese "parents," Okumura Keiko and Shinji. I also reserve special thanks to my colleagues (and close friends) Karl Ian Uy Cheng Chua and Kristine Michelle Santos in the Japanese Studies Department at Ateneo de Manila University in the Philippines, where I have been a regular visiting scholar and have worked on this (and other) projects.

This book would not have been possible without the immense assistance of the dedicated staff at University of Michigan Press. I wish to thank my editor, Christopher Dreyer, for helping me prepare this book and guiding me through the process of working with a university press for the first time. I especially thank Christopher for being willing to speak with me on the phone despite the challenging time difference involved. I also thank the anonymous readers of my manuscript who helped push the book in new and exciting directions. I thank Melissa Scholke, the project manager for this book, and Theresa Schmidt from the marketing team not only for their timely support but also for their willingness to answer my endless questions. Akiko Yamagata of Graphite Editing provided this book with one of the most thorough copy edits I have ever seen. I thank her profusely for improving the book's style and expression. I also extend my gratitude to Lori Morimoto, who assisted with the indexing.

My final thanks are reserved for my family, who have all supported me through my educational journey and instilled in me the values and ethics that continue to guide my practice as a scholar. I thank my father, Chris, and my mother, Pauline, for supporting me financially and emotionally, especially in times of hardship. Dad, who knew as we lay there in the lounge room reading encyclopedias when I was only a toddler that I would one day write my own book? Mum, a special thank you for letting me be myself and always being there for me whenever I need to get something off my chest. Thanks to my sister, Kate, for brightening up the world with her smile and passion and for fighting the good fight every day of her professional and personal life. Sam, my twin brother, I am especially indebted to you for all the intellectual and emotional encouragement you have provided me over the years. I miss our nightly walks each and every day.

Portions of chapter 3 were previously published as an article titled, "Japanese Gay Men's Attitudes to 'Gay Manga' and the Problem of Genre" in the *East Asian Journal of Popular Culture*. I thank the journal editors for granting me permission to reproduce and expand this article within the pages of this book.

## Notes to Readers

I follow the Hepburn transliteration system to present Japanese language terms except for words and place names that have gained wide currency in contemporary English. I follow the Japanese convention of placing family name before given name for all Japanese authors whose work I cite, unless an author presents their name otherwise in published materials (such as in English language works). Likewise, I follow author preference for instances when an author's preferred rendering of their name differs from Hepburn transliteration. All translations of Japanese language material into English in this book are my own, unless otherwise acknowledged.

Finally, I wish to convey to readers that in providing illustrative figures for this book, I needed to consider the ethics of reproducing photography of a district that is a safe space for a community that still experiences significant discrimination in Japan. Likewise, I needed to consider whether it was appropriate to reproduce images of pornographic material which, if made public, may cause harm to the performers who appear within it. As such, I have regrettably kept images to a minimum despite recognizing that written descriptions of body types may not be as useful as illustrative figures for the purposes of accessing my arguments. I hope readers appreciate the reason why I have chosen to do this.

# Introduction

One night in July 2013, after many hours spent drinking and dancing in a club packed with shirtless men pressed together, swaying to the deep throbbing base of house music, I found myself browsing through magazines with a young man named Shōtarō in Lumière, one of Shinjuku Ni-chōme's cramped "gay shops." Shōtarō was a university student I had met a few nights earlier who identified as "gay" (gei) and who was quickly becoming a key contact who helped me navigate Shinjuku Ni-chōme's gay bar culture.[1] Flipping open the most recent issue of Bádi, Japan's highest-selling magazine produced for and by gay men at the time, Shōtarō began enthusiastically evaluating the scantily clad men pictured in the magazine's centerfold, trying to ascertain which ones were "my ideal Type" (risō na taipu). By this time, I had realized that this question was inevitable whenever young gay men gathered in Shinjuku Ni-chōme, and I quickly assured Shōtarō that I found the men within the magazine quite attractive. Pointing at a picture of the popular gay pornstar Koh Masaki, Shōtarō exclaimed, "Look how manly he is! There has never been a better-looking gay guy in Japan." With much enthusiasm, Shōtarō explained to me that men such as Koh were his own "ideal Type" even though he himself possessed a much slimmer and less rugged physique than the famous pornstar. With his short boxed beard, washboard abs, ripped pecs, and a sense of self-confidence that seemed to leap off the page, Koh appeared to be the very definition of an ikanimo-kei, the "Obviously Gay Type," which I was coming to understand represented the ideal of masculine beauty in contemporary Japan's burgeoning gay culture.

Having come to Tokyo to research how media consumption informed young men's understandings of their same-sex attraction, I decided to ask Shōtarō what magazines such as Bádi meant to him. I especially wished to find out what roles media played in his everyday life and how they informed his experiences of living as a gay man in Japan. After some reflection, during which he subconsciously ran his hand over the photo of Koh's muscular body, Shōtarō pensively responded. "I think it's great that *Bádi* exists. Magazines for gay men show us that we can be masculine (*otokorashii*) . . . that we aren't all like the *onē kyara* you see on TV," he explained, contrasting "masculine" men such as Koh with cross-dressing comedians known as *onē* implicitly understood as homosexual who regularly appear as objects of humor on Japanese variety television shows.[2]

Shōtarō's statement and his comparison of Koh Masaki and *onē kyara* reveal two central concerns of this book. First, they affirm the important role that engaging with gay media plays for young Japanese same-sex attracted men. In particular, Shōtarō's comments suggest how media produced for gay male consumption may provide men with discourses that appear to challenge the depictions of male-male homosexuality that circulate throughout Japanese mainstream media, a point well established within the previous literature.[3] Specifically, Shōtarō and other young gay men expressed a concern over a supposed tendency for mainstream media to position same-sex attracted men as somehow lacking *otokorashisa*, a term conventionally translated as "masculinity" but which may also be understood as signifying "male nature." Second, Shōtarō's statement shows that *Bádi* equips Japanese gay men with knowledge that allows them to negotiate the broader conceptualizations of sexuality that inform these negative depictions. *Bádi*, Shōtarō argued, instilled within him a sense of belonging and acceptance since the magazine ultimately presented gay desire as "natural" and "appropriate." Furthermore, as his comments regarding Koh Masaki clearly indicate, media such as *Bádi* allow Shōtarō to challenge normative assumptions that his same-sex attraction negates his claims to conventional masculinity. This was particularly important to Shōtarō and others since Koh deliberately identified as "gay" within his pornographic work and had therefore come to represent a role model of an explicitly "masculine" gay subject position for Japanese same-sex attracted men.

The narrative of Japanese gay media consumption that weaves this book together, however, is much more complicated than an initial emancipatory reading may suggest. Immediately after praising Koh Masaki and his "masculine" appearance when compared to the *onē kyara* who populate mainstream television, Shōtarō paused for a moment. A troubled look passed across his face as he returned his gaze to the issue of *Bádi* in his hands. He became visibly more subdued, and becoming concerned, I asked him to let me know if there was anything wrong. In a lowered voice, he replied, "Koh Masaki is just as masculine as any straight guy (*nonke*), maybe he's even more masculine . . . Looking at Koh-san, I feel like I need to work harder to become manly as well, just like Koh. I need to become more straight-acting (*nonkerashii*) so I will be more attractive." Shōtarō's discomfort appeared to grow out of a need to justify Koh's attractiveness to me with reference to the image of the heterosexual male, or *nonke*, in Japanese gay slang. While broadly affirming of his sexuality, Shōtarō's comments seemed to indicate that attractiveness was contingent on an implicit acceptance of the primacy of conceptualizations of gender embodied within the image of the *nonke*. Within his narrative, *otokorashisa* and *nonkerashisa* ("straight nature" or "straight-acting") were tied together, exposing how Shōtarō's understanding of masculinity was strongly influenced by Japanese society's privileging of the normalcy of heterosexual desire and the attendant marginalization of all gendered performances that fail to conform to socially dominant conceptualizations of the naturalness of active and reproductive sexuality.[4] His reliance upon the image of the *nonke* indicated that the discourses circulating throughout Japanese gay media may not have been as emancipatory as I had first envisioned, since these media appeared to be facilitating readings that resuscitated forms of masculinity based in patriarchal understandings of sex, gender, and sexuality.

Reflecting upon Shōtarō's reactions to *Bádi*, I found myself wondering whether being desirable in Japanese gay culture relied upon the reappropriation of masculinity (*otokorashisa*) from *nonke*. Shōtarō's comments clearly revealed that "true" masculinity was still ideologically tied to a remarkably patriarchal and conservative heteronormativity and its attendant gender regimes.[5] Perhaps gay men who visit the bars and clubs of Shinjuku Ni-chōme, I began to ponder, had retreated into conservative understandings and fantasies of masculinity to produce an affective shield designed to recuperate their abject positioning within Japan's highly heteronormative society. My seemingly casual conversation with Shōtarō in Tokyo's "gay town" of Shinjuku Ni-chōme came to represent an important transitional moment in my thinking about the experiences of same-sex attracted men in Tokyo and led me to consider what role Japanese gay media played in disseminating knowledge concerning sexual desire. Further, this discussion revealed to me that questions concerning the nature of masculinity remained intimately tied to understandings of same-sex attraction among young Japanese gay men, with many of those with whom I spoke expressing desires for "hard" (*katai*) and "rough" (*arai*) forms of masculinity that they believed were rapidly disappearing from contemporary Japan. Even though countless men explained to me that gay media affirmed their same-sex attraction, I became increasingly cognizant that these media were failing to challenge the common-sense understandings of gender that underpin Japanese society, since they catered only to desires for hard masculinity via fetishistic and often implicit fantasies of straight men. Indeed, my experiences with young gay men in Tokyo exposed the continued ideological strength of heteronormativity throughout sections of Japanese society.

As I continued to conduct fieldwork with Shōtarō; my other key informants Junho, Yōichi, and Haruma; and fifty other men, I became progressively more interested in how the young gay men I encountered in Tokyo appeared to conflate "desirability" with a heteronormative construction of masculinity that privileged certain desires and marginalized others. Fundamentally, I was intrigued by how various "regimes of desire" circulate throughout what I term the "Japanese gay media landscape," a transmedia space formed by several interrelated platforms explicitly produced for gay male consumption. I began to explore how these regimes of desire structured Shōtarō's and others' understanding of their desires and identities, producing a complicated political economy tied to aesthetic hierarchies that did not necessarily provide young gay men the agency to fully reject the heteronormative systems that position their same-sex attraction as problematic. Desire, I came to realize, was principally understood by the young men with whom I spoke as a hierarchical knowledge system that naturalized identity categories tied to heteronormative conceptualizations of masculinity embedded within postwar Japanese society for decades. The regimes of desire that circulate throughout Japanese gay media and which uphold these remarkably conservative understandings of masculinity ultimately produce complicated affective economies that compromise the emancipatory potential of the Japanese gay media landscape.

*Regimes of Desire* therefore aims to specifically investigate how consumption of gay media influences how young gay men who visit Tokyo's "gay town" of Shinjuku Ni-chōme understand their desires, with an emphasis placed on examining the ideological role heteronormativity plays in the development of this understanding. Based on ethnographic fieldwork conducted over several research trips between 2012 and 2017 in Tokyo's Shinjuku Ni-chōme neighborhood, this book recounts the story of young gay men who are consuming media during 21st-century Japan's so-called crisis in masculinity and reveals through a case study of their experiences that hard forms of masculinity remain a hegemonic fantasy for some groups in contemporary Japanese society. Through in-depth ethnographic analyses of the consumption of media, including gay pornography, manga comics, magazines, and online dating sites, this book reveals how a political economy of desire directly impacts young gay men's gender performances, simultaneously exploring heteronormativity's influence over aesthetic production and exposing the limits of neoliberalized identity management within Japan's gay media.

At this point, it is important to acknowledge that Japan's gay culture is not unique in its resuscitation of desires for heteronormative masculinity. After all, it has become common within gay male cultures across the so-called developed Global North to valorize heteronormative masculinity as desirable. Japanese gay culture's privileging of hard masculinity is reflective of this broader global trend. Such privileging forms part of a wider neoliberal politics that positions acceptance of sexual minorities as a marker of development and even "culture" itself, while failing to critique the capitalist systems that have historically marginalized certain groups who sit outside heteronormative, patriarchal, and racist social systems.[6] As Jasbir Puar has insightfully noted, the contemporary moment is dominated by a "terrorist assemblage" that conflates fantasies of development and tolerance with patriarchy, heteronormativity, and White supremacy, producing "homonationalist" affects.[7] Throughout this book, I seek to understand how a gay male community in Tokyo is becoming increasingly implicated within transnational, neoliberal gay media networks that sit at the heart of these homonationalist trends and which promote "homonormative" understandings of queer experience that "[do] not contest dominant heteronormative assumptions . . . but uphold and sustain them."[8]

*Regimes of Desire* thus investigates how the neoliberalization of Shinjuku Ni-chōme's gay culture renders desire just another commodity within Japan's hyperconsumerist society, made accessible to neoliberal subjects—those whom theorist Wendy Brown has termed *homo oeconomicus*, or "economic man"[9]—whose very subjectivity is formed through the consumption of commodities within restricted markets. As Brown has insightfully noted, neoliberalism's mandate is to limit choice in order to maximize profit potential at the same time as presenting consumers with a fantasy of expanded choice and increased agency. Alexandra Chasin powerfully suggests that recent gay and lesbian identity politics, as a neoliberal phenomenon, similarly limits the acceptability of certain gay desires and identities so as to better segment what she terms the LGBT market for the purposes of capitalist exploitation.[10] Chasin further notes that gay and lesbian media around the world are complicit in this process as they produce fantasies of queer emancipation via consumption. By critically engaging with these globalized processes of neoliberal commodification, I explore how the Japanese gay media landscape's stratification of desire ultimately produces "a privatized, depoliticized gay culture anchored in . . . consumption."[11] The ethnographic analyses presented in the following chapters deploys both "homonormativity" and "heteronormativity" as hermeneutic devices to argue that social stratification ultimately limits the agency of young gay men to explore their sexuality through the reinscription of hegemonic hard masculinity as desirable.

## Negotiating Gender within Japan's "Hetero System"

It is not at all surprising that Shōtarō and other young gay men were anxious about their own masculinity and that these anxieties influenced how they understood their same-sex attraction. After all, throughout most of Japanese postwar history, questions concerning the nature of gender and how it relates to same-sex attraction have been central to Japan's gay culture.[12] Indeed, musing over gender identity represents a common trope within memoirs produced over the past 30 years by same-sex attracted men, such as the late activist Tōgō Ken,[13] former radio DJ and activist Ōtsuka Takeshi,[14] gay cultural critic Fushimi Noriaki,[15] former gay magazine editor Ryū Susumu,[16] influential activists Itō Satoru and Yanase Ryūta,[17] and erotic artist Tagame Gengoroh.[18] Throughout these memoirs, a common trope that emerged was the supposed failure of gay men to meet the gendered ideals of Japanese society. As these memoirs sensitively explore, same-sex attracted men were—and continue to be—positioned as what one of my informants termed "failed men" (*otoko shikkaku*). During my own discussions with young gay men in Tokyo, similar sentiments were often shared, revealing that possession of same-sex attraction is widely perceived as excluding or disqualifying men from normative masculinity.

To understand why gay men are considered failed men, it is important to unpack how sexuality and gender are conceptualized in contemporary Japan. But in order to do this, it is first necessary to explore how I theoretically define these key terms within this book. In *Regimes of Desire*, I take a social constructivist approach that emphasizes that both sexuality and gender are "expressed in situationally varied everyday behavior . . . [as] the products of earlier experiences and learning."[19] Importantly, I draw upon post-structural approaches central to queer theoretical work, including Judith Butler's seminal theory of performativity, to destabilize simplistic thinking that links gender identity to biology. Following Nakamura Momoko's sociolinguistic elaboration of Butler's theories in the Japanese context, I view gender as a "discursive resource" derived from the repetition of socially meaningful performances attached to idealized gender roles.[20] Gender is thus utilized in the fluctuating construction of an individual's subjectivity and deployed to make sense of their sexuality. I recognize that gender represents a social category as opposed to a biological essentialism, despite heteronormative assumptions to the contrary, which are common in Japan, with one's status as a "man" or "woman" socially derived and performed.[21] As sociologist Raewyn Connell has famously stated, "Gender, even in its most elaborate, abstract or fantastic forms, is always an 'accomplishment' . . . gender is something actually done; and done in social life, not something that exists prior to social life."[22]

Around the world, heteronormativity operates as a "regulatory" knowledge system that privileges heterosexuality as "natural" and "correct,"[23] and Japan is no exception when it comes to conceptualizations of gender and sexuality. Philosopher Michel Foucault has famously posited that the origins of heteronormativity can be traced to Western Europe, where industrialization and the attendant growth of population in the late 18th to 19th centuries led authorities to consolidate their control of society by policing sexual knowledge and behavior.[24] Foucault persuasively argued that the new "sexual knowledge" (*scientia sexualis*) primarily produced at this time through medical science and the emerging field of psychiatry led to the formation of new subject positions such as the sodomite and sexual deviant. In creating these subject positions,[25] Foucault argues that "sexual knowledge" produced discourses that "naturalized" heterosexual desire by excluding homosexuality as deviant and unnatural.[26] Terming this process "bio-political" control, Foucault believed that heteronormative discourses normalized and hence revived the Judeo-Christian sexual morality that had been embedded within Western European society for almost two thousand years.[27] According to Mark McLelland, this heteronormative bio-politics subsequently emerged within Japan during the late 19th to early 20th centuries as the Japanese government imported Western (particularly German) sexological literature as part of its strategic campaign to borrow Western knowledge to improve Japan's industrializing society.[28] As Sabine Frühstück insightfully notes within her history of sexual knowledge in modern Japan, the new science of sexology was deployed by Japanese leaders to manage the population and thus develop a modern state based in a "normative sexuality . . . viewed as existing between women and men."[29]

Cultural critic and gay activist Fushimi Noriaki, in reflecting on the "question of desire" within his writing, has insightfully noted that the routine conflation of biological sex and gender within Japanese society has led to the development of a "hetero system" (*hetero shisutemu*) that systematically marginalizes same-sex desiring men and women.[30] Fushimi argues that this "hetero system" promotes heterosexual, cis-gendered men as the default Japanese social subject, effectively excluding gay men from the cultural domain of Japaneseness. Without explicitly doing so, Fushimi thus evokes the concept of sexual citizenship and preempts the writings of scholars such as Claire Maree in acknowledging that Japanese citizenship ideologically privileges heterosexual subjects.[31] Like Fushimi, feminist historian Vera Mackie has also argued that "the archetypical Japanese citizen is a *male, heterosexual*, able-bodied, fertile, white-collar worker," revealing that this symbolic citizen strengthens the patriarchal conservatism that sits at the heart of contemporary Japanese culture.[32] Under the hetero system and its privileging of heterosexual men as "natural," same-sex desiring men (and women) are conceptualized as dangerous social elements because of the supposed non-reproductive nature of their sexual practices.[33] Fushimi persuasively argues that it is the nonreproductive nature of his and other gay men's desires that ultimately renders them "failed men," since their masculinity is compromised by their rejection of heterosexuality.

As the above discussion makes evident, the notion that sexual desire and biological sex are intimately linked is integral to the hetero system.[34] This heteronormative logic also underpins Japanese mainstream conceptualizations of sexuality more broadly. Nakamura Mia suggests in her queer sexological studies that contemporary Japanese attitudes toward sexuality are firmly situated within a highly essentialist paradigm that constructs an individual's gendered and sexual identities as equivalent to their biological sex.[35] This conceptualization of sexuality is one of the many legacies of the sexological management of the Japanese population during the late 19th and early 20th centuries that adopted pronatalism,[36] constructing gendered ideologies that positioned women as mothers and wives and men as fathers and husbands. Responding to this history, Fushimi notes that the hetero system purports that there are only two static genders—the "male role" (*dansei*) and the "female role" (*josei*)—and that this sexual ideology promotes a rigid, heteronormative "system of gender/sexual duality" (*seibetsu nigensei*) where men actively desire women and women are rendered passive objects of men's desires because of the influence of pronatalist logics.[37] Here, drawing on the earlier work of activist and social critic Tōgō Ken, Fushimi engages in wordplay to stress the constructed nature of these sexual roles. Rather than employing the standard Japanese orthography for the terms man (*dansei* 男性) and woman (*josei* 女性), Fushimi replaces the typical character 性 (*sei*) with the homophonous character 制 (*sei*), meaning "regulation," "law," or "rule," to create a neologism that reveals how gender represents a "role" that individuals play in society, once again implicitly evoking the work of Butler.

Within the hetero system, "passive desire" for other men is coded as feminine and is "naturally" attached to those bodies understood to be biologically female.[38] On the other hand, to be masculine is to be active, heterosexual, and sexually (re)productive. Therefore, the hetero system conflates gay men's desires with the desires of heterosexual women, and both gay men and women are thus understood as passive in their desires for heterosexual men, whose desires are consequently positioned as active.[39] The system of gender/sexual duality promoted by the hetero system ultimately constructs gay men as inherently possessing "womanly" attributes, with same-sex desiring men subsequently understood as effeminate (*joseiteki*).[40] Fushimi refers to this process as "androgynification" (*chūseika*).[41] Because of the androgynification of same-sex desiring men inherent to the hetero system, the common image most Japanese people have of gay men is one of women "trapped" in men's bodies. In this sense, Japanese gay men are understood to be "gender inverts" that disrupt the logics of the hetero system. This is what makes them particularly threatening.

As briefly indicated above, Japan's mainstream media is awash with depictions of same-sex attracted men that reinforce this view of them as "gender inverts"; the *onē kyara* whom Shōtarō criticized is just one example. Japanese popular culture has a long history of depicting gay men through an almost transgendered paradigm, with one particular image, the *okama*, holding a central position within Japanese conceptualizations of male-male homosexuality. The conventional image of an *okama* is a cross-dressing male who employs a stereotypically feminine linguistic style known as *onēkotoba* (variously translated as "queen's language" or "camp language"), who enacts a highly parodic performance of so-called feminine body language and who is understood as possessing same-sex desire.[42] The *onē kyara* who commonly appear in mainstream media represent a humorous parody of this *okama* stereotype and serve a largely comedic function on television, their inability to pass as women (their "unnaturalness") consistently portrayed as a source of humor.[43] The main difference between *onē kyara* and *okama*, however, is that *onē kyara* are understood to be performing a role, whereas an *okama* is instead simply a woman trapped in a man's body.

Overtly antagonistic and explicitly derisory attitudes toward *onē kyara* are relatively scarce in Japan, although the ambiguous positioning of them as objects of humor is based on a belief in the supposed abnormality of their same-sex desires. In fact, the heterosexual consumers of Japan's mainstream media, particularly young heterosexual women, mostly view *onē kyara* with good-natured condescension and affection.[44] Nevertheless, many gay men in Japan view the heteronormative positioning of *onē kyara* and *okama* as objects of ridicule, and they view as highly stigmatizing the simplistic reduction of gay experience to transgenderism that lies at the heart of depictions of *okama*.[45] Likewise, there have been high-profile debates among Japanese gay activists concerning use of terms such as *okama* to describe gay men, most notably in 2001 when, in response to an article published in the weekly magazine *Shūkan kin'yōbi*, a roundtable was convened to discuss whether the term *okama* is discriminatory.[46] Overall, whether terms such as *okama* are discriminatory, the heteronormative positioning of gay men as somehow transgendered that underlies such terminology effectively silences gay men's desires, illegitimating their same-sex attraction and constructing gay desire as unnatural and abnormal.[47]

The hetero system explored within this section represents one of the chief regimes of desire that my interlocutors navigated as they consumed gay media and made sense of their same-sex attraction. As I demonstrate throughout this book, notions of the inherently active and productive nature of masculinity remain central to notions of desirability within Japan's gay media landscape as well as the bars and clubs of Shinjuku Nichōme. In fact, *Regimes of Desire* reveals how gendered knowledge within Tokyo's gay social spaces remains fundamentally binaristic and that it is the rigidity of this binary that limits the agency of young gay men to explore their desires and identities. Nowhere is this more evident than in young gay men's responses to both the images of hegemonic masculinity that circulate throughout wider society and the aesthetic logics that structure these images.

*The Rise of Precarious Japan and the Crisis in*
*Hegemonic Masculinity*

There is a strong perception within contemporary Japanese society that masculinity is in crisis because of recent shifts in the socioeconomic and cultural life of the Japanese nation-state.[48] My discussions with young gay men occurred during the final years of Japan's Heisei period (1989–2019), a time when intense experiences of precariousness became the norm among young people—especially men—who increasingly found themselves excluded from the traditional support systems that had evolved in postwar Japan. The Heisei period represented a moment of economic stagnation brought about by the collapse of the Japanese postwar economic miracle and the bursting of Japan's hyperinflated 1980s bubble economy. These economic disasters, in turn, produced a so-called fertility crisis as the socioeconomic precarity of contemporary Japan has made it increasingly difficult for young people to enter into long-term relationships and eventually have children.[49] This has led conservative voices throughout Japanese society to begin vocally advocating for a return to traditional forms of manhood and womanhood based in patriarchy, with same-sex attracted men coming to represent "failed men" who threaten governmental efforts to reinvigorate Japan's postwar economy. One particularly salient example of such criticisms is Liberal Democratic Party lawmaker Sugita Mio, who argued in 2018 that sexual minorities did not deserve state welfare because of the supposedly unreproductive nature of their sexual practices.

Furthermore, neoliberal reforms designed to reinvigorate the economy and encourage spending introduced by various governments throughout the first years of the 21st century have also destabilized traditional notions of work and leisure, strongly impacting perceptions of men's role in Japanese society. Previous postwar guarantees of economic stability via lifetime employment rapidly eroded as the workforce increasingly casualized, disallowing most men from entering the corporate world to which normative notions of masculinity remain tied.[50] For cultural anthropologist Anne Allison, the final years of the Heisei period were thus typified by a sense of hopelessness brought about by the inherently alienating effects of neoliberalization.[51] This hopelessness was further strengthened by the 2011 Greater East Japan Earthquake and subsequent nuclear catastrophe at the Fukushima Daiichi Nuclear Power Plant, which increased young people's beliefs that Japan has become a society that is teetering on the edge of catastrophe. The increasingly precarious nature of employment and the millennial fear brought about by nuclear disaster, Allison argues, have produced feelings of *ikizurasa,* or "painful living," tied to anxieties related to Japan's imminent demographic collapse and the weakening of patriarchal authority.[52]

As David Slater and Patrick Galbraith note in their analysis of mass media responses to the 2008 Akihabara Massacre—where an irregularly employed young man named Katō Tomohiro drove a truck into the crowds amassed in the busy entertainment district of Akihabara and subsequently murdered ten people—the destabilization of Japan's traditional corporate culture has engendered a panic that society itself is collapsing.[53] The blame for this collapse, Slater and Galbraith reveal, is placed squarely at the feet of individuals such as Katō who fail to enter into full-time work and hence become responsible citizens or "full members of society" (*ichininmae no shakaijin*). Within alarmist accounts of the massacre, which spread throughout Japanese media, Katō's lack of a (heterosexual) relationship, his position as an irregular worker, and the massacre's occurrence within a space linked to the *otaku* (geek/nerd) subculture of obsessive fandom for anime characters were all highlighted as indicating a "crisis" in contemporary Japanese masculinity. Analyzing the discourse surrounding this event, Slater and Galbraith argue that the media representations of Katō that emerged in 2008 as society tried to grapple with the tragedy in Akihabara ultimately revealed the "persistence of middle-class masculine ideals" within recessionary Japan. That is, Katō emerged as a symbol of a pathologized, failed masculinity because of his inability to enter full-time employment and maintain a "healthy" heterosexual relationship.

But how is the exceptional experience of one troubled young man such as Katō relevant to an ethnographic investigation of young Japanese gay men's understandings of their desires and identities in Shinjuku Nichōme? The Akihabara Massacre and the media's subsequent positioning of Katō as a failed man who is symptomatic of a broader societal collapse reveal another important regime of desire with which young Japanese gay men must contend—that masculinity remains ideologically tied to understandings of economic as well as sexual productivity. That is, to be a successful man within contemporary Japanese society is still connected to an expectation that a man will be gainfully employed through the postwar system of lifetime employment. This form of "successful" masculinity is embodied within the ubiquitous image of the "salaryman" (*sararīman*), the stereotypical corporate warrior who "came to be regarded as the 'everyman' of Japan's postwar landscape."[54]

The salaryman is primarily constructed with reference to heterosexuality, drawing upon men's economic role in the family.[55] Sociologist Romit Dasgupta, through ethnographic study of salarymen working in medium- or small-size firms in the late 1990s, has suggested that the discourse of the salaryman is intimately tied to maturational understandings of manhood, expressed through the metaphor of the *daikokubashira*—literally "the pillar supporting the roof of the home," but more idiomatically translated as "breadwinner."[56] The informants in Dasgupta's study reported that they derived a sense of "masculinity" (*otokorashisa*) from being able to support their family and viewed their identity as salarymen to be linked to their ability to economically provide for their wife and children. Ultimately, the salaryman image promotes an understanding of masculinity that is firmly situated within discourses of "strength" and "activity" that have become consolidated within the idea of the "corporate warrior" (*kigyō senshi*), who was the ideological backbone of the postwar Japanese economic miracle. Further, the fact that the salaryman ideology contains within it an implicit understanding that to be a successful man is to be married with a wife and children demonstrates, according to leading feminist theorist Ueno Chizuko, the privileging of heterosexuality and the so-called nuclear family in Japanese society.[57]

Mainstream media, particularly film and television, promote an idealized, romantic image of the salaryman as working hard and sacrificing his time for the sake of his family. As a cultural touchstone for "successful" masculinity against which all other masculine performances (such as Katō Tomohiro's or that of my young gay informants) are judged, the salaryman represents the form of masculinity that is hegemonic within Japanese society.[58] Within every society there are myriad ways of being and crafting masculinity, and Japan is no exception. These masculinities "respond to various cultural, economic, political and other conditions" with hierarchies of power defining the relationships between them.[59] This leads to some ways of enacting manhood being rejected as nonnormative, while others gain ideological currency as the "correct" or hegemonic way to be a man.[60] Importantly, while hegemonic masculinity is not always the most common form in a given society, it typically exerts a powerful and often implicit influence over all other expressions of masculinity.[61] In other words, hegemonic masculinity forms another regime of desire that conditions the understandings of gendered and sexual identity that gay men must navigate in contemporary Japan. Indeed, although the salaryman is considered to be ubiquitous in Japanese society, in reality most Japanese men do not work in elite corporations and instead work in smaller firms, engaging in both white- and blue-collar work.[62]

As a result of the collapse of lifetime employment, young people in contemporary Japan evince a growing rejection of the salaryman ideal and its attendant hegemonic privileging of a hard or stoic form of masculinity. Jan Bardsley notes through an analysis of fashion advice literature that recent years have even seen the emergence of a discourse that weds the salaryman to the "uncool" (*dasai*) image of the "old geezer" (*oyaji*). Conceptualized predominantly within popular culture texts targeting young women, the salaryman is presented as a relic of Japan's problematic patriarchal past.[63] Likewise, through the careful semiotic and discursive examination of young (heterosexual) women's popular culture—including manga comics and "idol" boy bands—scholars such as Yumiko Iida, Fabienne Darling-Wolf, Jennifer Prough, and Sharon Kinsella note a growing privileging of a supposedly "softer" masculine ideal tied to the image of the *bishōnen*, or beautiful male youth, at the turn of the 21st century.[64] Within her influential ethnography of Japan's late 1990s aesthetic salon industry, linguistic anthropologist Laura Miller suggests that this privileging of a so-called soft masculinity within women's texts impacted heterosexual men's beauty norms. What emerged was a new form of disciplined aesthetics based in slimmer physiques and emotionally expressive faces, which challenged the harder aesthetics and ideals tied to the salaryman image.[65] For Miller, the collapse of lifetime employment and the neoliberalization of Japanese society had the positive effect of dislocating the centrality of the salaryman and allowing soft masculinity to emerge as a potential new hegemonic form in contemporary Japan.[66] Recent ethnographic work by Alexandra Hambleton in Japan's "female-friendly" pornography industry, however, challenges such emancipatory readings, suggesting that depictions of masculinity within young women's popular culture remain implicitly patriarchal despite their supposedly softer veneer.[67]

Many subcultures have also emerged among young men themselves that challenge the hegemony of the salaryman. Some of these alternative masculinities include that professed by *otaku*, referring to obsessive fans of Japanese animation (anime) and female idols;[68] *furītā*, young people who are not employed full-time and take on minimum wage, part-time work in order to support their lifestyles;[69] and "herbivorous boys" (*sōshoku-kei danshi*), a male subculture that rejects heteronormative understandings of Japanese manhood through a commercialized engagement with fashion, beauty, and being "cute" (*kawaii*).[70] A significant body of scholarship has emerged in recent years to explore how members of these specific subcultures exercise their agency, taking advantage of the neoliberalization of contemporary Japanese society to develop identities and communities which allow them to cope with rising precarity. In rejecting the normative masculinity attached to the middle-class values of the salaryman image, men who subscribe to these subcultural identities are also often positioned as "feminized."[71] Furthermore, these subcultural groups' rejection of hegemonic masculinity through so-called feminized behavior is often pathologically positioned by mainstream society as another contributing factor to Japan's crisis in masculinity and the subsequent collapse of patriarchal authority.

Despite the sophisticated critiques of contemporary Japanese masculinities presented in previous research—especially studies arguing that so-called soft masculinity represents a newly emergent hegemonic masculinity—I follow Dasgupta and Fushimi in arguing that the salaryman remains the dominant ideological image defining what it means to be a man in Japanese society. Although I recognize that "socio-economic and corporate culture upheavals and shifts over the post-Bubble era" may have destabilized the lived reality of salarymen,[72] the understanding of the salaryman as a hard worker who can support his wife and children rather than just his own lifestyle still underlies contemporary understandings of "successful" masculinity. Anthropologist Ian Condry argues in his work with *otaku* men that the discourses of "manliness" surrounding subcultural figures such as the *otaku* still "share a common assumption with salaryman masculinity, namely that value (a man's worth) tends to be grounded in productivity."[73] For these reasons, *Regimes of Desire* continues the project of investigating how the young gay men I encountered in Tokyo engage with the heteronormative, hegemonic discourse of masculinity as it is tied to identity categories such as the salaryman. Further, as I reveal throughout this book, in many ways, Japan's gay media has failed to capitalize on the crisis in masculinity in broader society to renegotiate the privileging of hardness. Unlike young women's popular culture, where a supposedly softer alternative masculinity has emerged, the binary logics that structure gendered knowledge in the Japanese gay media landscape reinforce the desirability of hardness and demonstrate the continued prevalence of hegemonic and patriarchal understandings of masculinity tied to productivity. Whereas precariousness has produced challenges to Japan's hetero-normative gendered order in some social spaces, I ultimately reveal in this book that responses to the crisis in masculinity found within Japan's gay media have merely bolstered hegemonic masculinity within Tokyo's "gay town" of Shinjuku Ni-chōme, producing complicated political economies that in turn produce homonormative affects.

*A Cultural History of Male Same-Sex Desire in Japan:*
*Cycles of Booms and Busts*

At the same time as young gay men must negotiate hegemonic concep-tualizations of masculinity in the context of an increasingly precarious Japan, they are also currently witnessing dramatic changes in society's understandings of what it means to be a same-sex attracted person. The Heisei period was, in many ways, a historical moment when queer vis-ibility rapidly developed as a consequence of bursts of attention paid to gay men by the mainstream media in the early 1990s and of increased engagement with sexual minority politics throughout the 2010s. The his-tory of male same-sex desire in both the pre- and postwar periods has been typified by a cycle of such "booms," which have been strongly tied to Japan's industrialization and integration into global capitalist systems over the past 150 years. This history affirms that American historian John D'Emilio's seminal argument concerning the influential role of capitalism in producing queer sexual culture holds true in the Japanese context, but with some important caveats.[74] These booms include the first gay boom of the 1950s, the second gay boom of the early 1990s, and the recent LGBT boom of 2015. For literary theorist Keith Vincent, this cycle of booms pro-duces disjunctive knowledge systems within which identity-based con-ceptualizations of homosexuality deriving predominantly from Western sources come into conflict with Japanese nativist understandings of same-sex attraction based in desire.[75] As I explore below, desire rather than identity has represented the chief paradigm within which Japanese men have conceptualized their same-sex attraction.

Japan has a long tradition of male homoeroticism. One of the earliest discourses of male same-sex desire emerged in the sixth century within Buddhist monasteries.[76] Known as *nanshoku* (male-male erotics), this system of male homoerotic practice typically involved the penetration of the *chigo*, a young boy between the ages of 13 and 18, by the *nenja*, an older and superior monk typically in his 30s or 40s. *Nanshoku* propagated two specific discourses of masculine aesthetics that dominated conceptualizations of male homoeroticism throughout Japan's premodern eras; the *chigo* became linked to a discourse of idealized masculine youth and beauty, while the *nenja* was viewed to be the embodiment of "the masculine as educator."[77] It is important to note, however, that *nanshoku* never represented a locus for identity construction, with terms like *chigo* and *nenja* instead acting as labels for culturally understood acts associated with age rather than subject positions based in sexual desire.[78] More than anything, *nanshoku* was an important aesthetic discourse that strongly influenced premodern conceptualizations of masculinity and pleasure. Although viewed as a normative practice, particularly as it became intertwined with popular culture forms such as kabuki theater and literary texts such as the oeuvre of Ihara Saikaku in the Edo period (1600–1868), *nanshoku* was still understood as societally unproductive, and heterosexual relationships were thus more highly valued because of their ability to produce children.[79]

Understandings of homoeroticism changed greatly, however, after Japan's encounter with the West and the nation's subsequent industrialization as a result of the 1868 Meiji Restoration. The Meiji government attempted to modernize the nation through the strategic adoption of Western knowledge, and *nanshoku* subsequently came to be downplayed in an effort to hide Japan's "shameful" premodern past.[80] The importation of Western sexological science during this period, discussed previously as a cornerstone of the hetero system, played an important role in pathologizing male homoeroticism. The neologism *dōseiai* (homosexuality, literally "same-sex love") entered into Japanese medical language along with the adoption of pathologizing discourses of same-sex attraction from European medical texts.[81] Until the 1920s, however, *nanshoku* remained the dominant system of knowledge attached to male-male desires within popular discourse, although it was increasingly judged as "backward" and "unnatural."[82] The continued relevance of *nanshoku* during the Meiji period (1868–1912) is evidenced by a popular literature boom that explored homoerotic themes. Within this literature, *nanshoku* played a foundational role in the development of discourses concerning the *bishōnen*, who eventually became central to Japan's postwar young women's popular culture.[83] In particular, *nanshoku* was employed throughout this literary boom within a dualistic categorization of newly emergent modes of modern masculinity. As depicted within Mori Ōgai's seminal modernist text

*Vita Sexualis*, the practice of *nanshoku* was tied to a so-called hard faction (*kō-ha*) of rough and "barbaric" Japanese men linked to the premodern past. Contrasted with a heterosexual and cosmopolitan "soft faction" (*nanpa*), this hard faction began to index a strong masculine past among some thinkers (although not Mori).[84]

It was roughly toward the end of the 1920s that newspapers began to use the term *dōseiai* instead of *nanshoku* when discussing male same-sex attraction, reflecting a paradigm shift in conceptualizations of homoeroticism in mainstream Japanese society.[85] This paradigm shift is evidenced by the explosion of Japanese popular sexological literature published during the Taishō period (1912–1926), wherein *nanshoku* was increasingly reinterpreted through the lens of pathologized homosexuality and was resignified as either *dōseiai* or *sodomiya* (sodomy).[86] Homosexuality came to be conceptualized as a "perverse desire" (*hentai seiyoku*) that motivated individuals to commit socially unproductive and "deviant" acts.[87] During the early Shōwa era (1926–1989) and war years, as Japanese society became increasingly militaristic, the Japanese government progressively sought to control the sexual lives of its citizenry, leading to the establishment of a pronatalist state.[88] Because of this pronatalism, sexuality became increasingly conceptualized as purely heterosexual, lending further credence to the pathologizing discourse of homosexuality that circulated in wider society.

McLelland argues that the defeat and subsequent Occupation of Japan by the US-led Allied powers promoted a democratization of sex as censorship of sexual materials was relaxed.[89] During the Occupation, the notion of *seiyoku* (sexual desire) came to be linked with the liberal ideas of freedom and *asobi* (play) at the same time as discourses of *shutaisei* (selfhood) and individuality were similarly promoted.[90] Yet sexual desire under the Occupation was also still firmly rooted in heteronormativity and pronatalism. Despite the outwardly liberal nature of Occupation-era rhetoric, love and sexuality were increasingly understood via the commercialized paradigm of "pure love" (*junsui na ai*), a heteronormative system that constructs men as the possessors of both romantic and economic capital.[91] Although commercialized love was still heteronormative, the concomitant commercialization of sex allowed for the reintegration of "perverse desires" (*hentai seiyoku*) such as sadomasochism and homosexuality into the sexual marketplace as objects of consumption.[92]

This consumerist discourse was most evident within the vast subcultural "perverse press" (*hentai zasshi*), which sought to satisfy the demand

for male and female homoerotic content. McLelland has identified publication of these materials as representative of Japan's first postwar gay
boom, a moment when knowledge production concerning same-sex
desire reached unprecedented highs.[93] Perhaps the most influential magazine from this perverse press was *Adonis*, which sociologist Maekawa
Naoya argues was the first magazine to specifically promote a sense of
community—albeit a private and secretive one—among same-sex desiring men in Japan.[94] This community was, however, based less in a specific shared identification with male same-sex attraction than it was in the
possession of nonnormative desires in general. Indeed, because systems
of homosexual desire were presented in magazines also aiming to supply
sadomasochistic content, homosexual desire was also often conflated with
sadomasochism, with men's uncontrollable urges being violently enacted
upon the passive and willing bodies of other weaker, "feminized" men.[95]
This postwar perverse press had little effect, however, on mainstream
understandings of same-sex attraction. Rather, it was the emergence in
the 1960s of transvestite performers known as "gay boys" (*gei bōi*) within
Japan's burgeoning postwar sex entertainment industry that played a significant role in structuring mainstream conceptualizations of same-sex
attracted men.[96] This discourse ushered in the ascendancy of the transgendered understandings of male homosexuality central to what Fushimi
Noriaki terms the hetero system.

In reaction to mainstream discourses of gay men as effeminate, the
1970s saw the development of what Jonathan Mackintosh and Maekawa
Naoya have both termed *homo* magazines, named after a newly emerging subject position that sought to emphasize hypermasculinity.[97] These
magazines included *Barazoku*, the first commercially published magazine aimed at a male homosexual audience in Japan, as well as Minami Teishirō's *Adon* and the sadomasochistically themed *Sabu*.[98] While
doing little to reformulate wider society's conceptualization of same-sex
attracted men as transgendered, these *homo* magazines deliberately sub-
verted such tropes through their valorization of hypermasculinity in the
form of extremely muscular, savage, and sadistic men. Furthermore, the
*homo* magazines also played a crucial role in introducing Western (typically American) "gay rights" understandings of homosexuality to Japan as
evidenced by adoption of the term *homo*, then widely used among same-
sex attracted men in the US as an in-group marker.[99] Through *Barazoku*,
Itō Bungaku also attempted to popularize the notion of a nationwide
community of male homosexuals, which he believed were unfairly alien-

ated from Japanese society at large. His philosophy, known as "solidarity" (*rentaikan*), played an influential role in instilling a sense of community among Japanese same-sex attracted men.[100]

The development of this communal feeling was enhanced by Minami Teishirō's increasingly explicit engagement with gay rights discourse in *Adon* in the early 1980s. The spread of the "Western" gay rights discourse in Japan was also particularly aided by Minami's decision to join the International Lesbian and Gay Association (ILGA) and to subsequently found a "European-style gay rights advocacy group" in Osaka named ILGA Japan.[101] The North American gay rights model of "queer community" explicitly linked sexual attraction with identity; this discourse was adopted by a new generation of young activists and cultural critics representing the genesis of communal and personal "gay" identities in Japan.[102] Throughout the 1980s, and well into the 1990s, Japanese same-sex attracted activists increasingly engaged with North American and European discourses of gay rights and identity politics, although certain sections of Japan's gay culture rejected this model of identity, criticizing it as "Americanisation."[103]

Importantly, because of the influence of earlier lesbian activist organizations formed in the 1970s such as Wakakusa no Kai (Young grass group),[104] the notion that lesbian and gay men shared a similar "same-sex desire"— once again labeled *dōseiai*—led to a decrease in the use of the term *homo* among Japanese same-sex attracted men.[105] This in turn brought about a wider acceptance and use of the term *gei*/"gay" and a move away from the hypermasculinity of the *homo* discourse. Integral to this shift was the affirmation drawn from the supposed Western gay identity politics of the normative masculinity of gay men and the concomitant pressure for gay men to adopt heteronormative identities.[106] Concurrently, the long-running daytime variety show *Waratte iitomo* (It's okay to laugh) began to provide a platform for certain *okama* and "gay" activists to voice their critiques of Japanese society.[107] The "Mister Lady" segment on this highly popular program, which featured transgendered talents (many of whom did not identify as same-sex attracted), promoted the use of the term "new-half" (*nyūhāfu*) as a label for transgender performers. Throughout mainstream society, the transgendered discourses explicitly attached to the term *gei* began to diminish as new terms for transgenderism such as "new-half" became common in Japanese society.

The 1990s ushered in a veritable explosion of interest in male homosexuality throughout wider society, starting with the women's magazine

*CREA*.[108] This second gay boom included not only articles in magazines but also numerous homoerotic movies and TV shows.[109] In many ways, Japan's mainstream media was adopting similar tactics to those found in North America and Europe where investment in queer visibility represented a strategic targeting of an audience of same-sex attracted men and young women, two groups who had emerged in the 1990s as important consumers of popular culture products. The 1990s gay boom also saw the rise of high-profile activist cases, such as when the gay rights organization OCCUR successfully sued the Tokyo Metropolitan Government over a number of cases of discrimination.[110] The second gay boom was almost immediately followed by the advent of relatively inexpensive internet access through mobile telephony and other increasingly sophisticated technological developments, and the subsequent popularization of the internet in Japan. The internet radically changed Japanese gay men's patterns of socialization, leading to the development of a deeper awareness not only of a nationwide community of gay men but a "global" gay culture.[111] Yet throughout this period, tensions still existed concerning the nature of same-sex attraction as a locus for identity production, with pioneering sociological research by Lunsing, McLelland, and Yajima into the life stories of gay men suggesting that the vast majority continued to conceptualize their desires as behavioral and rejected political activist positionings of same-sex attraction as the basis of an identity.[112]

Throughout the first decades of the 21st century, same-sex desiring men continued to be involved in activism at the same time that a burgeoning gay media landscape developed. From the mid-2000s until today, Japan has seen a rising number of gay pride parades and other activist events across the country designed to raise the visibility of same-sex desiring and gender-nonconforming communities among the general public. Perhaps the largest of these events is Tokyo Rainbow Pride, a weeklong festival that often attracts sponsorship from major national and international corporations and which has become a major event in Tokyo's calendar due to its being held over the Golden Week holiday period in late April to early May. In the second half of the 2010s, partly in response to the growing visibility of explicit LGBT rights politics in Japan, a third mainstream media boom occurred that has come to be termed the LGBT boom by activists and scholars alike.[113] Broadly speaking, this LGBT boom referred to trends in media reporting that are typified by the explicit use of the LGBT acronym when discussing Japan's minority queer communities rather than the previous practice of utilizing phrases such as *sekushuaru mainoritī* or *seiteki shōsūsha.*[114] This boom developed following Japanese media reporting of the 2015 US Supreme Court decision to extend same-sex marriage across the whole US as well as the much-publicized decision in the same year of Tokyo's Shibuya Ward to begin issuing symbolic "certificates acknowledging marriage-like relationships" (*kekkon sōtō pātonāshippu shōmeisho*) to same-sex couples. The major difference between the contemporary LGBT boom and previous gay booms is that the latter had less to do with rights than with visibility, whereas the LGBT boom focused on the broader queer community and is explicitly focused on rights-based understandings of gay male experience as a discreet identity.[115] The LGBT boom occurred at the same time as the latter stages of my fieldwork, and I discuss it in greater depth in this book's conclusion as the vast bulk of my data predates this seminal event in recent queer Japanese history.

## Desire is a Social Construct: Unpacking Regimes of Desire

Most of the young men with whom I spoke in Shinjuku Ni-chōme framed their discussions with me largely through the tropes of "sexual desire" (*seiyoku*) and "attraction/longing" (*akogare*), although various subject positions known colloquially as "Types" were also central to their narratives. Studying desire, then, is integral to understanding how cultural codes of sexuality influence young Japanese gay men's engagement with media since desire is fundamental to their experiences of subjectivity. The social constructivist approach to sexuality deployed within this book understands desire as a primarily discursive phenomenon, challenging the psychoanalytic notion that desire represents the origin of behavior or a "drive" typified by notions of "lack" found within classical Freudian or Lacanian theory.[116] A social constructivist approach privileges the idea that desire is in fact a series of dislocated affects and ideologies, which interact in a nonhierarchical, multivariate manner. For Gilles Deleuze and Félix Guattari, traditional psychoanalysis places too heavy an emphasis upon identifying the origin of desire; they suggest instead that it would be more beneficial for scholars to engage with the multifaceted directions in which desire flows.[117] Carole Vance likewise argues that social scientists must now seek to "map" how desire is socially produced to understand exactly how it influences the expression of an individual's subjective experiences.[118] Furthermore, following theorist Sara Ahmed, queer desires such as same-sex attraction must also be recognized as a primarily affective phenomenon experienced through the body as an intensity that often frustrates or destabilizes social knowledge systems, particularly heteronormativity.[119]

Placing desire as the focus of investigation allows for the study of human sexuality to distance itself from an approach that privileges the a priori existence of what Butler has termed an "epistemological subject."[120] An epistemological subject denotes an almost metaphysical subject "thought to have a kind of stable existence prior to and outside the cultural field that encompasses it."[121] For linguists Deborah Cameron and Don Kulick, the epistemological subject is problematic as it represents an always already existing "I," an entity that can paradoxically draw from ideologies external to itself in order to determine "what best corresponds with its (already somehow established) sense of self."[122] Butler argues that there is a need to shift the focus of analysis away from the epistemological subject and to adopt an approach which "locates the problematic within practices of *signification*."[123] Butler's approach to subjective experience is particularly useful when studying sexuality in Japan, as critical theorists Karatani Kojin and Masao Miyoshi have both persuasively argued that Japanese systems of thought have traditionally lacked epistemological conceptualizations of subjectivity (*shutaisei*). Indeed, these two critical theorists have both argued that the notion of individual personhood emerged in Japan only during the late 19th century after encountering Western Enlightenment thought and that such ideologies still remain fraught in contemporary Japan.[124] Rather than identity, anthropologist Karen Kelsky has argued that subjectivities in Japan are often phenomenologically experienced through *akogare*, a "yearning" or "longing" that reflexively shapes an individual's subjective relationship with the world via the projection of desire onto an Other.[125] This was certainly true of my informants, for whom desiring others was integral to their sense of self.

Within Butler's conceptualization, a gay identity is not essentially linked to same-sex desire but emerges from an individual's performative relationships with their same-sex attraction, their gendered experiences, and societal understandings of sexuality, gender, and desire. Cameron and Kulick suggest that situating desire as the object of analysis "acknowledges that sexuality is centrally about the erotic."[126] It must be noted, however, that taking desire as the object of analysis does not preclude the study of gay subject positions, nor does it disavow those who choose to align themselves with such identity categories.[127] Following Butler, such an approach enriches the study of identity categories by encouraging researchers to attend to how the subjective experience of same-sex attraction motivates individuals to align themselves with socially constituted categorizations, facilitating the investigation of how these categories are born out of engagement with the cultural codes of sexuality disseminated throughout society. In many ways, this process of alignment resonates with Ahmed's notion of sexuality as a phenomenological process of "orientating" oneself to social expectations.[128] Within Ahmed's influential "queer phenomenology," queerness is understood as a deliberate decision not to "orientate" oneself to patriarchal and heteronormative conceptualizations of sex and gender, with desire representing the phenomenological "surface" across which subjective experience is both mapped and felt. Heteronormativity is likewise conceptualized as a "straightening out" of queerness to better align with the social privileging of heterosexual desire. I argue throughout this book that the regimes of desire inherent to the Japanese gay media landscape ultimately operate to "straighten out" gay desires through the production of heteronormative hard masculinity as desirable.

By recognizing the fundamentally ideological nature of desire, this book foregrounds "the extent to which our erotic lives are shaped by forces which are not wholly rational and of which we are not fully conscious."[129] Studying desire recognizes that representations of same-sex attraction are often inherently paradoxical and that conflicting discourses about what it means for men to desire other men may exist in the same discursive spaces. For these reasons, Regimes of Desire follows Cameron and Kulick in investigating the various social semiotic systems that represent "set[s] of meaningful resources that both constrain and enable the choices individuals make when they communicate desire."[130] Furthermore, I pay particular attention to individual engagements with these discursive systems in order to theorize the complex ways in which individuals understand what it means to desire the same sex, "chart[ing] the way [desire] moves, acts and forms connections" in a constant process of being "dis/re/assembled."[131] Throughout Regimes of Desire, I discuss how individual desire, as neither conscious nor rational, can complicate, frustrate or deconstruct the very socio-semiotic systems with which individuals engage to make sense of their subjective experiences.

As an ideological and affective system, desire is neither neutral nor divorced from social concerns. Particularly within systems of neoliberalized capitalism where desire is strategically managed for the purposes of economic exploitation,[132] it is important to recognize that desire possesses a political economy. Following recent trends within queer studies that have adopted an "affective" approach, this book specifically seeks to chart how the ways desire moves throughout society and between desiring subjects is controlled by structures that produce both social and aesthetic knowledge. That is, normative understandings of what is and is not desirable in both the Japanese gay media landscape and the bar culture of Shinjuku Ni-chōme shape and direct how individuals perceive their sexual desires, drastically impacting their sense of self. As Ahmed has highlighted, "Emotions work to align some subjects with some others and against other others," creating economies of affect that hierarchize values through "the very intensity of their attachments."[133] Likewise, desirability as it is chiefly linked to aesthetic notions of taste exerts symbolic power over how individuals choose to position themselves within Japanese society, producing what Lauren Berlant has termed "cruel optimism." In thinking through notions of symbolic power and images of "the good life" in contemporary Europe and the US, Berlant argues that to desire is fundamentally cruel within late capitalism, for the objects of one's desire are always already unattainable as capitalism requires excessive and endless consumption in order to fulfill its logics of accumulation.[134] Following Berlant's theorization, *Regimes of Desire* examines how the promotion of heteronormativity is similarly "cruel," since Japanese society continues to fundamentally position same-sex attraction as outside the realm of the normal, thus necessitating fantasies of hard hegemonic masculinity that are also never truly attainable.

## Toward a Queer Ethnography of Desire in Shinjuku Ni-chōme

*Regimes of Desire* ultimately interrogates how consuming gay media influences young men's understandings of their desires, critically exploring how desire's political and affective economies resuscitate heteronormative logics and produce homonormative cultures of consumption. I focus upon engagement with media not only because Japan's explicitly gay media represent a significant industry with estimated annual revenues of several trillion yen[135] but also because previous research has indicated that these media represent an important "gateway" for men seeking to understand their same-sex attraction.[136] I draw upon an ethnographic study of media consumption as it is tied to a particular space in Tokyo: Shinjuku Ni-chōme, the historically significant gay district introduced more thoroughly in the following chapter. My methodology couples participant observation and interviews conducted during a number of fieldtrips to Tokyo between 2012 and 2017 with discursive analyses of various gay media content. My analyses of these media texts are situated specifically within a cultural studies framework that critiques the role of power and ideology in the production of cultural representations. Furthermore, following seminal cultural studies theorist Stuart Hall, I recognize that individual consumers of texts "decode" these representations and their politics in culturally situated ways.[137]

This marriage of discursive cultural analyses of media texts and field-based participant observation of Shinjuku Ni-chōme's material environment represents what influential theorist Jack Halberstam terms a "queer methodology." As a "scavenger methodology that uses different methods to collect and produce information on subjects who . . . have been excluded from traditional studies of human behavior,"[138] my mixed-methods approach eschews the fixed and classical methodologies of social scientific practice. Furthermore, my discursive analysis of Japanese gay media takes inspiration from what Louisa Schein has referred to as an "ethnotextual approach," a method that calls for the "close reading" and "situated interpretation" of media texts whereby ethnographic research into the production, distribution, and consumption of texts informs discursive analysis.[139] My textual and discursive analyses are thus intimately tied to the lifeworlds of the young gay men with whom I spoke during my visits to Tokyo, and it is their voices that I channel in my theorization of the regimes of desire at the heart of this book. My arguments are therefore not "clinical," and I am thus not a "social science voyeur" who simply diagnoses what I observe in texts and through participant observation.[140] Rather, as in all good ethnographic projects in which the process of writing the ethnography is an important aspect of the analysis, my theorization in Regimes of Desire relies upon a constant reflexive practice where the development of critical theory is firmly tied to the experiences of those individuals with whom I engaged in the field.[141] The analysis is thus historicized to the life-stories of my interlocutors and situated within the broader historical processes elucidated in this chapter.

Through several recruitment methodologies, including field-based interviews, recruitment via online noticeboards, and snowball sampling, I interviewed for this project a broad sample of 50 young gay men who regularly frequent Shinjuku Ni-chōme. These 50 men were all active in the neighborhood's gay bar culture and were all engaged at the time of first interview in some form of tertiary education (whether vocational college or university). As frequent participants in Tokyo's gay bar culture and as self-professed heavy consumers of various gay media, which they often purchased, these young men all also possessed significant economic capital, and it is safe to say that they were all at least middle class. I focused my recruitment on such young gay men, all in their 20s, because previous analyses by the sociologist Moriyama Noritaka had indicated that such men represented the target audience of the majority of Japan's gay media.[142] Over the seven years that I conducted fieldwork, I interviewed these 50 men once or twice either on the spot in gay bars and clubs, during the day at cafés or family restaurants near Shinjuku Ni-chōme, or sometimes in the evening while walking around the gay district and observing the neighborhood together. Formal interviews with 23 of these men were audio recorded and transcribed for later analysis, but most interviews were simply transcribed in a research journal because they occurred in busy bar environments where recording was not feasible.

While recruitment was initially challenging, my status as a White, gay man facilitated access to one particular population of Japanese gay men—five men who were primarily interested in dating White men (known as *gai-sen* in Japanese gay slang)—and my experiences interviewing this cohort helped build the cultural capital I required to negotiate my entry into other Shinjuku Ni-chōme "scenes." I found that my ability to speak Japanese and the fact that I was of the same age group as many of the men with whom I spoke also encouraged those uninterested in White partners to also participate in the project; the other 45 informants identified as such. Following anthropologist Margot Weiss, I thus mobilized my own queerness as both a non-Japanese outsider and a same-sex desiring man to develop solidarity and rapport with young Japanese gay men based in our shared "queer desires . . . to know and inhabit a different way of thinking, a path of solidarity" that relies on "the vulnerable and queerer work of trying to know another."[143]

Although my analysis throughout *Regimes of Desire* is tied to the interviews with this broad sample of 50 young gay men, I privilege the experiences of four specific key informants with whom I developed significant rapport during my initial fieldwork in 2013—Junho, Yōichi, Haruma, and Shōtarō. These four men's highly subjective understandings of their desires thus ground much of my discursive analysis of the Japanese gay media landscape. My decision to focus on these four men's experiences has less to do with positivist notions of their generalizability than with the fact that these young men's complicated musings concerning desire quickly emerged during fieldwork and writing as central to my own understandings of what I had observed in Shinjuku Ni-chōme. I draw upon these specific young men's experiences since they were intimately tied to my own reflexive processes of theorization. Whereas I sometimes interviewed the other informants only once or twice—it is partly for this reason that I do not name them in the body of my book, since our engagements were often ephemeral—I was able to have numerous formal and informal interviews with Junho, Yōichi, Haruma, and Shōtarō over a period of seven to eight years. In fact, I was able to record and transcribe 17 interviews with these four men, and these interviews strongly guided my analysis of the ideologies of desire appearing in Japan's gay media landscape.

Drawing upon the life-stories of these four young men in particular, my ethnographic analysis adopted a case study approach that focused on the specific individuals and which centered the particularity of their experiences as critical sites for theorization. As has become common in recent cultural anthropological literature, my ethnographic investigation of Shinjuku Ni-chōme thus does not set out to present my field in totalizing, positivist terms. I thus resist the "representational" urge of traditional ethnography and instead engage with a methodology that is sensitive to the lifeworlds of the four principal informants whose experiences naturally emerged as significant to my theorization during both the process of conducting my field observations and writing the subsequent ethnographic analysis. Taking inspiration from anthropologist Tom Gill's ethnographic study of an individual day laborer in Yokohama,[144] I situate the experiences of my four principal informants Junho, Yōichi, Haruma, and Shōtarō within an ethnographic web of media analysis and urban research to theorize how Japanese gay media consumption directly impacts the highly personal and subjective process of conceptualizing same-sex attraction. In so doing, I engage with the radical and transformative power of ethnographic participant observation whereby working closely together with key individuals helps unlock knowledge concerning broader cultural systems.[145] In the spirit of the queer "scavenger methodology" that guides my project, I resist the notion that an ethnography should be generalizable or representative and celebrate the messiness of theory produced through careful attention to four individuals' lives. In chapter 2, I provide more reflections on the nature of this approach to ethnographic analysis that focuses on case study; I also introduce the four key informants' life-stories in that chapter.

As a methodology, ethnography is a fundamentally reflexive practice, and there is recognition in the theoretical literature that the ethnographer is heavily implicated in the production of knowledge through the writing of their fieldwork experiences.[146] Critical reflexivity concerning similarities and differences between the experiences of the researcher and their interlocutors sits at the heart of ethnographic practice and is often where theory is developed. Thus, while my informants and I certainly experienced what Weiss terms "queer solidarity" given our shared same-sex attraction and similar age, I recognize that my cultural experience as a White Australian differs greatly from that of my Japanese informants. But these differences and my cultural ignorance during the initial stages of my fieldwork in Tokyo were highly productive in generating knowledge concerning the Japanese gay media landscape and its ideological privileging of heteronormativity. Furthermore, I undertook an ethnography that was not only longitudinal, working with the four key informants over seven years, but also material and mobile in order to productively address the cultural differences between myself and my interlocutors. My ethnographic practices and the subsequent discursive analysis of media texts were thus informant-led. In particular, I went on "strolling tours" of Shinjuku Ni-chōme together with 16 of my initial informants in July 2013, conducting interviews "on the go" in the district's material environment. It was through this process that I initially learned about the social stratification of desire within the district. As Tamás Szabó and Robert Troyer note, "walking ethnographies" such as this allow researchers to act as a "directive agent in the conversation" who is not "detached from the ongoing situation."[147] Furthermore, walking ethnography also allows both the researcher and participants to lead discussions in a way that respects the informants' role as cocreators of scholarly knowledge.[148] These initial ethnographic experiences helped inform both the later discussions I had with my interlocutors and the ethnotextual analyses of the regimes of desire that condition knowledge about same-sex attraction within the Japanese gay media landscape.

## Structure of the Book

I now present a brief overview of the book. Chapter 1 analyzes Shinjuku Ni-chōme's role as a discursive space that propagates the heteronormative understandings of desirability and masculinity structuring Japan's gay media landscape. I especially interrogate how this impacts young gay men's attitudes toward the space and their use of it through my ethnographic interactions with the 50 informants whom I interviewed over several research trips to the district. In focusing upon the regimes of desire that circulate throughout the district, and which these young gay men consume, I pay attention to the role of a socio-semiotic system known as "Typing" (*taipu*) in the production of knowledge about sexuality, gender, and desirability. In chapter 2, I introduce the psychobiographies of Junho, Yōichi, Haruma, and Shōtarō to explore the role that visiting Shinjuku Ni-chōme and consuming gay media played in the development of their understandings of their gay desires and identities. I argue that while all four men first came to experience same-sex attraction through a process of "awakening" tied to their *hatsukoi* (first loves), Japanese gay media quickly came to influence their attitudes to their gay desires. I also explore the four principal informants' patterns of gay media consumption, arguing that their consumption is typified by high levels of convergence across genre and media platform. Chapter 3 then turns to explore and problematize the valorization of hard masculinity in Shinjuku Ni-chōme, critically examining how the regimes of desire that circulate throughout both the neighborhood and the broader Japanese gay media landscape have led to a retreat into fantasies of a lost masculine past to cope with the rise of a supposed soft masculinity in mainstream society.

Chapter 4 specifically examines the four principal informants' consumption of Japanese gay pornographic videos, known colloquially in Japanese as "GV." I demonstrate through an investigation of the four men's patterns of pornographic consumption that Junho, Yōichi, Haruma, and Shōtarō did not initially view Typing as a locus for identification but rather as a way to categorize individuals based upon their physicality. I suggest that through their consumption of pornography, the four men became aware that desire for "heteronormatively masculine" gay men is considered normative in Shinjuku Ni-chōme and explore the implications of this on the four men's initial understandings of their desires and identities. Importantly, I also reflect on how consuming GV instills the idea that this heteronormative masculine ideal represents a supposed "Japanese" expression of gay masculinity among the men I interviewed. Chapter 5 then focuses on the four principal informants' consumption of *Bádi* magazine, exploring how their experiences with this print media introduced them to the idea that Typing could represent a locus for individual and community identity creation. I examine how consuming *Bádi* reinforced the regimes of desire and led the informants to interpret the commodified lifestyles promoted within the magazine as representative of the *ikanimo-kei*.

In chapter 6, I explore the four principal informants' use of online dating services to understand the limits of agency within the marketplace of desire; I further investigate the informants' attitudes toward online dating and their need to strategically manage their identities online. First, I examine the representational strategies adopted by users of online dating services in Japan through a case study of the gay dating site JP MEN'S CLUB and demonstrate that gay men in Japan are required to situate their identities within highly rigid meta-discourses of "hunkiness" (*sawayaka*) and "cuteness" (*kawaii*). I then explore the principal informants' use of location-based dating apps in Shinjuku Ni-chōme and reveal that the choice of a particular service is also read as revealing one's Type. In chapter 6, I also briefly reflect on how the Japanese gay media landscape's regimes of desire produce ideologies concerning the intersections of race and sexuality in Shinjuku Ni-chōme.

In the conclusion, I then reinterpret the analysis presented in the previous chapters through Berlant's theory of cruel optimism. In so doing, I draw upon later stages of my fieldwork conducted after the 2015 LGBT boom to investigate how young gay men are challenging the heteronormative regimes of desire that contour knowledge of gay identity in Shinjuku Ni-chōme via new discourses based in aspirations and hopes for a better future.

This chapter has detailed the ideologies of sex and gender that have produced fantasies for heteronormative masculinity in Japan's gay media. Throughout this book, I argue that these heteronormative understandings are promoted as desirable through various regimes of desire circulating through the Japanese gay media landscape, influencing how young gay men who frequent Tokyo's "gay town" of Shinjuku Ni-chōme conceptualize their same-sex attraction. Through the discursive analyses of gay pornographic films, magazines, manga, and online dating services, which I present in the following chapters, I elucidate how the figure of the heterosexual male is fetishized in Japanese gay cultural production and reveal how this fetishization specifically situates discourses of desirability within a heteronormative gendered binary that valorizes hard masculinity. Ultimately, *Regimes of Desire* reveals that homonormative practices promoted in Japanese gay media have limited the agency of young gay men, and it explores why men such as Shōtarō whose experiences opened this book continue to turn to fantasies of heteronormative masculinity to make sense of their positioning within contemporary Japanese society.

ONE

# Shinjuku Ni-chōme
## *Typing, Media, and the Commodification of Desire*

In this chapter, I draw upon my participant observation of media consumption in Shinjuku Ni-chōme and my initial discursive analyses of gay media to explore the role that a socio-semiotic system known as "Typing" plays in the management of desire in Japan's gay culture. I draw upon strolling interviews with sixteen young gay men to present a preliminary investigation of the regimes of desire that inculcate heteronormative attachments to "hard" masculinity among frequent visitors to the district. In so doing, I lay the groundwork for the more sophisticated analyses of heteronormativity and homonormativity presented in later chapters of this book. Typing, this chapter reveals, is central to how young gay men who visit Shinjuku Ni-chōme conceptualize their same-sex attraction under conditions of neoliberalism wherein desire becomes explicitly commoditized for the purposes of economic exploitation and capitalist accumulation.[1] Before launching into this analysis, however, I first draw upon numerous "intercept interviews"[2] with many young gay men that I conducted in gay bars and other venues between 2012 and 2017 to paint a picture of Shinjuku Ni-chōme's importance to Japan's gay culture. I reveal that Ni-chōme, as the district is affectionately known, broadly operates as a "queer space" that supports same-sex attraction, providing gay men an escape from the relentless heteronormativity of mainstream Japanese society. That being said, within this chapter I then nuance the overtly emancipatory readings of Ni-chōme that have tended to dominate Japanese-language scholarship on the district. I thereby complicate the emancipatory potentials of this communal space through my discussion of Typing and its links to the heteronormative regimes of desire that circulate throughout the Japanese gay media landscape.

## *Shinjuku Ni-chōme as a Queer Space*

Nestled between Yasukuni-dōri to the north and Shinjuku-gyōen Park to the south, Ni-chōme is a city block (*chōme*) to the east of Shinjuku railway station, depicted in figure 1. In the early morning, the streets of Ni-chōme are relatively quiet, populated only by the previous night's revelers. By noon, gay businesses open, and the district begins to get a little livelier. But it is in the evening that the neighborhood is at its busiest, when gay men from all over Tokyo and outlying regions visit Ni-chōme to socialize together in the various drinking establishments. These bars are highly important to the structuring of Ni-chōme, for the district purportedly contains the highest concentration of gay bars in the world. Sociologist Ishida Hitoshi estimates that there are approximately 300 exclusively gay bars in the neighborhood.[3] Upon emerging from exit C8 of Shinjuku San-chōme subway station, the standard entrance or "gateway" to Ni-chōme, one comes across not only gay bars but also bookshops, host clubs, sex entertainment venues, DVD stores, love hotels, massage parlors, and saunas, all catering to a gay male clientele. Other businesses and organizations found in the district include a community health center named akta, which is highly active in HIV advocacy, as well as convenience stores, coffee shops, and family-style and ethnic restaurants catering to both the district's residents and its gay visitors.

In the contemporary mainstream imaginary, Ni-chōme is quintessentially linked to Japanese gay culture. This is despite the fact that in the early postwar years, the neighborhood was set aside for female sex workers, known as "pan-pan girls," who were frequented primarily by American soldiers.[4] Thus, historically, Ni-chōme initially emerged as a heterosexual pleasure district. As a result of the Anti-Prostitution Law of 1958, however, the pan-pan establishments of Ni-chōme were forced to close.[5] Their closure led individuals "who found that the long established 'hidden' nature of the district worked in favour of those who wished to keep their sexuality secret" to open businesses catering to same-sex attracted men in their stead.[6] Since the 1970s, Ni-chōme has represented not only Tokyo's but also Japan's most visible and important "gay town" (*gei no machi*), and it has developed notoriety in mainstream media as a salacious "hidden district" for gay men to pursue their supposedly hedonistic pleasures.[7] While mainstream media often narrowly focuses on the district as a space where sex between men is negotiated, gay activist Ōtsuka Takeshi's mem-

Figure 1. Shinjuku Ni-chōme (used under Google creative commons license).

oir highlights that Ni-chōme more importantly represents a site for developing friendship networks and community support systems among gay men.[8] Even today, there is more to the district than the simple pursuit of sex, although sexual encounters were privileged by some of the young men I interviewed.

The development of this gay district, as can be seen above, is intimately tied to the development of Japan's postwar marketplace. The emergence of Ni-chōme thus echoes broader trends within the history of gay male spaces in North America where the development of urban markets in major cities played a crucial role in the development of sexual minority community cultures.[9] As John D'Emilio argues in his seminal history of the emergence of homosexual identities in North America, the development of industrial capitalism and the concomitant urbanization of society divorced sex from the private sphere, as both working and sexual lives became separated from the home.[10] This allowed same-sex desiring men and women to explore their desires in public urban settings, and a number of businesses—particularly bars and clubs in cheaper ghettos throughout major cities such as New York and San Francisco—emerged to cater to this new market. These queer urban centers only grew during the immediate postwar period as migration to urban centers increasingly became the norm within the United States. Cities therefore became linked to a queer imaginary of liberation within which urban centers were understood as spaces that facilitated the exploration of same-sex desire. It is important, however, to note that queer districts that emerged throughout this period faced increasing surveillance and suppression from police because of the criminalization of sex between individuals of the same sex.[11] Throughout the 1990s, as queer rights became increasingly mainstream via the enactment of various public ordinances designed to protect same-sex desiring individuals in public, queer districts, or "gayborhoods," have emerged as central to the economic lives of major US cities and have even become important tourist attractions.[12] This process has, according to Alexandra Chasin, co-opted the traditionally radical nature of queer urban space and developed a neoliberalized gay culture that simply promotes consumption divorced from politics. For Chasin, this neoliberalization is the driving force behind the collapse in recent years of "gayborhoods" throughout the United States, many of which are increasingly "disappearing" because of rising gentrification driven by middle-class desires to move into "hip" gay neighborhoods.[13] While Ni-chōme has yet to face such challenges, it is very clear that a similar neoliberal culture of consumption has emerged in the neighborhood.

Figure 2. Advertisements on the walls of Lumière in Ni-chōme (April 2017).

Like most districts in Tokyo, Ni-chōme is saturated with advertising media, some of which targets mainstream, putatively heterosexual audiences (principally found along the fringes of Ni-chōme) and some of which directly targets a gay male audience. An example of such advertising targeting gay men can be found in figure 2. Most of the media that constitute the Japanese gay media landscape—magazines, pornographic videos, advertising, websites, social networking services, and other print, video, and digital media—are visible and obtainable in Ni-chōme. There are also many guides to the area online, and people frequently come to the district because of their interaction with this online media. Overall, Ni-chōme appears typical of the *sakariba* entertainment districts integral to the development of Japan's mass consumer culture, in which everything from food to leisure to sex and intimacy is for sale.[14] As a *sakariba*, Ni-chōme is ultimately a space where desire is commoditized.[15]

Gay bars are crucial to Ni-chōme's status as a *sakariba*, providing spaces where gay men may socialize and seek advice and aid from others under a limited anonymity. Interviews with the young gay men I met in these bars over the years revealed that they do indeed view the bar culture of Ni-chōme incredibly positively. The men variously described the gay bars as possessing a "gay feeling" (*gei no kanji*) or "gay resonance" (*gei no hibiki*), revealing a particularly affective relationship with Ni-chōme as a male homosocial space that provided them comfort and support. The district as a whole represents an important safe space for Japan's stigmatized queer communities, and many young men described Ni-chōme during interviews as their *ibasho*, a space where they feel they belong. In his longitudinal ethnography of the district's gay bars, anthropologist and activist Sunagawa Hideki also presents Ni-chōme as the gay community's *ibasho*, contending that the production of spaces where gay desire is welcomed and supported renders the district a utopic space where all gay identities ultimately become socially acceptable.[16] Sunagawa explicitly contrasts this with Tokyo's wider cityscape, which he argues overwhelmingly disenfranchises queer subjectivities through the normalization of heterosexual desire.[17] For Sunagawa, Ni-chōme is thus a "communal space" where gay men go to "share their lives."[18]

In an earlier literary study, queer theorist Katsuhiko Suganuma developed similar ideas to Sunagawa, examining how Ni-chōme is utilized as a discursive trope in the production of knowledge concerning public space and public values in two explicitly "gay" texts.[19] He highlights that Ni-chōme is utilized throughout a guidebook and a gay activist's memoirs to criticize heteronormative values and to demonstrate how public space can be reappropriated by sexual minorities in order to create safe spaces.[20] Suganuma persuasively argues that Ni-chōme provides a site from which "to challenge the structures that configure non-normative sexualities as perverted,"[21] suggesting that the district typifies what Lauren Berlant and Michael Warner term "queer counterpublic space." According to Berlant and Warner, queer counterpublic spaces such as Ni-chōme are visible platforms from which sexual minorities challenge the social systems that implicitly mark their desires as deviant, perverse, and dangerous to public morality.[22] In the terms of Sara Ahmed's phenomenological conceptualization of queerness, Ni-chōme thus represents a "surface" upon which orientations that deviate from heteronormativity can flow, producing liberating affects among same-sex desiring individuals.[23] As a queer counterpublic space, Ni-chōme thus represents a liminal space that emerges through social processes challenging the default, heteronormative nature of urban space through the "unsanctioned" use and subversion of space by those who are excluded from full participation in the public sphere.[24] Ni-chōme is ultimately a "queer space" that affirms same-sex desire, although Suganuma cautions that "there are diverse interpretations of the space according to numerous points of view."[25]

For many, Ni-chōme represents more than just a "gay neighborhood" in Tokyo but also operates as a broader symbol that represents a suppos-edly "national" gay culture. Sunagawa notes in his ethnography of the dis-trict that links made between Ni-chōme and the struggle for gay men's rights in Japan solidified in the early 2000s as a result of prominent pride events hosted within the neighborhood, including the Rainbow Festival of 2002 and the recent Tokyo Rainbow Pride events of the late 2010s.[26] Noting that the neighborhood has increasingly come to be ideologically mobilized within LGBT activist work surrounding "gay community" in Japan, Sunagawa reinforces a narrative I often encountered during field-work, that the district could act as a "model" for the rest of Japan's stigma-tized queer communities.[27] This narrative evokes a common trend within Japanese culture whereby the experiences of Tokyo as the nation's "metro-politan center" come to be privileged as representative of Japan itself.[28] For activists and theorists like Sunagawa, Ni-chōme thus sits at the heart of a broader Japanese gay culture that responds to the ideologies produced and circulated within the district. On the other hand, sociologist Jane Wallace's recent work among LGBT activists in the Kansai region of western Japan has suggested that while the knowledge produced in metropolitan urban centers such as Ni-chōme may be privileged outside Tokyo, it does not always reflect the experiences of LGBT individuals living in other areas of Japan.[29] For this reason, the positioning of Ni-chōme as a "national sym-bol" for gay culture should be viewed with skepticism, even if the men I met in Ni-chōme accepted the district's role as a "model" for the rest of Japan without question.

There have been some studies that have revealed a darker side to Ni-chōme and that have also sought to demonstrate that the district may hin-der the development of a comprehensive and progressive queer activist community. For instance, Wim Lunsing has suggested that since the focus of Ni-chōme is to provide a space for gay men to "play around," the district is not ideally situated to allow for the development of a robust and dynamic gay community that can truly subvert Japanese society's inherent hetero-normativity.[30] Lunsing highlights excessive consumerism as key to Ni-chōme's inability to make meaningful interventions that could potentially push forward LGBT inclusivity in wider society.[31] Ryū Susumu, one of the editors of the 1970s *homo* magazine *Barazoku*, has likewise criticized the rampant consumerism characteristic of contemporary Ni-chōme, arguing that the district is becoming "clubified" (*kurabu-ka*).[32] Ryū has also controversially contended that young Japanese gay men, who have grown up in an age when their desires can easily be satisfied over the internet, fail to respect and acknowledge the importance of the district's history.[33] Ryū ultimately believes that Ni-chōme is in danger of disappearing because of a newly emergent focus on the hedonistic pursuit of pleasure among the gay bars' clienteles, leading to a decline in supportive communication between gay men.[34]

While the majority of the young gay men I interviewed over the years did not generally criticize Ni-chōme along these lines, they did feel anxious about the district's future. During my 2013 fieldwork, for instance, some expressed a fear of "losing" Ni-chōme after the Tokyo Metropolitan Government announced that a "clean up" of Shinjuku was necessary in preparation for the Summer Olympic Games, originally scheduled to be held in Tokyo in 2020.[35] It was not clear to me who exactly would be "stealing" Ni-chōme in these informants' narratives, and I believe these fears are not necessarily directed at any specific group. Rather, these anxieties represent an existential fear that has emerged from the precarious nature of living as a young gay man in Japan's increasingly isolating and alienating society.[36] Sensitivity to potential processes of social exclusion within Ni-chōme was thus borne out of these individuals' existential dread, and I interviewed many young men—although not representing most of my interlocutors—who questioned the district's status as a gay utopia. Specifically, some men, while broadly viewing Ni-chōme as an important space in Tokyo that supported their gay desires, questioned the notion that all desires are considered equal within the district's bars. To lay the groundwork for an investigation of these conflicting attitudes, I now turn to an ethnographic description of a typical day in Ni-chōme to explain the role gay media plays in structuring the district as a queer space.

*Media and the Emergence of Queer Space:*
*A "Typical" Day in Ni-chōme*

The following ethnographic vignette presents a typical visit to Ni-chōme which is drawn from a compilation of my own observations, the strolling interviews I conducted with 16 young gay men in July 2013, and the reported experiences of other men I met in gay bars over the duration of this project. While there is no single experience of the area, the composite description I present here demonstrates the liminality of Ni-chōme and its media as they change during the day. These quotidian changes have an important impact on the media that are visible within the space and are thus important to the broader arguments concerning how desire is discursively circulated throughout the Japanese gay media landscape. From midday, Ni-chōme transforms from a sleepy quarter of the larger Shinjuku area into a highly concentrated space for gay men. I argue that this transitionary period is intimately linked to media. Indeed, right from its awakening, gay media play an important role in the social organization of the district as Ni-chōme emerges as a queer space.

During the daylight morning hours, Ni-chōme is relatively quiet and deserted until approximately noon. According to a group of men with whom I strolled through the district one morning, there is very little about Ni-chōme that "feels gay" at this time and the district is practically indistinguishable from the other parts of Shinjuku that surround it. Many men explained that, during the morning, Ni-chōme formed part of the "normal world" (*futsū no sekai*) as opposed to "this world" (*kono sekai*). "Normal" (*futsū*) is typically utilized as a euphemism to discuss the wider heteronormative society of heterosexual men and women and does not index an "abnormality" in the gay community as such.[37] On the other hand, gay men commonly utilize *kono sekai* to refer to the Japanese gay culture in a way that somewhat hides its queer status,[38] implicitly marking the space as the gay community's *ibasho* through explicit world-building that separates the space from so-called "normal" society.

At approximately five o'clock in the morning, a group of people whom the young men termed "normal people" (*futsū no kata*) start to enter the district on their way to work. Although some gay men are present in the area during the morning—mostly stragglers from the previous night's entertainments—the vast majority of people passing through the district appear to be on their way to the office buildings that surround Ni-chōme or are heading to the subway station located on the district's southwestern periphery. One man in his late 40s that I intercepted one morning in 2013 to ask about his perception of the district, and who insisted quite strongly that he was a "normal" heterosexual salaryman, stated that he felt a need to rush through Ni-chōme each morning on his way to work. He explained that he did so to avoid the stigma of being in a gay area despite living nearby and passing through every day. This demonstrates that, despite the fact that during the morning gay men may view the space as not yet part of "their world," heterosexual men passing through the district may view it as such and use the term "normal" to position themselves positively against Ni-chōme as a potentially dangerous and perverted "gay" space. In fact, young gay men described Ni-chōme in the morning to me as forming part of the "normal world" due to the presence of such people. Within this sleepy district, however, a potentiality for a queer space exists, and the group of gay men with whom I strolled together through the district one morning reported that the "true" Ni-chōme lies underneath the surface of this "normal" space.

From morning until noon, very few of Ni-chōme's gay businesses are open to customers, although there are sometimes preparations occurring behind closed doors. The streets are almost deserted, and few people can be found on Naka-dōri, the district's main street. Some are gay men who are loitering in the district and who will start work later in the afternoon. At noon, however, the *gei shoppu*—some of the most important businesses in the district—open for business. The *gei shoppu*, a Japanese rendering of "gay shop,"[39] can chiefly be found on Naka-dōri or on the corner of Naka-dōri and one of the many alleys that crisscross Ni-chōme. These stores represent the chief distributors of two important media within the Japanese gay media landscape: gay magazines and pornographic DVDs. They also sell queer literature, adult toys, exotic underwear, and a variety of other bric-a-brac as well as maintaining noticeboards where one can collect pamphlets concerning that week's latest gay club events.

The importance of these businesses to Ni-chōme is indexed not just by their physical centrality in the district but also by the importance placed on knowing how to navigate *gei shoppu* presented within Japan's gay literature. A representative example of such a discourse can be found in gay activist Fushimi Noriaki's *Introduction to Homosexuality*, where *gei shoppu* are described as places to find "positive resources" to educate oneself and others about "the experience called being gay."[40] Describing such stores as the "heart of the district," one store owner argued that most *gei shoppu* are centrally located in Ni-chōme because visiting these establishments to buy gay media represents many men's primary reason to come to the neighborhood. Speaking in front of Lumière, the largest *gei shoppu* in Ni-chōme (pictured in figure 2), one man in his late 20s informed me that if there were no *gei shoppu* in Ni-chōme, he would never visit the district. Another man I spoke to near Check, a smaller *gei shoppu* a few doors down from Lumière, said that he "didn't have the courage to visit gay bars."

The *gei shoppu*, he explained, were the only places where he could satisfy his desire "to look at attractive men" in a safe space. Many men substantiated the initial store owner's claims that visiting *gei shoppu* was central to any visit to Ni-chōme. One young man even mentioned that he could not imagine coming to the district and not "dropping by Lumière" to flip through gay magazines and check out the newest gay pornographic video releases. Another pointed out that some *gei shoppu* such as Lumière acted as "cruising sites" where men can meet other men and arrange to have sex in one of the many love hotels in Ni-chōme. Fushimi also makes note of this practice, arguing that their use as cruising grounds adds another layer of importance to *gei shoppu* as sites for gay male socialization.[41]

Generally, when the *gei shoppu* open at noon, the shop clerks place posters and flyers promoting the latest issues of magazines or pornographic films into the streets. These advertisements are forms of explicit gay media that frame the *gei shoppu* as spaces for gay men, typically featuring images of men in various stages of undress in highly eroticized poses. Furthermore, the sexually explicit nature of the advertisements signals to the men who visit Ni-chōme that the *gei shoppu* represent spaces where one's sexual desires may be satisfied through purchasing their goods. Over the years I visited Ni-chōme, I often observed men unassumingly strolling through the district suddenly make beelines for various *gei shoppu* when these advertisements were placed in the streets. At around two to three o'clock in the afternoon, more advertising begins to fill the sidewalks of Naka-dōri and the surrounding alleys as workers from the hundreds of bars in the neighborhood set up impermanent advertising noticeboards that promote their services for the evening. These impermanent boards, similar to the advertising put out by *gei shoppu* earlier, often feature shirtless and heavily muscled men in salacious poses. According to men with whom I walked through the neighborhood streets in the afternoon, the setting up of this advertising ultimately signals the moment when Ni-chōme emerges out of the "normal world" as a queer space.

These same informants explained that they viewed advertising media for gay businesses, the majority of which feature highly sexualized images of the male body, as integral to the status of Ni-chōme as a space for gay men. Young gay men view gay media—particularly advertising media that is sexually explicit—as the feature of Ni-chōme that most drastically differentiates the district from the rest of the heteronormative cityscape. This is because Tokyo represents a space where sexualized images of the female body are incredibly prevalent, with highly sexually suggestive images of women plastering the walls of buildings, covering the advertising found on trains, and permeating popular media such as television serials, anime cartoons, and manga comics.[42] Although my informants understood the domination of Ni-chōme by heterosexual men and women during the morning as detracting from the district's status as a queer space, they often considered this as causing less of an impact than the lack of explicitly gay images. The gradual influx of gay media transforms the district into a space specifically for gay men, allowing the "true" Ni-chōme mentioned above to emerge from the "normal world."

From approximately six o'clock in the evening until nine o'clock, Ni-chōme becomes increasingly crowded as gay men converge on the bars to relax, meet friends, drink and dance, or search for dates. After nine o'clock, however, the district truly comes alive as the Ni-chōme regulars descend on the neighborhood to, as one such regular put it, "party the night away." This is particularly true of Friday and Saturday nights, when Ni-chōme is at its loudest and busiest. It is during the evening that the young gay men who represent the target audience of most Japanese gay media—and the specific focus of this book—descend on the district. These young men congregate in groups in the street, and men of all age groups frequenting the larger venues centrally located along Naka-dōri spill out into the street during the warmer months, giving the whole district a carnivalesque atmosphere. The emergence of Ni-chōme from the "normal world" is now completed through the domination of the space by the bodies of gay men and explicit gay media. Many of these men identify as "regulars" (*onajimi*) at various establishments and often head straight to their favorite bars to meet friends or search for romance and sex. Other men instead come to the district equipped with information gleaned off the internet, particularly social media services such as Twitter. They also make heavy use of location-based dating apps on their smartphones to quickly meet other men present in the district.

Indeed, use of gay dating apps such as the US-produced Grindr and Jack'd or the Japan-produced 9monsters is incredibly prevalent in Ni-chōme among all age groups, augmenting socialization and connecting men in the district virtually. Social media services such as Twitter and Instagram, as well as instant messenger apps such as LINE, are also interestingly repurposed as "hookup" apps by some of the gay men I observed. These online media services are also utilized for a very specific purpose central to the social practices of young gay men: to track *hayatteru ikemen*, "hot trending guys" who move through the bars and clubs of Ni-chōme. *Hayatteru ikemen* represent attractive men who have developed a certain celebrity among those who frequently visit Ni-chōme. Examples of *hayatteru ikemen* who were active during my fieldwork in 2013 included many of the erotic dancers from the gay club event Shangri-La@AgeHa, the gay pornstar Koh Masaki and his Chinese boyfriend Tian Tian, and various gay male models who had appeared on the cover of *Bádi* magazine. *Hayatteru ikemen* often use Twitter, Facebook, and Instagram to promote their lifestyles to others, and many of these young men have amassed large social media followings. *Hayatteru ikemen* are thus similar to so-called media influencers, "everyday internet users who accumulate large followings on blogs and social media through the textual and visual narration of their personal lives and lifestyles."[43]

During busy Friday and Saturday nights, young men working for various bars and clubs circulate throughout Ni-chōme distributing flyers advertising parties and special events. Besides advertising material, the gay bars themselves are also filled with gay media, and many of the prominently located bars on Naka-dōri contain small libraries of gay magazines and literature. Some smaller bars have one or two issues of gay magazines such as *Bádi* and *G-Men*, and some bars even have pornography available. One prominent venue that is renowned for its large amount of advertising material is CoCoLo Café, a café centrally located on the intersection of Naka-dōri and Hanazono-dōri. In fact, this café is referred to as "a sort of information center for Ni-chōme" in a Japanese-English bilingual guidebook written by Morimura Akio.[44] Figure 3 presents a typical example of a pamphlet advertising an event at a gay club just outside Ni-chōme, sponsored by the international gay dating site Manhunt.net. Many men arrive in the district in the evening and draw upon such advertising to orientate themselves around the various events occurring that night in Ni-chōme. Importantly, one man I met in CoCoLo Café indicated that he would scan these pamphlets to assess whether the pictured models were desirable, and this assessment would determine whether he would subsequently visit the bar or event. It was not only young gay men in their 20s whom I observed reading these advertisements, but men of all age groups. While this practice was extremely common when I first began conducting fieldwork in December 2012 and in mid-2013, the practice had somewhat declined by 2015 as online social media increasingly came to replace the importance of physical advertisements such as that depicted in figure 3.

At midnight, there is a mass exodus from the district as men hurry to catch the last train at Shinjuku San-chōme subway station. Many men,

Figure 3. Pamphlet advertising a gay club event, collected in Ni-chōme during a July 2013 research trip.

predominantly those in their 20s but also of other age groups, continue to party in the district. After the bars have closed, from around three o'clock in the morning until five o'clock, those men remaining in Ni-chōme typically congregate in the *gei shoppu*—many of which remain open until five in the morning—or in 24-hour convenience stores or family restaurants to kill time. Some take a room at one of the various low-cost "love hotels" in the district. One such venue, 24 Kaikan, is also a notorious cruising ground, and some men spend the late evening and early morning hours searching for sex in this establishment, usually with the aid of gay dating apps. Many men choose to walk to Shinjuku station and spend their time waiting in the station district to the west or Kabuki-chō to the north, as these spaces have comparatively more 24-hour establishments than Ni-chōme. According to some informants with whom I strolled away from Ni-chōme during this early morning period, it felt like they must return once again to the "normal world" where they are required to suppress or hide their same-sex attraction. This causes feelings of disorientation, and one man went so far as to describe it as "traumatic" as we walked together toward Shinjuku station one early morning. As the gay men leave the bars for the first train, and as "normal people" begin to increasingly enter and dominate the space, staff at gay businesses throughout the district quickly take in their advertising boards, returning Ni-chōme's outer appearance to that of a standard residential district in inner Tokyo.

### "There Is No Rubbish Thrown Away in Ni-chōme": Is Ni-chōme a Gay Utopia?

The ebb and flow of gay media, and the emergence of queer space, is ultimately cyclical, repeated every day with very little variation. It is evident that two kinds of establishment—the *gei shoppu* and the gay bars—play a crucial role in producing a sense of queer space. Building upon the ethnographic vignette presented above, I now turn to the examination of my 50 interlocutors' specific attitudes to the district and the role Typing plays in contouring knowledge about desire within both the bars and clubs of Ni-chōme specifically and the Japanese gay media landscape more broadly.

Japanese queer literature has tended to promote Ni-chōme as a utopic safe space where all gay identities are validated. Guidebooks written for newcomers to the neighborhood often advise those who are nervous about visiting the district for the first time that "no rubbish is thrown away in Ni-chōme" (*Ni-chōme ni suteru gomi nashi*),[45] a phrase that a number of men also enthusiastically said to me during fieldwork in the neighborhood. Use of the phrase "rubbish" here is ironic and humorous: it reappropriates mainstream discourse that positions Ni-chōme as a "rubbish bin" within which perverts are thrown and instead emphasizes that the space is accepting of all whom society positions as outside the normal. Further, as one young man explained to me, this humorous phrase ultimately suggests that since all desires and men are accepted, Ni-chōme is not truly a "rubbish bin" but is instead a supportive environment for same-sex attracted men. Within guidebooks, and for many young gay men active in the district, the existence of gay bars that cater to men who desire all kinds of clientele thus renders Ni-chōme a space where all desires are accepted. A representative example of this utopic discourse can be found in *Guiding Your Friends Around Shinjuku Ni-chōme in English*, a Japanese-English bilingual guidebook written by the gay activist Morimura Akio. Morimura introduces both foreigners and Japanese "newcomers" alike to the vast number of "Types" to which the bars cater through the following dialogue between two fictional characters:

MIHO: The gay world sure runs deeper than I thought, what with people's preferences (*konomi no taipu*) being broken down by age and body type and all that!

MASASHI: And that's not the end of the story, by any means. There's also the wolf fetish (*okami-sen*) for slim but hairy types, and the bear fetish (*kuma-sen*) for fat, hairy guys . . . the suits fetish (*sūtsu-sen*) for guys who wear suits . . . [and] there's even an "anybody's okay" fetish (*dare-sen*) for guys who will sleep with anyone![46]

The guidebook goes to great pains to indicate that even "overweight men" (*debu*) and "old geezers" (*oyaji*) have a niche in Ni-chōme and thus should not be considered "rubbish."[47] For both foreigners and Japanese newcomers, the book stresses that "the Japanese gay world is broken down into unique communities representing people's different preferences (*konomi no taipu*) . . . even drinking establishments and events," but cautions that it is "unusual to meet people outside one's sphere."[48] The wealth of Types visible in the Japanese gay media landscape is truly staggering, but some of the most commonly visible include *ikanimo-kei* (Obviously Gay Type), *kawaii-kei* (Cute Type), *janīzu-kei* (Johnny's Type, who resemble the idols managed by the Johnny's and Associates talent agency), *debu-*

*kei* (Chubby Type), *gaten-kei* (Physical Laborer Type), and *oyaji-kei* (Old Geezer Type). There are also so-called *gai-sen*, or "Foreigner Specialists," who prefer White, Western men and whom I discuss in more depth below, and *uri-sen*, who have sex with others for money.

During my fieldwork, I encountered a diversity of attitudes toward Ni-chōme among men who regularly frequented gay bars in the district. There were men who, similar to the stance explored above, believed that Ni-chōme represents a space where "no garbage is dumped"; they linked this idea to a democratic ideal where the commercialization of desire via bars catering to many varied Types ultimately promoted the creation of spaces where all identities would become desirable, at least to someone. There were other men who, echoing Ryū Susumu's critique,[49] believed that the increasing prevalence of sexually explicit imagery in the Japanese gay media landscape and heavy use of gay dating apps led to a sense of emotional superficiality, an eroding of ties between gay men and, ultimately, the social weakening of the gay community. Most of the young gay men to whom I spoke in Ni-chōme believed that the heavy concentration of media in the area for purchase and consumption "facilitated their exploration of their desires by providing resources they could draw upon to make sense of the Japanese gay culture. For these men, Ni-chōme represented a symbol of Japan's broader national gay culture since the media produced and distributed in the neighborhood was consumed across the rest of the country. There were, however, a few men with more ambivalent attitudes toward the area who were highly reflective about their participation in the district, rationalizing their presence there because of a perceived lack of other venues for gay men to gather in Tokyo. This latter group of critical men included two of my principal informants, Shōtarō and Haruma, whose experiences form the basis of the discussions found in the latter half of this book.

Most young gay men I interviewed viewed Ni-chōme as saturated with erotic, pornographic gay media. During a strolling interview one evening in 2013, I asked a group of three men to walk together with me through the neighborhood and show me just how prevalent advertisements containing semi-naked men truly were. As we walked through the space and I catalogued ads covered with men striking salacious poses, exposing their heavily muscular bodies, one of the young men explained to me that he believed all the media found in the district was becoming increasingly "pornographified" (*poruno-ka sareta*). This young man evoked Brian McNair's theory of pornographication, "the process whereby the once heavily stigmatized cultural form we call pornography has become fashionable" and is "routinely referenced, pastiched, parodied, analysed and paid tribute to" in traditionally nonpornographic media.[50] As I strolled through Ni-chōme with my three interlocutors, and later in bars as I browsed social media together with other young men, it certainly appeared true that Japan's gay media landscape had been saturated with pornographied content. According to my interviews, the majority of young gay men in Ni-chōme appeared to embrace pornographication as an empowering tool for self-discovery, just as young people have done in other national contexts.[51] There was a significant minority of young men, however, who viewed pornographication as leading to the erosion of romance and of a sense of gay community. Many young men explained that the prevalence of pornography both online and in print media also educated them about the specific vocabulary needed to discuss their desires in meaningful ways. Learning this vocabulary not only allowed these men to distinguish between different Types when speaking with others, it also provided them with a way to express their own desires. Furthermore, some men explained that the increasingly pornographic media found within Ni-chōme informed them how they can satisfy their desires, teaching them about sexual practice. As one man put it, somewhat naively, "I love porn because it teaches me how to fuck like a pro, and I can bring that back [to Ni-chōme] and to my sex friends."

Young gay men active in Ni-chōme's bar culture mostly believed that the pornographication of the Japanese gay media landscape created a space where any desire can become legitimate. These men presented Ni-chōme as a model for other "gay towns" across Japan to follow, although when I asked them why they thought this, many admitted that they did not have experiences traveling to other gay towns. In a representative example from my fieldwork, one informant with whom I wandered through the district as the *gei shoppu* opened in the afternoon pointed out a poster depicting an older, overweight male sensuously rubbing his hands over his naked body as evidence that Ni-chōme's pornographied media landscape targeted niche tastes such as *debu-kei*. This man repeated the discourse found in Japan's gay media concerning the equality of Typing, that "no rubbish may be thrown away" in Ni-chōme, although he candidly admitted that he personally preferred "muscular" men. This young man's logic stated that the commoditization of niche Types through pornographied media has led to an increase in visibility and acceptance, suggesting that desire had itself been democratized.[52] Another man in his late 20s suggested to me in 2013, during a conversation outside the *gei shoppu* Lumière, that the plurality of Types visible in Ni-chōme not only allows gay men to understand the niche within which their own desires sit but also gives them the knowledge necessary to make judgments about other peoples' desires. To a certain extent, he argued, the visibility of numerous Types provides men with the ability to read traits such as physicality, clothing, and hairstyle as a "symbol" of the Type to which another man belongs. For young gay men who visit Ni-chōme, Typing thus ultimately acted as a semiotic code that they deployed to classify desire.

## Commoditized Desire: Typing and the Marketization of Gay Identity

In her ethnographic study of the host clubs in Kabuki-chō, Shinjuku's most (in)famous *sakariba*, anthropologist Akiko Takeyama argues that during the culmination of Japan's economic miracle in the 1980s, Tokyo became "a 'hyper' urban stage, where actors ranging from political leaders to pop stars to consumers project[ed] politico-economic interests and sociocultural fantasies."[53] For Takeyama, the city itself has been rendered "an object of consumption," with *sakariba* entertainment districts representing sites where sexual pleasure, fantasy, and the erotic have become fetishized commodities.[54] This forms part of a broader social process that emerged after the collapse of the bubble economy and alongside the rise of neoliberal capitalism in recessionary Japan. Eventually, as corporations and advertisers caught on to the increased economic clout of subcultural groups, districts within Tokyo became tied to patterns of neoliberal lifestyle management, which Toshiya Ueno terms "media tribalism" where consumer identities are intrinsically linked to specific urban spaces.[55] Takeyama also highlights the important role that media play in contouring processes of fetishization that commoditize alternative forms of sexual pleasure, such as women's visits to host clubs or, I argue here, gay men's visits to the bars of Ni-chōme. Through her ethnographic study, Takeyama suggests that during Japan's contemporary "precarious" recession, media have sought to alienate Japanese men and women from their sexual agency by commoditizing desire through the promotion of idealized lifestyles, which are in turn indexed by the consumption of specific commodities.[56] The "media tribalism" that has spread throughout neoliberal Japan ultimately produces complex systems of social stratification tied to consumption practices, and Ni-chōme is no exception.

In his exploration of Japan's gay culture, Sunagawa argues that the gay bars in Ni-chōme construct spaces where certain desires become normative through the targeting of individuals professing an attraction for particular physical and personal traits, or a specific "Type."[57] Sunagawa also notes that the practice of Typing spread from Ni-chōme to other gay towns across Japan. Within the Japanese gay cultural context, Typing refers to the alignment of one's subjectivity to a stereotypical identity category based upon ideas of an idealized body type and specific modes of consumption.[58] The system of Typing has precursors in the perverse press of the 1950s,[59] but its terminology ultimately developed in the late 1970s within Japan's *homo* media, chiefly via the personal advertisements known as *buntsūran* published in *Barazoku*. Within these *buntsūran*, the vocabulary of Typing evolved as a method of targeting niche audiences based upon desires for certain physical traits, which were understood to index specific gendered, class, and age-group identities.[60] As recounted by Ōtsuka in his memoir, this system subsequently spread to the bars located in Ni-chōme and became widely popularized via pornographic videos in the early 1990s.[61] Kabiya Kazuhiko, writing in the late 1950s, however, highlights that Japan's immediate postwar gay bars also had a loose system of Typing, but it appears to have been nowhere near as complex as the system that currently typifies contemporary Japan's gay culture.[62] The social stratification encountered by Kabiya in the 1950s was mostly a classificatory system based around one's sexual role—that is, whether one is the "masculine, active penetrator" or "feminine, passive penetrated"—which were linked to relatively static notions of biological sex. Contemporary Typing, while still incorporating various gendered ideologies that make similar heteronormative assumptions, is much more nuanced. For all 50 of the young men I interviewed over the duration of this project, one's preferred sexual role had little to do with one's professed Type.

It is important to note that "Typing" itself is not necessarily unique to gay culture in Japan. In fact, use of the word *taipu* is common throughout Japanese society and is particularly prevalent as a way to describe preferences in a variety of situations, not all of which are romantic, sexual, or erotic. As John Clammer remarks in his seminal *Contemporary Urban Japan: A Sociology of Consumption*, differentiation of consumers via consumption behavior is a common feature of Japan's marketplace, and the segmentation and stratification of individuals into distinct "consumer tribes" plays an important role in marketing and advertising as a way to "sell" lifestyles and products.[63]

As revealed in the ethnographic vignette presented above, Ni-chōme is a marketplace constituted by gay bars and shops that are devoted to the buying and selling of gay men's desires. The district is dominated by various gay media companies that circulate pornography and promote a specific gay lifestyle based in discourses of youth, heteronormative masculinity, and constant partying. The media produced within, and circulated throughout, Ni-chōme play an important role in turning gay desire into a commodity, collapsing the satisfaction of one's sexual desire into a simplistic process of consuming media. Through his insightful analysis of Japanese gay magazine texts, Moriyama argues that gay lifestyles have in fact been completely reified into patterns of consumer behavior, with "identity" arising from the values associated with the clothes one wears, the bars and clubs one visits, and the music to which one listens.[64] Japan's long history of viewing understandings of same-sex attraction as based in desire and practice is therefore co-opted by neoliberal capitalism, with consumption coming to represent the basis for an identity-based understanding of same-sex attraction. As Chasin has insightfully noted in her critique of contemporary North American gay identity politics, this process of locating or constructing queer identity via consumption produces complex systems of social organization, which are then utilized by media producers to segment the same-sex desiring population for capitalist exploitation.[65] This, as theorist Wendy Brown has noted, represents the end game of neoliberalism, where a fantasy of expanded choice is presented to consumers in order to promote apolitical and acritical consumption which feels emancipatory but does little to challenge the status quo.[66] Likewise in Ni-chōme, gay bar owners ultimately deploy Typing to generate profit, perhaps unintentionally producing a fantasy of democratized desire into which many of the young men I spoke are inculcated through their consumption practices.

In my interviews with bar owners, I uncovered that almost all strategically utilized Typing to construct exclusive spaces where specific modes of being and consumption practices became normative. As most gay bars in Ni-chōme have a maximum occupancy of 10 to 15 patrons, the decision to target a particular Type is pragmatic for it allows bar owners to encourage certain clientele to attend and thereby maximize profits. That is, by targeting individuals who identify as belonging to a certain Type, or who identify as desiring certain Types, bars are able to attract individuals who align themselves with particular consumer behaviors to which the bar is better able to cater.[67] Ishida, through a sociological analysis of the economic practices undertaken in Japan's gay bars, notes that while similar practices are visible throughout Japan's hospitality industries, they have been specifically deployed in Japan's gay culture to strategically create spaces that facilitate gay male romance and socialization.[68] Interviews with bar owners revealed a normative assumption that individuals who subscribed to the same Type tended to flock together, and most of these smaller bars failed to construct spaces that facilitated the development of relationships across Types. A great many bar owners politely asked customers to leave smaller bars if they did not align with the bar's Type—something that I had experienced myself on occasion—producing very clear "tribes" among their clientele. In later fieldwork conducted in 2015 and 2017, however, I noted the emergence of larger "mixed bars" that seek to provide spaces for those refused service in bars with strict Types, but these bars still represent a clear minority in Ni-chōme. Furthermore, online gay dating sites and apps also explicitly challenge the narrow use of Typing in bars by facilitating relationships between specific Types. As I reveal in chapter 6, however, use of online dating services is not necessarily fully emancipatory.

As a system of identity categorization, Typing is complex because Japanese gay men use it not only to describe their own identities—that is, identifying directly as a particular Type—but also to categorize themselves via their desired others through identifying as desiring a particular Type. This is reflected within the vocabulary of Typing itself: gay men use the suffix *-kei*, meaning "style" or "form," to reference belonging to, or identifying as, a specific Type. Conversely, gay men use the suffix *-sen*, deriving from the term *senmon*, meaning "specialty" or "preference," to identify as desiring a specific Type. For example, *kawaii-kei* refers to someone who identifies as a Cute Type, whereas *kawaii-sen* (cute specialty) refers to someone who prefers *kawaii-kei* partners. Types ending in the suffix *-kei* are also used to position other men as a certain Type, whereas *-sen* can be used to describe the nature of another person's desires or to describe the normative clientele of a gay bar. This makes for a confusing system of identification, especially when another man ascribes a different *-kei* Type onto an individual than the one with which that individual may personally align. This was a common occurrence for many of my interlocutors. One young man explained to me in frustration over drinks in 2015 that, while he believed himself to be *kawaii-kei* due to what he termed his "cute personality," this was regularly dismissed by other men who positioned him as the stigmatized *debu-kei*. He believed this occurred since he was "chubbier than the *kawaii-kei* you usually see in a porno," despite being objectively slimmer than what he believed was the typical *debu-kei*. I note here that this young man's experiences spoke to a broader tendency I noticed during fieldwork for young gay men to utilize *kei* more frequently in discourse when making aesthetic judgments of individuals' identities. This is perhaps because use of *kei* to describe one's desires has a long history in the Japanese language. Ishida notes that the term *kei* ultimately derives from descriptions of the roles of kabuki actors in the 18th century and entered common usage in the 19th century. On the other hand, *sen* emerged in the immediate postwar period in the context of marketing as a method of classifying ideal consumer groups.[69]

At this point, it is necessary to discuss one particular *sen* Type that plays an important role in the politics of Ni-chōme's gay bar culture: the *gai-sen*, or "Foreigner Specialist." While this Type ostensibly refers to a preference for foreign men, the term *gaijin* on which it is based has typically been used in the Japanese context to refer to White men because of the racial politics of postwar Japan, in which foreignness has become ideologically linked to Whiteness.[70] Since the US-led Occupation of Japan, Japanese gay media have frequently presented the White male body in fetishistic ways, with Suganuma arguing that doing so has less to do with Japanese desires for White partners than with a strong sense that Japanese gay men possess an "equivalent Whiteness."[71] Nevertheless, *gai-sen* bars catering to Japanese men who prefer White partners have formed a conspicuous part of Ni-chōme since at least the 1960s, even though the vast majority of Japanese gay men do not identify as *gai-sen*.[72] The linking of Whiteness to Typing implicit in the *gai-sen* category, where an individual's ethnic background is presented as a Type, speaks to broader Japanese understandings of ethnicity and race. In Japan, the concept of *minzoku* entangles race, ethnicity, and nationality into a specific subjectivity, with the Japanese *minzoku* positioned as homogenous and monolithic.[73] One's racial background becomes linked to cultural identity in a totalizing manner, producing a regime of desire within which desire for a particular racial identity overrides desires for other characteristics. Ni-chōme has thus become "split" into spaces where desires for Whiteness have become privileged and spaces where desires for Japaneseness are normalized, with all other ethnicities rendered invisible. I discuss this racialization of desire more thoroughly in chapter 6.

Typing ultimately represents an ideological system of complicated semiotic resources where physical appearance and consumer behavior are viewed as indexing particular identity categories, marked through one's status as a Type through *kei* or desiring a particular Type through *sen*. It is thus possible for a young Japanese gay man to deploy both versions of Typing to make sense of their desires. For example, one young man I met outside the *gei shoppu* Lumière described himself as *kawaii-kei* because of his slim build and identified as *okami-sen* (Wolf Specialist) due to his strong *akogare* (yearning) for older, slimmer, and hairy men. This young man's evocation of *akogare* is important, as it demonstrates how the commercialized concept of Typing speaks to indigenous conceptualizations of desire and attraction. As indicated in the introduction, *akogare* represents a fundamentally reflexive process through which Japanese individuals make sense of the world via their relationship with a desired other.[74] Typing as a system ties this process of self-discovery, which has been fundamental to how Japanese people traditionally conceptualize their subjective experience, to neoliberal capitalism's management of the self. This connection is clearest in Ni-chōme's gay bars, where the practice of classifying a business as catering to a specific *sen* Type, or "Specialty," ultimately inculcates in consumers an understanding that to properly explore or experience their desires requires one to visit bars that align with their *akogare*.

Of course, not everyone to whom I spoke during fieldwork had positive attitudes toward Typing, with some men indicating that they viewed the categorization of human beings into rigid Types as enforcing harmful stereotypes. This was certainly the case for my principal informants Haruma and Shōtarō, whom I introduce more fully in the next chapter. Men who viewed Typing skeptically informed me during our conversations that the pornographication of the Japanese gay media landscape was causing gay life to become increasingly shallow and superficial. Within these men's narratives, Ni-chōme was placed as the source of a superficiality that was spreading out of the district into the wider gay culture via the gay media circulating throughout Japan. They rejected the vocabulary of Typing at the first instance, viewing the system as a marketing ploy that only created shallow identities. These men also rejected as a dangerously exploitative marketing tactic the notion that the only way to truly experience and understand one's desires was to visit the bar that matched your specific "Specialty." One man even stated that such practices "tricked people into wasting their money" without ever truly "learning about themselves or making meaningful romantic connections." Although gay men have the agency to reject Typing,[75] I must emphasize that to reject the system is to accept its discursive reality to some extent. I noticed during my extended visits to Tokyo that even those young gay men who refuse to ascribe themselves a Type are conscious of the semiotic clues that index Typing in Ni-chōme. In many ways, these men were also co-opted into the system since they paradoxically were more familiar with its nuances because of their efforts to debunk Typing both to me and to themselves.

During my interviews in Ni-chōme's gay bars, many men explained that they could discuss their identities and desires only via Typing, having lost the ability to explore their gay desires without recourse to the specialized vocabulary developed in the gay media. The minority of my interlocutors who viewed Typing as stereotypical and superficial pointed toward this phenomenon as evidence that young Japanese gay men were suffering from a loss of individuality. Some of my interlocutors stated that they viewed the patterns of socialization that normalized Typing as analogous to "brainwashing," with men becoming co-opted by a system that promotes certain Types as normative and desirable and others as illegitimate or undesirable. Indeed, as I reveal below, the Japanese gay media landscape as it is tied to Ni-chōme promotes the *ikanimo-kei* as the most normatively desirable Type in Japan's gay culture, producing a regime of desire with wide-ranging impacts on how young gay men understand their same-sex attraction. Typing, I reveal below, thus possesses a political economy that has not been fully unpacked in previous scholarly studies of Japan's gay culture.

*Typing and the Stratification of Desire: Privileging the* Ikanimo-kei

In Morimura Akio's guidebook, the *ikanimo-kei*, a term with "a positive connotation," is defined as "someone who is obviously gay" due to "*that* cap (*kyappu*) . . . *those* boxer briefs (*hāfupantsu*) and *that* muscular body (*ano gatai*)."[76] Moriyama Noritaka, in his sociological study of gay magazines, explains that the *ikanimo-kei* is defined by the clothes he wears (hence "*that* cap" and "*those* boxer briefs"), the music to which he listens, and the movies and TV shows he watches.[77] The identity category of the *ikanimo-kei* derives from patterns of material consumption, with certain brands of clothing such as fashion labels Abercrombie & Fitch, Calvin Klein, and the Japanese underwear maker Toot supposedly marking them as being gay.[78] This Type thus represents an important "tribe" within Japan's media marketplace. It is important to note that the *ikanimo-kei* is therefore not always understood as implicitly referencing young, desirable bodies as such, as the definition of an *ikanimo-kei* can be extended to men in their 30s and 40s who dress in an "obviously" gay way through certain branded clothing. Throughout my fieldwork, however, young gay men tended to equate *ikanimo-kei* with "hot, young guys" (*wakai ikemen*) who possessed "plenty of muscles" (*kinniku tappuri*).

These codes of desirability are tied to the broader, transnational "pink economy" that has emerged in recent years out of globally circulating gay magazines such as the UK's *Attitude*, Australia's *DNA*, and the US's *Out* that promote a certain middle-class, Euro-American, White gay male identity as normatively desirable.[79] For example, sociologist Travis Kong has investigated how gay men in Hong Kong similarly equate fashion brands such as Abercrombie & Fitch as indexing a normative gay desirability that is explicitly equated with cosmopolitanism and worldliness, ultimately indexing an idealized vision of the gay scenes in London and New York.[80] The *ikanimo-kei* is defined through consumption of specific brands and concomitant sartorial and other performances that are attached to these consumption behaviors. Indeed, the *ikanimo-kei*'s links with this transnational pink economy are made particularly clear when exploring how young Japanese gay men perceive it as tied to a cosmopolitan gay culture. According to the strolling interviews I conducted with informants, during which we discussed the semiotic strategies deployed on signage in Ni-chōme, many young men perceive the common use of English throughout the neighborhood's signs as tying Japanese gay culture to broader globalized flows.[81] During interviews, this English-language signage was linked to the *ikanimo-kei* since the informants perceived English to be "cool" and "exciting" in comparison to Japanese, which was positioned as "uncool" (*dasai*). Similar to Kong's informants, the young gay men I interviewed thus linked the *ikanimo-kei* to imagined notions of gay cosmopolitanism tied to fantasies of North America and Europe as symbols of queer development and implicitly evoked the homonationalist affective logics seminally critiqued by Jasbir Puar whereby development is symbolically tied to White supremacy and homonormativity.[82]

Desirable gay identity within Ni-chōme and the wider Japanese gay media landscape is thus grounded within the transnationalizing discourse of gay male identity described by theorist Lisa Duggan as "homonormative." Since identification as an *ikanimo-kei* is specifically based in "a privatized, depoliticized gay culture anchored in . . . consumption,"[83] I would argue that the *ikanimo-kei* represents the Japanese expression of global neoliberal gay culture. For many of the interlocutors with whom I conversed in 2013, to be *ikanimo-kei* is divorced from political and socially motivated activism, and many explained that a representative member of the *ikanimo-kei zoku* (Obviously Gay Tribe) would be more interested in circuit parties and club nights than attending pride parades or political events. This is not to say that all gay men in Japan professing an *ikanimo-kei* identity are politically apathetic—in fact, during fieldwork I often met *ikanimo-kei* men who were highly committed to Japanese LGBT political activism and were regular attendees of Tokyo Rainbow Pride, particularly after the LGBT boom of 2015 that I address in the conclusion—but it appears that the consumerist nature of the *ikanimo-kei* as image is largely apolitical. Some informants, particularly those who criticize Typing, argued that the *ikanimo-kei* represented the ultimate example of the superficiality sweeping through Japan's gay culture. Others, however, rated the image positively as exceptionally desirable and strived to adopt its normative physicality through extensive gym regimens in order to be considered attractive by others.

More so than the patterns of consumption that define the *ikanimo-kei*, it was in fact the ideal physicality of this Type that young Japanese gay men found desirable. The body type referred to by Morimura as typifying *ikanimo-kei*—the *gatai*—can be defined as a hypermasculine, rough, and heavily muscled body that is typically understood as resulting from intense gym training. The model depicted in figure 3 is particularly representative of this body type. Importantly, such a body contrasts significantly with the so-called *gaten* body of working-class laborers, which are also privileged within certain subsections of the Japanese gay culture, although they are more niche than *gatai* bodies. The term *gaten* indexes a muscular yet chubby physique known as *gachimuchi*. The *gatai* body, by contrast, refers to an athletic, gym-toned body that is more lithe and "sculpted," often described as *assari* (clean-cut) or *sawayaka* (fresh or "hunky") on gay dating sites.[84] The *ikanimo-kei* body is thus sculpted by choice and by aesthetic discipline, whereas the *gaten* body is understood as deriving naturally from labor. These two Types are thus inherently classed, with the *ikanimo-kei* representing those who possess the economic capital and leisure time to aesthetically sculpt their bodies. The importance of gym-based aesthetic discipline to the formation of *gatai* bodies is so strong that, within some Japanese gay media, such as pornographic videos, men who possess *gatai* bodies are also referred to as *tai'ikukai-kei* (Gym Type). It is important to note that this focus on gym-based training and bodily aesthetics forms a large part of the transnational, "homonormative" discourse of neoliberalized gay identity alluded to above.

For many informants, the *gatai* body was understood as being like an idealized *nonke* in appearance and gendered performance. In fact, it was highly common for informants to describe the *gatai* as *nonkeppoi* (like a straight man or straight acting). Through the conflation of the *gatai* body with straight men, the Japanese gay media landscape promotes the *ikanimo-kei* as desirable through the fetishization of straightness, producing a heteronormative regime of desire that circulates throughout Japan's gay culture. Interestingly, while conflated with "straight men," the *gatai* could be said to contrast quite significantly with commonly held assumptions concerning the notion that "softness" represents an alternative hegemonic masculinity that has arisen in recent years within some pockets of Japanese popular culture. The *ikanimo-kei* is broadly conceptualized as "hard," resuscitating the logics that sit at the heart of hegemonic salaryman masculinity according to which to be masculine is to be active and productive. The tensions between these two representations of masculinity are explored in greater depth in chapter 3.

Not only are *ikanimo-kei* understood to always have such gym-sculpted bodies, *gatai* bodies are consistently privileged throughout Ni-chōme as the most desirable. In a survey of 188 pamphlets for gay night club events that I collected in 2013, 56.9 percent of the pamphlets depicted *ikanimo-kei* bodies, followed by 23.4 percent for *kawaii-kei* and 12.2 percent for *gaten-kei*.[85] The *ikanimo-kei* is mostly presented as young, with the pamphlets I collected rarely depicting men who appeared to be older than their late 20s, except for a very few examples of middle-aged *gaten-kei*.[86] These young *ikanimo-kei* represent the target of advertising throughout the Japanese gay media landscape as well as its subject. Much as the *ikanimo-kei* body is conflated with an idealized image of the *nonke*, it was also paradoxically described by many during interviews as representative of desirable young gay men. Thus, through the image of the *ikanimo-kei*, it is apparent that to be desirable within Japan's gay culture relies on young men being both "obviously gay" and "straight-acting" (*nonkeppoi*). This somewhat contradictory definition of desirable young gay masculinity is not unique to Japan's gay culture and has been attested within gay cultures globally.[87] Indeed, this heteronormativity represents the end result of the depoliticized and neoliberalized gay culture critiqued by Duggan.[88] Viewed as the most desirable and normative end point for young Japanese gay men, becoming an *ikanimo-kei* represents "successful" socialization into the gay community.[89] Following Ahmed,[90] the regimes of desire that privilege the *ikanimo-kei* thus discipline queer desiring subjects to "straighten" their desires back into heteronormativity, frustrating the disruptive affective logics of queerness and stymying queer expression.

Although many informants believe that "there is no rubbish to be thrown away in Ni-chōme," and that the plethora of Types visible in the district leads to a utopic space where all desires become equal, this is certainly not the case. Despite images of *kawaii-kei*, *debu-kei*, and *oyaji-kei*, among others, that appear in certain niche bars, most media in Ni-chōme depict the *ikanimo-kei*. This creates a regime of desire that positions the heteronormative *ikanimo-kei* at the pinnacle of desirability, with all other Types sublimated to the normativity of this obviously gay yet somehow straight-acting Type. Rather than the salaryman (which is embodied within the so-called Salaryman Type, or *rīman-kei*), it is the *ikanimo-kei* that acts as the hegemonic form of masculinity within both Ni-chōme and the broader Japanese gay media landscape and against which all other forms of masculinity are judged. In fact, the discursive power of the *ikanimo-kei* is so strong within Ni-chōme that the topographical space of the district has become divided into specific regions that are coded as being the *ikanimo-kei*'s "home." This coding occurs because the businesses located within these regions, as well as the images of men depicted in the advertising circulating within these regions, act as semiotic resources that "code" the space as belonging to the *ikanimo-kei*.[91] Nowhere is this clearer than on the district's main street, Naka-dōri, where most large gay bars and *gei shoppu* are found. This central space is awash with images of the *ikanimo-kei*, exerting symbolic power over the rest of the district.

Regions coded for niche Types—that is, not catering to an *ikanimo-kei* clientele—are typically shunted to the perimeter of Ni-chōme. *Okama* bars containing cross-dressing male performers are located on the edge of the district or in neighboring Shinjuku San-chōme, and many are understood by the men of Ni-chōme as catering to heterosexual "tourists" (*kankōkyaku*) who wish to voyeuristically consume *okama* as a representative symbol of the Japanese gay culture. Within Shin Chidori-gai, a ramshackle collection of old buildings dating from the 1950s found in the alleyways behind Shinjuku San-chōme subway station (west of Naka-dōri), are dozens of bars catering to *oyaji-kei* and *debu-kei*. Within Shin Chidori-gai one may find flyers containing models deviating significantly from the *ikanimo-kei* ideal, including models conspicuously lacking *gatai* bodies. The outermost southeastern section of Ni-chōme contains "Lily Path" (*Yuri no komichi*) where lesbian bars, which commonly refuse entry to men, may be found. Interestingly, the *gai-sen* bars are mostly located on Naka-dōri, or on the periphery of the district near major thoroughfares, but this may be because such locations allow foreigners to avoid navigating Ni-chōme's maze-like web of back alleys, only signposted in Japanese, to find bars where they can meet Japanese (or other foreign) men. The primacy of *ikanimo-kei* to Ni-chōme is reflected not just in their prominent display in the busiest, central region of the district, but also by the fact that, unlike other Types, which are very rarely visible in media outside their niche area, images of the *ikanimo-kei* are visible in regions not specifically coded as *ikanimo-kei* space. There is thus a political economy underlying Typing within which the *ikanimo-kei* becomes imbued with symbolic capital throughout Japan's gay culture.

To conclude, I turn to figure 4, which contains a pamphlet and a fan advertising the Japanese gay dating app named 9monsters, which purportedly targets "the whole of Asia." I collected these while conducting fieldwork in July 2013, when these materials were not only being circulated within the gay bars of the neighborhood, but a version of this advertisement was prominently displayed on a large billboard in the center of Ni-chōme. This billboard was particularly eye-catching, and during strolling interviews, all of my interlocutors rated the models' physiques very positively as representative of desirable gay men. In fact, it was when encountering this billboard early in my fieldwork that I first heard "hardness" used to discuss desirability, as one young man rhapsodized over the models'*gatai* bodies. As a dating app, 9monsters allows users to choose "monsters," which are analogous to Types. Some of these "monsters" represent *ikanimo-kei* ideals of highly muscular bodies and brand fashion, while others represent the *kawaii-kei*, *debu-kei*, and *kuma-kei* (Bear Type), for example. The advertisements presented in figure 4, however, can be read as only depicting *ikanimo-kei* (obvious due to "*that* cap" and "*those* boxer briefs," their facial hair, and their *gatai* bodies), and informants certainly did read it that way. The fact that the fan depicted in figure 4 also includes popular pornstar Koh Masaki (second from the left) further indicates that these models were intended to be representative of the most desirable Type. This is a clear indication of an instance when the *ikanimo-kei* is presented as normative and desirable, with other Types and desires becoming marginalized by their erasure. In this regard, the 9monsters advertisement is representative of the Japanese gay media landscape. It is also an example of how the regimes of desire that privilege heteronormativity contour knowledge concerning desirability in the Japanese gay media landscape by specifically marketing the *gatai*, and hence the *ikanimo-kei*, as representative of Japanese gay culture.

Figure 4. Pamphlet and fan advertisement featuring an *ikanimo-kei* model for the 9monsters dating app.

## Conclusion

There is a common perception within Japan's gay literature and among the men that I met during fieldwork that Shinjuku Ni-chōme represented a space where "no rubbish is thrown away." That is, there is a broad belief that the neighborhood supports all expressions of same-sex desire within a society where such desires are typically positioned as perverse and even dangerous and that Ni-chōme thus represented a supposed model for gay districts across Japan. While this chapter has demonstrated that Ni-chōme certainly does represent a space where gay desire is normalized and that the district provides important opportunities for gay men to socialize, a political economy exists that privileges desires for heteronormative masculinity as embodied within the figure of the *ikanimo-kei*. Although it was certainly the case that Ni-chōme emerges from the broader cityscape of Tokyo as a queer space awash with gay media and viewed positively by young gay, this media provided a homogenous view of what it means to desire the same sex. The democratization of desire that is often celebrated in Japanese queer literature is thus ultimately illusory. Overall, this chapter has problematized the utopic reading of Ni-chōme that has dominated previous research; it has nuanced our understanding of this crucial district and revealed that significant inequalities exist in Tokyo's most important "gay town."

Further, this chapter has argued that the Typing system that has emerged in Ni-chōme as a method of classifying desires represents a neoliberal strategy designed to segment the community of men who visit the district for the purposes of economic exploitation. Thus, Typing commoditizes desire as part of a broader phenomenon in recessionary Japan where consumer tribes are tied to specific urban spaces in order to promote endless consumption. The privileging of the *ikanimo-kei*, I argue throughout this chapter, must be understood within this broader social context where gay experience is homogenized in order to better produce particular consumer behaviors that benefit the businesses active in the neighborhood, such as bars and *gei shoppu*. Typing, as well as the broader pornographification of Ni-chōme, thus produces a homonormative culture that limits agency, and many men I met found it hard to make sense of their desires without relying upon the commercialized logics that dominate the district. The regimes of desire, identified throughout this chapter, valorize and resuscitate heteronormative conceptualizations of masculinity tied to neoliberal cultures; and these are promulgated via the gay media that are centered within Ni-chōme but which also circulate nationally. Throughout the rest of this book, I chart how four individuals navigate these ideologies as a focused lens through which to analyze the impacts of consuming such media. It is to these four men's experiences that I turn in the following chapter.

# TWO

# Four Young Men's Transformative Engagements with Gay Media

Of the 50 men from a variety of backgrounds I interviewed in Ni-chōme while conducting my fieldwork, I developed particularly strong relationships with four young gay men named Junho, Yōichi, Haruma, and Shōtarō.[1] These four men quickly emerged as key informants in my study, and throughout the rest of this book, I focus my analysis on their highly subjective, yet incredibly complex and fascinating, relationships with the gay media that they consume. In so doing, I develop in-depth case studies of these four young men's patterns of consumption to chart the impacts of the regimes of desire circulating throughout the Japanese gay media landscape. All four men identified as "young gay men" (*waka gei*), with the youngest being 20 and the oldest, 24 years of age when I first met them in 2013. They were thus representative of the ideal target audience of the Japanese gay media landscape identified in the previous chapter. Furthermore, they were all regular consumers of gay media, although their patterns of use differed considerably; and all four men visited Ni-chōme with varying levels of frequency, with media engagement playing an important role in their visiting the district. Three participants joined my project after I met them in Tokyo. Junho and Yōichi initially made contact with me independently in Ni-chōme's gay bars, while Shōtarō contacted me after seeing an advertisement, which I had posted on an online forum, calling for volunteers to participate in my project. The fourth participant, Haruma, was part of my extended network of Japanese acquaintances and joined my project after having heard about it from a mutual friend while he was in Australia.

Each of these four men has traveled abroad, including to East and Southeast Asia, Australia, and Canada. They all have international experiences and express an interest in cosmopolitan, international lifestyles in line with prevailing values in Japan, where international travel is fast becoming viewed as integral to young people's social development.[2] Haruma and Shōtarō in particular enjoyed visits to "multicultural" places such as Australia. The four men's familiarity with and interest in multiculturalism, as well as their previous experiences with foreigners living in Japan, many of whom they had met in Ni-chōme, may have motivated them to contact me. Additionally, all key informants appeared to be highly introspective individuals and indicated during interviews that they had often reflected on their consumption of media and their gay desires. Coupled with their interest in cosmopolitanism, the four men's prior reflection on gay desire and media consumption may have motivated them to participate in my research.

To make sense of the transformative role that consuming gay media plays in the lives of these four men, I draw upon the notion of the "psychobiography," defined by Derek Layder as "a linked series of evolutionary transitions, or transformations in identity and personality at various significant junctures in the lives of individuals."[3] Episodes such as when one first realizes one's gay desire, when one comes out to others about one's sexuality, when one first consumes gay media, and when one first sees gay men depicted in mainstream media represented significant junctures in the four men's psychobiographies. Rather than a purely narrative approach to recounting an individual's life story, the psychobiography actively maps "the changing contours of self and behaviour over time . . . stressing how the person is individuated within a social context."[4] As an analytical tool, the psychobiography emphasizes that each individual's social experiences and engagement with the world are "entangled in webs of social relationships which are unique both in terms of their quality and in terms of the personalities and behavioural patterns of those involved with them."[5] Transitions are central to an individual's psychobiography as they represent the moments when individuals ask questions about "who they are, what they have become and what they want to achieve."[6]

In tracing these four men's psychobiographies, I reiterate that my aim here is not to present a "positivist" narrative that seeks to present my principal informants' experiences and beliefs as representative of all young gay men who frequent Ni-chōme. Rather than focusing on generalization, my analysis instead celebrates the particularity of each of these four men's psychobiographies as a window into the highly subjective processes of meaning-making that represent the focus of this book. I thus pay attention to their highly personal encounters with Ni-chōme and gay media as sites for developing a targeted analysis of the impacts of media consumption on knowledge concerning gay desire and identity. I follow sociologist Richard Stake in recognizing that case studies represent a fruitful avenue for qualitative study because of their detailed focus on an individual's life-worlds, especially if this individual's experiences are somehow unique or exceptional.[7] Further, considering the broader "ethnoliterary" thrust of the analysis in subsequent chapters, in which the investigation of media is purposefully guided by the views, values, and experiences of specific media consumers, a detailed focus on these four men's cases is necessary. As anthropologist Louisa Schein acknowledges in her writing on ethnoliterary methods, such an ethnographic approach works best when engaging with a smaller sample as the aim is not to represent a community but to provide theoretical explication of an individual's media practices.[8]

## The Four Young Men's Psychobiographies

The following psychobiographies were written to privilege the four key informants' own descriptions of their lives; they focus upon our initial conversations in 2013, but I have supplemented each man's narratives with details uncovered during later periods of fieldwork where relevant. Importantly, I have included only those transitions that these men themselves indicated were formative to their lives as gay men and to their own understandings of their gay desires.

### Junho

Junho was 20 years old when I first met him in 2013 and identified as a fourth-generation *zainichi kankokujin*, a term referring to the resident Korean community in Japan, established by laborers before and during World War II. Many members of this community are not citizens of Japan, but are "special residents" with access to residence and employment. Like many *zainichi*, Junho has naturalized,[9] as have his mother and father, whereas his surviving grandfather maintains his special resident status as a Korean passport holder. Junho uses his naturalized name "Junpei" in wider society, but goes by his Korean name in Ni-chōme and with certain close friends. Because Junho uses his Korean name while participating in Ni-chōme's gay scene, I have chosen to use it in this study as he believes his Korean name is more pertinent to his life as a gay man.

Growing up in Tokyo, Junho lived in a bilingual Korean and Japanese environment and is thus fluent in both languages. Junho's family is aligned with the South Korean community in Japan, and they visit family in South Korea every year during the Golden Week holiday period starting April 29, which includes four national holidays. Junho, along with the rest of his family, is a member of a Korean Anglican Church near Tokyo's Koreatown of Shin-Ōkubo. Junho described his family as devout and conservative, and for this reason, he has no plans to reveal his same-sex attraction to them. He is, however, out among his friends in Ni-chōme as well as those at the vocational school that he attended between 2013 and 2014.

During his childhood and adolescence, Junho was consistently criticized by his father and grandfather for having "feminine features," causing Junho much anxiety, as these were aspects of his physical appearance that he felt he could not change. Indeed, Junho faced much pressure from his conservative family to adhere to heteronormative gender roles. Junho has subsequently developed two "masks": at home he is introverted and tries his best to be normatively masculine, but outside the familial sphere, he has developed an outrageous personality heavily influenced by *onē kyara* that he saw on television with his family. His decision to mimic *onē kyara* derives in part from the scorn for them displayed by the other males in his family, and his adoption of an almost *onē kyara* style performance himself outside the familial sphere is due to his desire to silently rebel against his family's heteronormative gender expectations. Although he does occasionally cross-dress on rare occasions while in Ni-chōme, Junho has never considered himself as similar to an *onē kyara* despite viewing these figures positively.

Junho reported that, at the age of 13, he fell in love with another boy at his school with whom he used to walk home every evening, referring to this boy as his "first love" (*hatsukoi*). It was this moment when Junho realized he was attracted to men. At the time, Junho was attending an ethnic Korean school, but when he was around the age of 14, his parents decided to naturalize (which led to Junho's naturalization), and he moved to a Japanese public high school. Throughout his time at this school, Junho dated a number of his female classmates and gained a reputation as a "playboy," partly as an attempt to assert a "masculine" identity such as preferred by his father and grandfather. When I interviewed him in 2013 (and again in 2015), Junho retrospectively labeled himself as bisexual during his adolescence because he was able to date and have sex with these women, but he explained that since growing up, he could only feel "true romance" with a man and continues to view his first love as a "perfect romance." During his adolescence, while simultaneously dating female classmates, Junho regularly consumed gay pornography online, from both Japan and the US and Europe, and continues to be an avid consumer today.

Junho began to visit Ni-chōme once a month when he was 16, pretending to be an 18-year-old (the age of consent in Japan; 20 is the legal drinking age) and using a fake ID he had bought through an online forum. (It is common for the larger clubs in Ni-chōme that Junho hoped to frequent to check for ID upon entrance.) He learned about Ni-chōme from the *onē kyara* variety programs he used to watch, and despite the negative images of the district that these shows often depicted, Junho came to feel that Ni-chōme was a "wonderful place," and he was desperate to visit as soon as he was able. Although he reported that he would often "fool around" with men in bars and clubs, he would never have sex or buy (or even drink) alcohol because he was afraid that he would be caught using a fake ID, and this would lead to his parents discovering his visits to the district. When Junho turned 18, he moved out of his family's home into his own apartment in order to attend a vocational school near Shinjuku, and he received his very own smartphone for the first time from his parents. With his access to Ni-chōme facilitated by this new independence, Junho began to visit the district every weekend and most weeknights, making friends with many young men in his favorite bars. One of these friends, Yōichi, is also a participant in this study. After turning 18, Junho reported that he "made up for lost time" by "sleeping with as many guys" as he possibly could. This was facilitated by his discovery of location-based dating apps, which allowed him to easily meet men for sex whenever he visited Ni-chōme. It was also at this time that Junho began to buy copies of gay magazines such as *Bádi* and *G-Men*, which he continued to buy and read diligently every month, until both ceased publication in 2019 and 2015, respectively. His experiences in Ni-chōme, Junho argued, eventually "turned [him] fully gay," and he no longer considered himself bisexual.

At the time of our last 2013 interview, Junho stated a desire to find a steady, exclusive partner whom he "can love." He had also been considering finding a "fake girlfriend" so that he can get married in the future, give his parents grandchildren, and find a way to hide his gay desire from his conservative family and church group. If he does marry a woman, however, Junho explained that he still intended to visit Ni-chōme in order to "play around" with men and would even potentially find a male lover to spend time with "on the side." When I reconnected with him in 2015, however, Junho had abandoned these fantasies of a double life and decided to eventually come out to his family.

Yōichi

Yōichi was a 21-year-old university student when I met him in 2013. He was a close friend of Junho and used to work both as a bartender at Junho's favorite bar and as a part-time clerk at an upmarket clothes store in Ginza. Yōichi grew up in a single-parent household in Chiba Prefecture; he explained that his father had divorced his mother and moved away during his childhood. He had not seen much of his father since the divorce and described him as both a drunkard and a "failed" man. His mother raised Yōichi with help from her own mother, who would babysit him while his mother worked late nights at a Japanese-style pub. Yōichi's mother also occasionally worked as a "hostess" at a club during times of financial hardship, although Yōichi stressed she never sold sex but "companionship."[10] Yōichi has a strong sense of gratitude to his mother and grandmother, and his motivation for attending university is to earn a stable income so that he can take care of them in their old age. His attitude toward his father is very negative, and he is motivated to take care of his mother and grandmother to make up for the "failures" of his father as a man.

During middle school, Yōichi began to develop an attraction to the boys in his soccer club, and believing that this was "not normal," he asked his grandmother for advice. She explained to him that "some men like other men" and told him not to tell his mother to avoid worrying her. His grandmother, outside of his friends in Ni-chōme, is the only person who knows that Yōichi is gay. Upon reaching high school, Yōichi strove to maintain what he termed during our conversations a "manly" exterior so that he would not be under suspicion of being gay. He understood being gay as "effeminate," demonstrating that his understanding of gay desire was firmly situated within mainstream society's heteronormative positioning of gay men as gender inverts. He continued to be an active member of his senior high school's soccer club, began to use a community gym for weight training, and would go for long runs every second morning. This was a fitness regime that he continued throughout his late teens and early 20s.

After graduating high school, Yōichi worked a number of part-time construction jobs until he was 19 in order to save up money, a job trajectory that is becoming increasingly common for young people in Japan's "precarious" economy.[11] He also attended a cram school to prepare for university entrance examinations, as he had been unsuccessful in passing these examinations during his final year of high school. During that period, Yōichi also used to watch a lot of gay porn in secret as a way to relieve his stress, but he also expressed that he often felt shame afterwards. After sitting and passing entrance examinations a year after leaving high school, Yōichi decided to travel extensively throughout East and Southeast Asia before he commenced university life. While traveling, Yōichi began to visit gay clubs overseas, and finding that "Japanese guys were really popular among Asians," Yōichi began to learn a little about the Japanese gay scene, which prior to his trip overseas had been restricted to knowledge of the *onē kyara* that he saw on variety programs and despised.[12] While he was in Thailand, some young Thai men apparently mistook Yōichi for the popular gay pornstar Koh Masaki, who was coincidentally in the country at the same time. Both Koh's appearance and success made a great impression on Yōichi, who began to make a concerted effort to style himself after Koh because of his belief that this was "the most popular Type."

Upon returning to Japan and moving away from his mother's home in order to attend university in Tokyo, Yōichi began to frequent Ni-chōme in order to hook up with Asian tourists, for whom he had developed a liking overseas. Yōichi made use of smartphone apps in order to meet Southeast Asian tourists for casual sex. It was around this time that he first took a position as a bartender at a bar in Ni-chōme, and he supplemented this income by working as a host in one of Ni-chōme's host clubs. Yōichi became quite popular among many of Ni-chōme's regulars and eventually became one of the *hayatteru ikemen*, whose social media was avidly consumed by fans of the *ikanimo-kei*. He also began to occasionally purchase copies of *Bádi* so that he could stay informed about the styles popular among young gay men so he could better attract other men for sex. Interestingly, as his popularity as a *hayatteru ikemen* grew, Yōichi explained that he began to have sex with more Japanese and Western men, and fewer East and Southeast Asian men. At the time of our final interview, he identified as exclusively attracted to other Japanese men, noting that it was the most "appropriate" choice for Japanese men to desire each other.

Around his 21st birthday, Yōichi became worried that his high visibility in the Japanese gay media landscape could lead to him being outed to his university friends and mother. He subsequently deleted his Twitter and LINE accounts and started to visit Ni-chōme less frequently. Yōichi was also greatly affected by the death of his gay idol Koh Masaki, who passed away in 2013 at the age of 29 from complications relating to surgery for peritonitis.[13] When I last spoke with him, Yōichi had been thinking about revealing his sexual orientation to his mother and had attended a workshop at a community center about coming out. He had distanced himself from Ni-chōme, stating that he wanted to develop a "romantic relation-ship" with a steady partner as opposed to having indiscriminate sex with multiple partners. Since completing my initial fieldwork in 2013, I have unfortunately been unable to reestablish contact with Yōichi, particularly as he cut ties with Junho after ceasing to visit Ni-chōme. Therefore, I am unaware of the results of his decisions to come out and search for a roman-tic partner.

## Haruma

Twenty-four years old when I met him in 2013, Haruma was completing graduate studies at a highly prestigious university in Tokyo. He is origi-nally from the city of Kagoshima in Kyushu, and his parents and older sister still live in their family home. Haruma moved to Tokyo in order to commence studying at university with a full scholarship. In 2013, he was working part-time as both a research assistant at his university and as a tutor at a cram school.

During his childhood, Haruma spent a lot of time playing with his older sister and her friends, and it was through them that he began to gain an interest in "all things cute and sweet." He was sometimes teased by the boys in his elementary school class because he was smaller and more "womanly" (*onnappoi*) than them, but he soon began to play soccer in a school club and became popular because of his skill at the game. During middle and senior high school, Haruma dedicated himself to his study and was no lon-ger able to play soccer with his friends or even visit with them. He became highly reclusive and was obsessed with gaining entry to a prestigious uni-versity in Tokyo because of pressure from his parents. At this time in his life, Haruma felt no particularly strong attraction to either men or women, although he did watch heterosexual pornography online to relieve stress and watch "the men's techniques." He stated that, although he felt aroused while watching these films and was able to reach orgasm, he did not feel particularly sexual at the time and believes that he "may have been asex-ual." For Haruma, asexuality referred to his inability to become attracted to men or women, but this did not mean he refrained from sexual behavior for he reported that he had been able to become aroused and masturbate by watching the act of sex itself and the men's techniques.

Upon moving to Tokyo to attend university, Haruma began to dedi-cate less time to study, partly because he became busier with his new part-time job as a tutor, but also in part because of a desire to spend time "having fun." At this time, Haruma was increasingly being drawn into the herbivorous boy (*sōshoku-kei danshi*) lifestyle of pursuing individual pleasure through consumption of branded fashion and a lack of interest in the opposite sex. Haruma began trying to "become cute" like a typical herbivorous boy, specifically through grooming and wearing fashion drawn from herbivorous boy blogs and guidebooks. In his pursuit of this lifestyle, Haruma explicitly rejected heteronormative understandings of masculinity.

In his second year of university, after having received top marks for his first year, Haruma traveled to Australia in order to study English at an Australian university for two months. He spent a lot of his time in Australia "playing around on the beach" with his new friends, the majority of whom were also Japanese. While in Australia, Haruma developed a "few confusing crushes" on some of his fellow Japanese male classmates, which produced feelings of shame. Upon his return to Japan, he quickly repressed these emotions and focused on his studies, refusing to consider his same-sex attraction as part of his identity. After returning to Japan and graduating from his undergraduate degree, Haruma continued on to graduate school. During his first year of graduate studies, Haruma began to feel strongly sexually attracted to other men, something he described as "sudden and unexpected." He quickly turned to the internet to find out what was happening. The more he read on various advice websites, the more he realized that he was in fact "something called 'being gay'" and that his lack of desire for women was "indicative of [his] desire for men." The information he read online pointed him to Ni-chōme, but he was not interested in visiting, as he thought of it as a "scary place." He also began viewing gay pornography online, which he quickly found he enjoyed. He came out to his female friends at university and turned to them for advice.

One of these friends introduced Haruma to her gay friend named Akito.[14] Akito soon took Haruma to visit Ni-chōme. Their relationship became sexual after one month, and Haruma subsequently became Akito's boyfriend. Akito also introduced Haruma to *Bádi*, which they would read together. It was only after consuming media containing images of *ikanimo-kei*, typically pornographic imagery in *Bádi* or online videos, that Akito would become aroused and have sex with Haruma. Haruma reported that he had ambivalent feelings toward these media, although he did develop an interest in the manga, known as *geikomi*, appearing in *Bádi. Geikomi* (gay comics) is a genre of manga produced for and by gay men, typically including depictions of hypermasculine characters engaging in rough sex.[15] The manga in *Bádi* also led Haruma to an awareness of Boys Love (BL) manga, which he would read on his own, outside his relationship with Akito. BL represents homoerotic manga typically written for and by heterosexual young women.[16] These two genres of "gay manga" are discussed in much more detail in the next chapter.

Throughout their relationship, Akito tried his best to teach Haruma what he thought it meant to be gay, impressing upon Haruma that being gay and coping with heteronormative society meant adopting a "masculine and straight" attitude. Haruma reported feeling particularly powerless in the relationship; he believed that Akito was trying to change him as Haruma wanted to maintain his herbivorous boy identity. After approximately half a year, Akito became dissatisfied with Haruma's explicit unwillingness to adopt a supposedly more masculine identity, and he broke up with Haruma via text message. Akito's callous treatment caused Haruma to become depressed, and he took a break from his studies and returned to Kagoshima. While there, Haruma came out to his parents and sister, who have been mostly supportive; his father believed Haruma's homosexuality merely represented a "phase" from which Haruma will eventually "return to being straight." Part of his recovery involved a lengthy period of reflection on what it meant to be gay. Haruma decided that he and Akito were incompatible because of Akito's insistence on "acting straight" and that Haruma, who was "at heart still an herbivorous boy," did not meet this ideal. Haruma's rocky relationship with Akito has led him to reject all the media that he once consumed with Akito, describing them as "poison."

Haruma had returned to Tokyo when I reconnected with him in 2015. At the time of writing, he now spends a lot of time with some *kawaii-kei* friends he had made in Ni-chōme and has started to frequent bars targeting *kawaii-kei* to make more gay friends. He reads a lot of BL manga, which validates his desire for "romantic" as opposed to "sexual" relationships, but he continues to read *geikomi* as a fan, having gained a "taste" for them. He avoids the bars that he used to visit with Akito and is gradually coming to terms with his sexuality.

## Shōtarō

At the time of my first interview with him in 2013, Shōtarō was 24 years old and had just completed his final year at university, where he was working part-time as a research assistant for one of his former professors. He reported a lack of interest in an academic career, however, and was instead trying to break into the creative industries. As a big fan of manga and anime, and as an amateur author of manga comics, Shōtarō wished to work in global promotions for an anime firm. His job hunting had not been going well when we first met.

Shōtarō is an only child who was still living with his parents in his family home in Saitama Prefecture, near Tokyo, during my initial fieldwork. Shōtarō has known that he desired men since he was ten years old, when he started to become attracted to the other boys in his class. In particular, Shōtarō became excited during gym class where he was able to view the bodies of the other boys. Shōtarō kept his sexuality hidden from those around him throughout his schooling, coming out only to a few of his close female friends in senior high school. It was roughly around this time when Shōtarō began to consume Japanese and Western gay pornography.

All of Shōtarō's female friends were fans of BL manga, and when they learned that Shōtarō was gay, they began to lend him BL manga to read. Like Haruma, Shōtarō continues to read these manga to this day and credits them with stirring his interest in a career in manga and anime. During his senior high school years, Shōtarō believed that homosexual relationships were "exactly the same" as those typically depicted in BL, in which one partner is usually presented as passive and effeminate (called the *uke*) and the other is presented as active and masculine (called the *seme*).[17] He identified with the *uke* characters and was attracted to the *seme* characters. In high school, Shōtarō developed a crush on his senior classmate in the basketball club. Thinking that this senior was also gay because his mannerisms resembled those of a favorite *seme* character in a certain BL manga, Shōtarō confessed his love, which was not reciprocated, as his senior was "just a normal, straight guy."

Throughout university, Shōtarō continued to keep his sexuality hidden, except from a few close friends. In his second year, he tried to date some women, but this was unsuccessful as he was unable to have sexual relationships with them. As part of his degree, Shōtarō studied for one year at an Australian university, where he focused on improving his English. While in Australia, Shōtarō decided to cease hiding his sexuality. His decision to come out was not just due to Shōtarō's perception that Australia—"the home of the Sydney Gay and Lesbian Mardi Gras"—was a more open and tolerant space than Japan to reveal his sexuality but also due to a bout of depression he attributed to hiding his sexuality and his "true self." At this time, Shōtarō serendipitously discovered the genre of manga known as *geikomi* while surfing the internet for "gay manga" in English. He began to consume it online and, when he returned to Japan, also began consuming *geikomi* in gay magazines such as *Bádi*. His consumption of gay pornography increased during this period as well, and he also began briefly experimenting with what he termed "Western, English-language gay dating apps."

Upon returning to Japan, Shōtarō continued keeping his sexuality hidden from his family but began to venture out to Ni-chōme occasionally in order to meet men. He first went to the district with a straight female friend of his, and he felt dissatisfied by his visits since his association with his female friend meant he did not interact with any gay men. He started to visit the district's *gei shoppu* in order to read the gay magazines and learn more about *geikomi*, but he did not feel comfortable buying them and bringing them home, where they may be discovered by his parents. He was also disappointed by what he saw as a mindless pursuit of sex and pleasure among the gay men he encountered in Ni-chōme. Like Junho and Yōichi, Shōtarō used a variety of dating sites and apps on his phone to make more gay friends and find a boyfriend. Through these media, he went out on a few dates with an Italian man, but this ultimately ended in rejection. This experience led Shōtarō to become disillusioned with Ni-chōme, and he blamed the prevalence of pornographic media for the frivolous behavior of the men there who "just wanted to play." Disappointed by the men he had met in Ni-chōme, Shōtarō indicated during our final 2013 interview that he was preparing to go on student exchange to Canada, where he hoped to meet "romantic" gay men. He has since settled in Vancouver, where he is in a steady relationship with a Chinese Canadian man at the time of writing.

Table 1 summarizes each principal informant's demographic information at the time of initial interview in 2013. In particular, it presents demographic information that all the informants stressed was important, such as their age or whether or not they had come out and to whom. Other important demographic factors, such as education and employment, are also presented. Through the self-narratives presented above, it is clear that these four men have diverse ideas, derived from their unique life histories, about what it means to be gay and to desire the same sex.

Table 1. Informants' demographic details at first interview

| Informant | Age | Ethnicity | Education | Employment | Came out | Travels abroad |
|---|---|---|---|---|---|---|
| Junho | 20 | Korean-Japanese | Enrolled at a vocational school | At his parents' Korean restaurant | To friends, but not to family | Korea |
| Yōichi | 21 | Japanese | Enrolled at a university | At a gay bar, and in high-end retail | To his grandmother and friends in Ni-chōme, but not to everyone else | Southeast Asia |
| Haruma | 24 | Japanese | Graduate student | Tutor at a *juku*, research assistant | To family and friends | Australia and China |
| Shōtarō | 24 | Japanese | University graduate | Research assistant, searching for work in the *anime* industry | To certain female and foreign friends and friends in Ni-chōme | Australia (living in Canada at time of writing) |

## *Desire before the Media: First Loves and the Awakening of Gay Desire*

None of the key informants indicated that engaging with gay media (or even mainstream media) revealed to them that they desired other men.[18] All of them did, however, first become aware of the existence of gay men via mainstream televised media, such as variety shows starring *onē kyara*, but this did not "awaken" their gay desires. Junho and Shōtarō had always held positive views of gay men thanks to their consumption of *onē kyara* variety programs, whereas Yōichi particularly disliked such shows and they subsequently inculcated in him a negative perception of gay men. For Haruma, *onē kyara* eventually came to represent a positive image of gay identity, which he drew upon to reaffirm his identity as an herbivorous boy, but his first encounter with them during his childhood was mostly ambivalent. All four informants found it very difficult to identify an exact moment in time when they first realized their same-sex desires, although they were all adamant that media played no role. This indicates that although media may influence how Japanese gay men understand their desires, for some men, the awakening of desire is not always dependent on media and is often stimulated through interactions between individuals.

All four men could recall their *hatsukoi* (first love), and they drew upon this experience not only to provide a reference point for when they first began to desire other men but also to conceptualize the nature of this desire as innate and embodied. This is a discourse of desire that is particularly hegemonic in the Japanese gay media landscape, forming part of the regimes of desire that contour understandings of sexuality and gay identity in Japan. The four men suggested that their desires were "awakened" by their *hatsukoi*. When asked to comment on his use of the metaphor of "awakening," Haruma, whose realization of gay desire came relatively later in his life, discussed how his same-sex attraction had "lain dormant for a long time inside" until it finally "revealed itself" as a consequence of external stimulation. Junho and Shōtarō made similar remarks, believing that their gay desires were "innate" and "natural." For Junho, his "innate desires" were "activated inside him" after he "first fell in love." Yōichi stated that there "must have been something inside [him]" that made him desire men, but he did not realize this until he experienced same-sex attraction in his soccer club.

Drawing upon the concept of *hatsukoi* to make sense of one's romantic and sexual history is relatively common practice among Japanese of all sexual orientations, and many of the young men I met in Ni-chōme's gay bars also used this narrative to make sense of their desires during our conversations. The "first love" is foundational to the commercialized discourse of love that developed in the postwar period. As Sonia Ryang notes, the concept of *koi* (sensual love) has historically been utilized to make sense of the "captivating sense of the other."[19] For Haruma, *koi* is an immediate bodily response to an attractive person that is marked by "the erection of the penis" and "the quickening of the heartbeat," and many other young gay men I met expressed similar opinions. Ryang further suggests that conceptualizations of *koi* are embedded within broader discourses of maturation toward *ren'ai* or *romansu* (romantic love) which index a more spiritual or emotional ideal.[20]

Under the heteronormativity that structures Japanese society, even gay men—by virtue of their male sex—expect to follow the process of sexual maturation epitomized by the progression of *koi* to *ren'ai*. This maturational discourse is strongly heteronormative, with progressing from *koi* to *ren'ai* ultimately leading to marriage and the societal recognition of a man's adulthood.[21] *Hatsukoi* is also the initial prelude to the *hatsutaiken*, or "first sexual experience," which is privileged in both mainstream romantic media and gay media and is also often being seen as a stepping stone toward heterosexual maturation. All four young men's understanding of the innateness of their desires reflects the dominant discourses concerning sexuality and desire found in Japanese society. It thus appears that all four subscribe to the normative view of sexual desire promoted in Japan via mainstream and gay media, defining it as a completely embodied phenomenon. However, the men also tended to link love and desire, which is counter to these normative Japanese sexological discourses that typically tend to separate love as a spiritual and emotional state from sexual desire as an animalistic passion.[22] Junho, who had a knack for wordplay, particularly criticized this conceptual division, drawing upon the neologism *dōseikoi* to state that "it's called 'homophilia/same-sex love' (*dōseiai*) and not 'homocarnality/same-sex lust' (*dōseikoi*), so of course the loving of men (*otoko o ai suru koto*) is part of the desire."

For the four men, the various gay media they consume played an important role in providing a conceptual vocabulary and framework to justify their belief in the innateness of their gay desires. One such framework is Typing, as discussed in the previous chapter. But the realization of same-sex desire and the development of an understanding of it as "innate" and "natural" reportedly occurred before their first exposure to gay media. It was only some years later that they came to justify this understanding of their desires through recourse to discourses appearing in various gay media, and they would draw on these discourses "after the fact" to make sense of their initial feelings and memories. Indeed, our conversations in 2013 about their pasts represented an example of how these four men drew upon their current knowledge to reconceptualize and make sense of their past desires and experiences. Shōtarō pieced together his understanding from information found on various Japanese gay websites during his early 20s. Haruma reported reading discussions about the innateness of desire on a gay-themed thread on the popular *Ni-channeru* bulletin board system (BBS). Junho and Yōichi both mentioned that they encountered similar discourses in *Bádi* and in discussions they had with gay friends in Ni-chōme.

Sometimes the delay between the *hatsukoi* and the encounter with a justifying discourse in gay media was considerable, with Shōtarō encountering these discourses almost 10 years after his gay desires were awoken during his childhood. Regardless of when the men encountered justifying discourses within gay media, the key informants' *hatsukoi* remained an important source of experiential knowledge that they drew upon to make sense of what they were encountering in the Japanese gay media landscape. As Shōtarō succinctly phrased it, without having "the experience of the first love," he never would have searched for affirming discourses in the first place, nor could he have "made sense of them." The other informants made similar claims, demonstrating the importance of the *hatsukoi* as a point of reference that mediates how they apply the discourses appearing in gay media to their own experiences. It also reiterates the fact that certain understandings of their desires come from a time before their engagement with media.

The discourse of the innateness of gay desire is an important facet of both Western and Japanese queer identity politics.[23] These young men's engagement with and internalization of this discourse differentiates them from participants in previous studies. As mentioned in the introduction, both Mark McLelland and Yajima Masami argue that their informants, gay men of varying ages living in Japan during the early to late 1990s, did not adopt Western notions of queer identity politics, nor did they view their gay desire as an "integral part of their identity," instead viewing it as "play" or as "hobby."[24] For the four young men participating in this study, however, as their desires were viewed as innate, they also viewed them as being an important aspect of their selfhood, although not in all spheres of their lives. This is true not only of these four men but for all the young men I met during my fieldwork for this project. Furthermore, as summarized in table 1, not all of these four men are out to all members of their social networks. Coming out is a cornerstone of the framework of queer identity politics advocated in much gay media, including in Japan,[25] and the principal informants' reluctance to come out in certain parts of their lives demonstrates a level of discomfort with this discourse. The motivating factor, according to Junho, Yōichi, Haruma, and Shōtarō, is the idea of privacy. Although their gay desires are an integral aspect of their selfhood, they also believe their desires are private and not relevant to all spheres, including the familial sphere.

Finally, all four informants indicated that although their desire for men was "awoken" by their *hatsukoi*, the Type of men to whom they have subsequently become romantically and sexually attracted has changed over time. Shōtarō in particular explained that the gay media that he now consumed had affected his desire for certain Types of men, leading him to reject the idealized depictions of men found in BL manga. Junho mentioned that his *hatsukoi* was not like the Types of men to whom he was now attracted, because of his consumption of gay pornography and his experiences in Ni-chōme. Here we can see the explicit influence on

Junho's desires of the regimes of desire that circulate in the Japanese gay media landscape. Haruma, however, stated that although he was sure that the media he consumed had an unconscious effect on the Type of men he liked, he still had the choice of which media he consumed and this choice was made by his preexisting preference for certain Types of men. This is a tension all four men experienced, especially after they began to frequent Shinjuku Ni-chōme and explicitly engaged with the Japanese gay media landscape as it is anchored to the district.

## Becoming Socialized into Ni-chōme's Gay Bar Culture

After the awakening of their same-sex desires, all four men eventually made their way to Ni-chōme. As seen in the psychobiographies presented above, all but Haruma reported that their attraction to other men became evident during their childhood or adolescence. Thus, there was a significant delay between the realization of same-sex desire and the men's first visits to Ni-chōme.

Of the four principal informants, three learned about Ni-chōme from variety programs starring *onē kyara*. Shōtarō had known about the district for some time from watching these shows as a child but lacked the courage to visit Ni-chōme until after he returned from studying abroad in Australia. Yōichi also learned about the district through these programs, but he visited Ni-chōme only after returning to Japan from his holiday in Southeast Asia as it was his experiences abroad that led him to fully acknowledge his gay desires. For both these men, their discomfort with their gay desires and fear of the district delayed them from visiting. Junho, on the other hand, started to visit Ni-chōme when he was 16, after finding out at around the age of 14 or 15 about its existence via a segment on *Waratte iitomo*, the popular variety show featuring *onē kyara* celebrities. As well as being the youngest informant in this study, Junho was thus also the youngest when he visited Ni-chōme for the first time; the other informants first visited in their 20s. In contrast to the other three men, Haruma realized his same-sex desire relatively later in life and was guided to the space by his ex-boyfriend Akito. Interestingly, then, Haruma first visited Ni-chōme shortly after realizing his gay desire, after a period of approximately three or four months.

Reflecting on their first impressions of Ni-chōme, Junho and Shōtarō indicated that they were excited by the prospect of a safe space just in

Tokyo for gay men, although Shōtarō was reluctant to visit the district immediately, fearing that he would be outed. As stated above, Junho was particularly eager to visit, and even procured a fake ID through illegal channels, believing he needed it to gain access to the gay bars. Both Junho and Shōtarō subscribed to the utopic discourse of Ni-chōme discussed in the previous chapter, finding in the neighborhood a space that affirmed their same-sex attraction. Yōichi and Haruma, on the other hand, initially had largely negative impressions of the district. Yōichi, whose initial encounter with the space was influenced by his distaste for *onē kyara* variety programs, viewed Ni-chōme as a place for "effeminate *okama*." However, after he came into contact in Southeast Asia with "manly" discourses of gay desire, which affirmed his identification with heteronormative masculinity, he finally dared to visit the district after returning from his travels. Yōichi soon found Ni-chōme to his liking, especially because he was able to meet "lots of hot, manly guys" from all over the world with whom he could have sex. Haruma was also frightened by the space at first, perhaps because of lingering fears about his own sexuality. He gained the courage to visit Ni-chōme only in the company of his then boyfriend. As will become evident in later discussions, however, Haruma soon became a fierce critic of certain communities active in the district.

Ni-chōme came to represent a site that was immensely influential to the development of these four men's lives as gay men. In particular, visiting Ni-chōme highly influenced their patterns of gay media consumption, and the amount and content of gay media they consumed changed significantly because of their experiences within the space. Each informant began to regularly visit the district after first encountering Ni-chōme. There are important differences, however, in the frequency with which they visited. Of the four men, Shōtarō visited the district least often, once a month. Shōtarō began by visiting the district only once or twice a year, but only after making friends in the district and becoming socialized into certain bars' communities. This was facilitated by Shōtarō's frequent visits to the Shinjuku area in order to look for work. Junho and Yōichi visited Ni-chōme most frequently: every weekend night (including Friday) and most weekday evenings. Yet by the time I concluded my initial fieldwork and departed Tokyo in 2013, Yōichi had ceased visiting the district because he was concerned his gay lifestyle might be discovered by family and friends. Junho had also become somewhat less enthusiastic about visiting the district.

Similarly, Haruma used to visit the district quite frequently, going

Table 2. Frequency of informants' Ni-chōme visits and attitudes toward the district

| Informant | | Frequency of visits | Opinions of Ni-chōme |
|---|---|---|---|
| Junho | Very frequent | Every weekend night (Friday, Saturday, Sunday), most weeknights | Mostly positive; some negativity developed over time |
| Yōichi | Very frequent | Every weekend night, some weeknights | Mostly positive; some negativity developed over time |
| Haruma | Frequent | Before breaking up with Akito: every weekend night | Ambivalent, but became mostly positive after breaking up with Akito |
| | | After breaking up with Akito: once a week | |
| Shōtarō | Sometimes | Once a month, but less frequently before making friends in Ni-chōme | Somewhat positive, but became more negative over time |

to Ni-chōme at least once a week, usually on a Saturday night. Before his traumatic breakup with Akito, he would even visit Ni-chōme as frequently as Junho and Yōichi, spending every Friday, Saturday, and Sunday night in the bars Akito liked to frequent, large dance clubs catering to an *ikanimo-kei* clientele. Haruma's somewhat diminished frequency after breaking up with Akito is due partly from his wariness about encountering his ex-boyfriend in Ni-chōme and partly due to his desire to regain control of his life. Indeed, he previously visited the district with such high frequency because Akito was eager to spend time in Ni-chōme and was not necessarily out of his own desire to spend his weekend leisure time in the gay bars. Haruma's decreased visits to Ni-chōme were strongly linked to his growing distaste for the privileging of heteronormative masculinity in the gay media he consumed. Table 2 summarizes both the frequency of the men's visits to Ni-chōme and their overall attitudes toward the district.

Visiting Ni-chōme also played an important role in educating the men about the role of Typing in Japan's gay culture and how bars in the district represented "Typed" space. The four men had encountered Typing prior to coming to Ni-chōme via their consumption of gay pornography online. Yet this previous consumption introduced them to Typing only as a system of classification based on physical appearance, not as a semiotic system that managed and made sense of desire. Participating in Ni-chōme's bar culture also socialized the four men into a world where Typing represented a system of cultural knowledge that could be utilized to make sense of the media with which they were interacting. Indeed, Typing came to play a crucial role in how the four men accessed and understood the various discourses of desire circulating in Japan's gay media landscape, leading them even to read Typing into media where Typing was not explicitly present. Importantly, visiting Ni-chōme also greatly affected the four men's patterns of media consumption, expanding their engagement with the gay media landscape beyond their previously limited patterns of consumption.

### Visiting Ni-chōme and the District's Impact on Media Consumption

It was difficult to observe explicit instances of the informants consuming gay media during fieldwork because the most commonly consumed content was pornographic in nature and typically private. I was occasionally able, however, to observe the use of dating apps and the reading of magazines (particularly when we visited gay bars and shops). To uncover the media that the four young men consumed on a regular basis, I asked them to recall the media they had consumed on the day before each interview, as well as on the day of the interview itself. This method of focused questioning allowed the interviewees to provide specific answers based upon recent experience, presenting a rounded picture of the phenomenon under investigation as opposed to vague answers based on conjecture or distant memory.[26] Although I hesitate to present the four focal informants' patterns of media consumption as broadly representative of all young gay men who visit Ni-chōme, comparing their accounts with that of several of my other 50 informants seems to suggest a certain level of representativeness, particularly with regard to the prevalence of certain kinds of media content such as pornography and online dating sites.

Junho, Yōichi, Haruma, and Shōtarō all indicated that they broadly consumed gay media via three different platforms: online media, such as websites and dating sites (accessed using either computers or smartphones); print media, including gay magazines and manga comics (although some also consumed manga online); and non-internet based film media, such as DVDs and TV shows (especially *onē kyara* variety programs). The four men preferred online consumption; print media came second, and film media was quite rare except for Junho and Shōtarō. It is important to mention, however, that breaking down patterns of consumption into these platform-based categories is somewhat problematic as it does not show the true complexity of each individual's patterns of media consumption.

Media scholar Henry Jenkins argues that in today's hypermediated world, traditional media such as magazines and film have entered a state of "convergence" with new, online media. For Jenkins, convergence refers to "the flow of content across media platforms, the co-operations between multiple media industries, and the migratory behavior of media audiences who will go almost anywhere in search of the kinds of entertainment they want."[27] Patrick Galbraith and Jason Karlin suggest that Japan's contemporary media landscape is particularly influenced by media convergence, which they argue has become a "new normal."[28] A salient example of convergence can be seen in manga. Media such as manga that were once confined to printed magazines or books are now easily accessible online, through both official and unofficial distribution. Although Shōtarō reads BL manga in its printed form, he also thus frequently reads it through various online distributors, as does Haruma. This is largely because manga is often freely accessible online. Shōtarō chooses to read printed manga as some titles that he enjoys reading are too specialized to be distributed online and are available only in print form. Furthermore, purchasing printed copies is understood by Shōtarō (as well as Haruma) as a way to express one's loyalty to a particular artist. Such convergent media practices ultimately typify the four men's overall consumption of gay media.

The four men consume a wide variety of media content, often accessing the same kinds of content on a variety of different platforms. Thus an approach that is sensitive both to the mode of access (online or offline and via which technologies) and to the effects of the four men's psychobiographies on the content they selected for consumption presents a more useful and nuanced understanding of their overall patterns of media consumption.

## Consuming media before Ni-chōme

Before visiting Ni-chōme, the four men consumed a variety of gay media. Yet their overall consumption was somewhat limited. All four had been exposed since childhood to variety shows starring *onē kyara* celebrities. Although these shows are produced by and for largely heterosexual audiences, the four men all considered them to be "like a kind of gay media" and situated their consumption of these shows within their overall consumption of gay media. Both Junho and Shōtarō became fans of these shows: Junho drew on *onē kyara* performance tropes to silently rebel against his parents' heteronormative gender expectations, and Shōtarō came to identify certain *onē kyara* celebrities as role models in his life as a gay man. By contrast, Yōichi greatly disliked these shows, finding the *onē kyara*'s supposed "femininity" (*onnarashisa*) problematic as it reinforced beliefs he had internalized from wider heteronormative society that his same-sex attraction lessened his masculinity and rendered him effeminate. Haruma used to watch *onē kyara* variety programs but stated that he neither liked nor disliked them. After breaking up with Akito, however, Haruma has slowly started to spend time in Ni-chōme with men who identify with *onē kyara* tropes or specifically as *okama*. This has given him a renewed appreciation of *onē kyara* variety programs as promoting a legitimate form of gay experience that counters that in other Japanese gay media; his views are thus in direct opposition to Yōichi's.

After the four informants' gay desires were awakened by their *hatsukoi*, their first engagement with gay media was often online pornography. Although Haruma would often watch heterosexual pornography online before his gay desire was awoken, about a decade later than for the others, he focused his attention on "the men's techniques." At the time of our interviews in 2013, Haruma was unable to explain why he preferred to watch men, reflecting that it may have been "natural" because he identified with them as fellow men. The other informants, however, did not consume pornography before the awakening of their gay desires. Junho, Yōichi, and Shōtarō all began consuming gay pornographic videos to satisfy their growing need for sexual gratification after experiencing the awakening of their desires by their *hatsukoi*. Haruma reported similar consumption once he awoke to his gay desires. The men variously described their first encounter with gay pornographic videos as "liberating," "satisfying," "educational," and "fun." While the pornographic videos each man consumed differed, all men made use of unofficial video sharing websites known as tube sites. These tube sites, as well as pornography companies' official methods of distribution via their websites, represent the four informants' most common method of consuming pornography. The four men consumed pornography online almost daily, even to this day, and their overall consumption of online media was thus particularly heavy.

Beyond gay pornographic videos, Shōtarō also started consuming BL manga, lent to him by his close female friends before he began visiting Ni-chōme. Even though, somewhat similar to *onē kyara* variety shows, BL manga are largely produced by and for heterosexual women, Shōtarō viewed BL manga as a kind of gay media because he consumed them in the context of his life as a gay man.[29] This view was shared by the other informants and even Yōichi, who expressed little interest in BL manga beyond occasional casual consumption; they all believed that BL manga could be considered gay media. This suggests that for my informants, the definition of gay media rests on the presence of and focus upon gay men, relationships, and sex, rather than on whether or not the media is specifically intended for a gay audience. For these four men, this understanding of what constitutes gay media was developed just prior to visiting Ni-chōme, with their subsequent visits to the district merely reinforcing their definition of what constitutes gay media in Japan. I would thus argue that, for my principal informants, the presence of a same-sex desiring male character is enough to conceptualize media as distinctively gay. That being said, I explore in the following chapter how BL manga sometimes complicates this tendency.

## Consuming media after visiting Ni-chōme

The four informants' first visits to Ni-chōme represented an important transition in their psychobiographies that strongly affected their patterns of consumption, although they continued heavy consumption of online pornography. As Junho, Yōichi, Shōtarō, and Haruma started to visit Ni-chōme to meet sexual or romantic partners, they began to use a variety of online dating sites and location-based dating apps. Junho and Yōichi began to utilize online dating services not just to meet potential sexual partners but also in conjunction with their smartphones' inbuilt organizational tools, such as calendars and reminders, to help organize their increasingly busy lives within the district. McLelland reports in his study that the internet, and particularly internet-capable mobile phones, have revolutionized how Japanese gay men organize their love lives by facilitating almost immediate interactions between gay men,[30] and the four key informants' use of dating apps in conjunction with their smartphones to organize their busy schedules in Ni-chōme seems to reflect these experiences. The informants' heavy smartphone use was representative of broader trends among young gay men in Ni-chōme, as revealed in the previous chapter.

These four men used dating apps to facilitate interactions not only with potential dates but also with friends. As mentioned in the previous chapter, large multinational Western dating apps such as Grindr and Jack'd and websites such as Manhunt.com are commonly utilized in Japan, but Junho and Yōichi preferred Japanese-produced dating sites and smartphone apps. Western apps and sites typically lack an adequate Japanese-language interface and fail to adapt to the sociocultural specificities of the Japanese gay culture. Japanese companies such as 9monsters have subsequently developed Japanese-language dating apps and sites that build on the functionalities of Grindr and also explicitly employ sociocultural knowledge from the Japanese gay culture, such as Typing. These were not the only factors, however, which influenced Junho's and Yōichi's decision to utilize Japanese-produced dating apps. As I discuss in chapter 6, choosing to use a Western dating app is often a strategic decision: the majority of users of these apps are foreign men (understood to be White, Western men) living in Tokyo and Japanese men who desire such foreign partners.

Shōtarō explained that visiting Ni-chōme for the first time with a female friend made it difficult to meet men for romantic dates, so he began to use dating sites and the location-based dating apps Grindr and Jack'd on his smartphone to arrange rendezvous. Shōtarō expressed a preference for Western location-based dating apps, explaining that the experience of coming out in Australia made him feel more comfortable using Western-produced apps. Haruma, who first visited Ni-chōme in the company of his then boyfriend, started to use a dating site only after he broke up with Akito, but explained he used it to make friends. Because of his motivation to make friends, as opposed to meet men for sexual interactions, Haruma preferred a gay dating BBS that specifically facilitated making friends and which he accessed via his home computer. He avoided using location-based dating apps on his smartphone, believing they were used only by men seeking indiscriminate sex.

Importantly, visiting Ni-chōme was the first point of contact all four informants had with Japanese gay magazines, and all men explained that they had not encountered them online prior to visiting the district. Junho and Yōichi reported that they first encountered the magazines while visiting bars, whereas Shōtarō discovered them in *gei shoppu*. Haruma was introduced to Japanese gay magazines by his ex-boyfriend Akito, with whom he used to read them as a prelude to sex. Junho, Yōichi, and Shōtarō eventually developed a preference for *Bádi*; Junho was the only one who read another magazine (*G-Men*), and only rarely. Junho preferred *Bádi* as he was "attracted" to the models in its pages and because it had a "youthful feeling." Yōichi favored *Bádi* because it featured Koh Masaki more frequently than other magazines, and Shōtarō enjoyed its *geikomi*. Haruma also used to enjoy reading *Bádi* because of Akito, who presented the magazine as "like a bible" to educate Haruma about living as a gay man in a manner Akito deemed appropriate. Eventually, Haruma came to view *Bádi* as emblematic of Akito's attempts to force him to become "manlier" and rejected the magazine as "poison." He came to read *Bádi* very infrequently, consuming only very specific content, such as the *geikomi* drawn by one of his favorite manga artists. I explore this shift in Haruma's consumption of *Bádi* more fully in chapter 5.

Only Junho and Yōichi bought physical issues of *Bádi* magazine. Junho would buy each month's issue of *Bádi*, and occasionally issues of *G-Men*, and would avidly read them in his apartment. Yōichi also bought *Bádi* regularly, but not every month. He explained that he would first read copies in bars or *gei shoppu* and bought issues only when they featured content that interested him. Because he was interested primarily in Koh Masaki, he ceased buying the magazine upon Koh's passing in 2013. Shōtarō, who felt nervous about buying magazines and bringing them home where they may have been discovered by his parents, would instead read them in CoCoLo Café. This café in the center of Ni-chōme houses a large library of gay magazines and books, as well as displays event pamphlets. For all of these men, their physical discovery of the magazines, and *Bádi* in particular, while in Ni-chōme affected their online gay media consumption. Shōtarō, for instance, after discovering new *geikomi* series in *Bádi*, began to search for it online and became an avid consumer of this manga genre through unofficial distribution methods. Yōichi used *Bádi* as both inspiration for his personal fashion style and also as a way to ascertain which Japanese pornographic films were worth downloading and viewing each month.

Table 3 presents a summary of the patterns of content consumption, presented in order of overall frequency, from left to right. Online media constituted the most frequently consumed content; within this category, pornographic videos and dating sites occupied the top two positions. The next three items in the ranking are traditionally print-based media, although some of these were commonly consumed online. It must be noted that Haruma did frequently consume gay magazines while in a relationship with Akito, but after their breakup, he ceased consuming them entirely; this is reflected in the table. The least frequently consumed content was televised film media, such as *onē kyara* variety programs, which were typically watched on televisions in the home.

Table 3. Frequency of informants' gay media content consumption

| Informant | Pornographic videos | Dating sites | BL manga | Gay magazines | *Geikomi* | *Onē* programs |
|---|---|---|---|---|---|---|
| Junho | Very frequent | Very frequent | Rare | Frequent | Rare | Frequent |
| Shōtarō | Very frequent | Frequent | Frequent | Occasional | Frequent | Frequent |
| Yōichi | Very frequent | Frequent | Rare | Frequent | Rare | Never |
| Haruma | Frequent | Rare | Frequent | Never | Occasional | Rare |

*Note*: The informants are listed from most to least frequent consumer of media.

## Conclusion

In this chapter, I have explored the life histories of four principal informants in order to understand the role gay media played in their understandings of their desires and identities. Interestingly, I uncovered that for Junho, Yōichi, Haruma, and Shōtarō, gay media played no role in the awakening of gay desires, and it was rather interpersonal relationships with idealized romantic partners or "first loves" that revealed to these men the inherent nature of gay desire. That being said, the gay media they eventually encountered in Ni-chōme, accessed primarily through online means, provided them with justifying discourses for this knowledge, hence introducing them to the regimes of desire that came to strongly influence the four men's understandings of their desires. As typical young consumers, the discourses of desire they encountered, which circulate throughout Japan's gay media landscape, played a crucial role in the development of their lives as gay men. In particular, for all four men, it was the concurrent consumption of media and visits to Ni-chōme that introduced them to the privileging of hard masculinity throughout Japan's gay culture, and this discourse subsequently strongly contoured how they understood their same-sex attraction.

In my discussions with the four focal informants, it became increasingly apparent that Typing represented an important conceptual paradigm on which they drew to make sense of the diverse media they were consuming. Indeed, discussions of Typing dominated our interviews and even our more informal, casual interactions. This is unsurprising given the primacy of Typing in both Ni-chōme and the Japanese gay media landscape discussed in the previous chapter. As the following chapters reveal, the four men's attitudes to Typing gradually evolved as they consumed more and varied media content in conjunction with visiting Ni-chōme.

From initially viewing Typing as a classificatory system based in physicality, to eventually understanding Typing as a complex socio-semiotic system that could be used to construct and market various identities within Japan's gay spaces (both physical and virtual), the four informants' engagement with Typing in the media is complex. It is necessary to explore this engagement in some depth, as Typing represents the system through which the regimes of desire that contour understandings of gay desire and sexuality are disseminated throughout the Japanese gay media landscape. In the next chapters, I draw upon the psychobiographies presented in this chapter to reflect upon how the four men negotiate the privileging of heteronormative masculinities in Japan's gay media landscape. In so doing, I continue drawing on focused case studies as an approach to theorize what is, at heart, a highly personal and subjective cultural process.

# THREE

# The Curse of the Beautiful Boy

*Privileging Hardness, Rejecting Femininity*

Hard, rough, masculine. Throughout my conversations with young gay men over the years I visited Ni-chōme, these three words were repeated time and time again not only to describe an ideal partner but also to articulate the traits of the desirable men appearing within various forms of Japanese gay media. Of the four key informants introduced in the previous chapter, Junho, Yōichi, and Shōtarō certainly agreed that "hard" (*katai*) masculinity was especially desirable, whereas Haruma represented a dissenting opinion. In this book's introduction, I signaled that many of my interviews with young gay men focused upon anxieties relating to gendered performance and that ideas concerning masculinity (*otokorashisa*) were central to how they made sense of their same-sex attraction in contemporary Japan. As I strolled through Ni-chōme with 16 men in July 2013, seeking to learn more about the social organization of the district, my interlocutors consistently answered my questions concerning the signage I observed in the street: they insisted that the heavily muscled *ikanimo-kei* models depicted on these signs possessed a masculinity that was not only sexually attractive but also empowering. That is, the fact that these models performed a masculinity that these 16 young men identified as "hard" was viewed as a challenge to mainstream society's positioning of same-sex attracted men as both failed men and gender inverts. What was surprising, however, was their insistence that Ni-chōme somehow represented a bastion within which "true masculinity" (*hontō na otokorashisa*) resided. A belief that Ni-chōme's gay culture was somehow valorizing a form of masculinity that was once ascendant throughout Japan but that was now in decline represented a common trope during fieldwork interviews. Even Yōichi voiced such beliefs, despite his own concerns about how his same-sex attraction may threaten his status as a man.

Within the discourses of many young gay men that I met in Ni-chōme, there was a firm belief that mainstream society was becoming somehow weakened by a growing desire for "soft" (*yawarakai*) masculinity. The young gay men with whom I spoke tied this notion of softness to an image that many appeared to hold in some contempt: the *bishōnen* or beautiful male youth that represents the focus of young women's media.[1] By privileging hardness as desirable in their narratives, the majority of the young gay men who visited Ni-chōme thus appeared to position soft masculinity as a threat to the neighborhood, with the potential to disrupt the heteronormative masculinity that the Japanese media landscape privileged as ultimately desirable.

This chapter explores such beliefs by investigating the valorization of hard masculinity and how this is situated within a phenomenon afflicting contemporary Japan, referred to as a "curse of the beautiful boy" (*bishōnen no noroi*) by some young gay men. I particularly wish to tease apart how certain young gay men have come to conceptualize Ni-chōme as the last redoubt of a besieged hard masculinity and how such beliefs reveal the ongoing ideological power of hegemonic masculinity in some sections of contemporary Japanese society. In so doing, I investigate how my four key informants placed their own understandings of gay desire into dialogue with the privileging of hardness and rejection of softness found in Ni-chōme, exploring how this in turn influences their relationships with the media that they consume.

When I entered the field in 2013, I was admittedly unprepared to encounter such views among the men I met. As elucidated in the introduction, a vast majority of the research into masculinity in contemporary Japan has emphasized how the collapse of Japan's bubble economy and the concomitant rise of precariousness among young people have led to a destabilization of traditional gender norms. In her prescient ethnography of Japan's aesthetic salon industry, Laura Miller has persuasively argued that new forms of bodily aesthetics emerged in the late 1990s and early 2000s that focused upon softness because of a growing distaste among both heterosexual men and women for the hegemony of images such as the salaryman.[2] Miller reveals through her analysis of men's salons that a newly emergent aesthetic of lithe bodies, smooth faces, and long curly hair was explicitly derived from young women's popular culture, particularly *shōjo* manga (girls' comics) and the male performance idols from Johnny's and Associates talent agency.[3] Indeed, Miller demonstrates how one of these idols named Kimura Takuya emerged as a new aesthetic norm of so-called soft masculinity for young men not only through his domination of popular culture (including television serials) but also via his role as a style icon (as a frequent model in men's fashion magazines and the public face of a large male salon chain).[4] But the young gay men with whom I spoke in Tokyo presented opinions that differed greatly from Miller's experiences. Rather than adopting a supposed soft masculinity that challenged hegemonic forms—as Miller implies young heterosexual men were doing in Japan at the time of her fieldwork in the late 1990s and early 2000s—the young gay men I encountered in Ni-chōme during the 2010s appeared instead to be retreating into hegemonic fantasies of masculinity based in conservative understandings of gendered performance.[5]

One of this chapter's main aims, then, is to nuance the increasingly axiomatic view that Japan's social precarity during the Heisei period always already produces desires for "softness" and that experiences of anxiety inherently destabilize social norms. Adopting a less optimistic reading of contemporary masculinity than does Miller, I argue in this chapter that precariousness has instead led Ni-chōme to retreat into fantasies of a lost masculine past linked to a valorization of hardness, which has in turn produced a regime of desire. As I reveal through the remaining chapters, the neoliberal and homonormative social systems that underpin the Japanese gay media landscape resuscitate heteronormative masculinity through the production of these fantasies of hardness. After exploring in more detail young gay men's attitudes toward the desirability of hard masculinity, I demonstrate how such views have a long history in Japan's gay culture and are tied to a broader distrust of the feminine (*onnarashisa*) as a consequence of the mainstream positioning of same-sex attracted men as gender inverts. I then specifically investigate the notion of a "curse of the beautiful boy" and untangle how my interlocutors understood the relationships between Ni-chōme and mainstream society through the trope of masculinity. I expose how the young gay men with whom I spoke criticized the supposed feminization of Japanese popular culture and how Japan's gay culture—and specifically Ni-chōme, which they positioned as representative of a broader national experience—represents a challenge to this spreading "curse" of softness and weakness. To conclude the chapter, I explore gay men's attitudes toward a specific form of young women's popular culture known as Boys Love, discussing it as a site within which these debates become especially explicit and central to Junho, Yōichi, Haruma, and Shōtarō's understandings of desirable masculinity.

*Hard Masculinity: Desires for Hegemonic Masculinity in Ni-chōme*

When two young gay men meet in Ni-chōme for the first time, it is common for them to inquire about each other's preferences in a partner as part of the broader process of getting to know each other. Likewise, when I conducted brief interviews in gay bars or on the streets with young gay men, I would often commence the discussion by asking them to tell me about their "ideal Type" (*risō na taipu*), just as Shōtarō had done when we first visited Lumière together early in my fieldwork. Invariably, the most common response to my question would be that young gay men found "masculine" (*otokorashii*) individuals particularly attractive, with almost all of the men with whom I spoke indicating at some point in our ice-breaking conversations that they were attracted to "masculine" men. Delving deeper into what this specifically meant revealed how the young gay men with whom I spoke remained firmly influenced by the hetero system critiqued by Fushimi Noriaki that produces two binary and mutually exclusive genders, the "male role" and the "female role."[6] To be masculine was variously defined as being "hard," "rough," "active," "strong," "serious," "stoic," "disciplined," and "reliable." As indicated above, "hard" and "rough" were the two most frequent adjectives used by my interlocutors to make sense of masculinity. One young man I met in a large *gai-sen* bar in the center of Ni-chōme also rather flippantly defined masculinity as anything that was not "like a woman" (*onnappoi*). In fact, many of the men I met in Ni-chōme found questions about how they understood masculinity difficult to answer and preferred to list what masculinity was not. In doing so, such men often drew upon the trope of "femininity" (*onnarashisa*). Thus, through conversations with young gay men, I learned that desirable masculinity in Japan's gay culture was neither "cute," "soft," "sweet," "playful," nor "emotional." As can be plainly seen, my interlocutors drew upon gendered stereotypes to make sense of the masculinity that they positioned as desirable and ideal, juxtaposing it with an implicitly undesirable femininity, which I unpack further below.

I was particularly interested to learn more about my informants' opinions concerning hard masculinity and often asked the men with whom I conversed in bars and *gei shoppu* to more concretely define hardness and to explain why they found it desirable. For one young man with whom I chatted outside Lumière in 2015 as we looked at a poster depicting heavily muscled *ikanimo-kei* models, "hardness" referred both to the desirable bodily aesthetics of an ideal man as well as to his "determination to work hard and be the best that he can be." Pointing to the models on the poster, this young man explained that a gym-trained *gatai* body was desirable specifically because it was produced through disciplined training, hence revealing the inner "strength"—both physical and mental—of an ideal man. "Masculinity" was often tied to a desire for "seriousness" (*majime*) and "hard work" (*doryoku*) among the men I interviewed, with the *gatai* body representing a broader index of more spiritual traits often linked to notions of masculine power. As another informant explained to me in 2013, the *gatai* body was not necessarily desirable in and of itself, but rather came to be viewed as desirable since possession of such a hard body revealed that an individual's personality conformed to normative understandings of masculinity as strong and dedicated. Further, hardness was often linked in my interlocutors' narratives with a desire for rough and violent sex, and the *gatai* body once again represented an index for a man's ability to "fuck vigorously," as Junho put it during one of our early conversations. Overall, hardness was conceptualized as a descriptor for a specific physical appearance, personality traits, and behaviors that together formed an image of ideal masculinity conforming to heteronormative and hegemonic logics circulating throughout mainstream Japanese society.

For many men, this sense of "hardness" was the indispensable quality that rendered the *ikanimo-kei* the most privileged Type in Japan's gay culture. Simply put, one could not be considered *ikanimo-kei* unless one possessed the hard masculinity that the young men with whom I spoke understood as normatively desirable in spaces such as Ni-chōme. It was for this reason that the *gatai* body had come to be linked to the *ikanimo-kei* in young gay men's imaginaries, and this Type in turn represented the epitome of the hardness valorized throughout the Japanese gay media landscape. In fact, when I asked informants who identified as *ikanimo-kei* what it meant to be this Type, almost all took this question as an opportunity to describe their extensive gym regimes, which many followed religiously in order to maintain their *gatai* bodies and hence their desirable status. Yōichi, as a *hayatteru ikemen*, was one such individual, justifying his extensive fitness regime as necessary to maintain a "masculine" physique that would allow him to attract potential men with whom he could have sex. Further, I met many men dissatisfied with their body image who also viewed their gym training as a way to develop a "hard" masculine bodily aesthetic and thus become an *ikanimo-kei*. Indeed, Shōtarō was one of the young men I met during fieldwork who engaged in such aspirational practices. He reported on many occasions that he was dissatisfied with his progress, lamenting that his body remained "soft, weak, and effeminate."

This privileging of gym training among the young gay men I met in Tokyo demonstrates links to the same kinds of normative body types and related fitness practices that are privileged within the homonormative gay culture critiqued by Lisa Duggan.[7] For radical queer theorist and activist Mattilda Bernstein Sycamore, the gym-trained bodies that have emerged as hegemonic within global gay culture represent a homogenization of gay male experience, privileging American gay culture's middle-class values and consumerist culture.[8] The desires for hardness reported by my interlocutors in Japan may thus emerge from Ni-chōme's interactions with global gay media circuits that produce neoliberal consumerism as the basis for gay identity. Further, recent years have seen an increase throughout Japan in health manuals for young men focusing on "muscle training" (*kintore*) and bodybuilding. Sociologists Jesper Andreasson and Thomas Johansson argue that these publications are being spurred by the global "male aesthetics" movement, and it is highly likely that the young men I met in Ni-chōme were influenced by this broader social movement as well.[9] What is clear from my discussions with young gay men is that such gym regimes were designed to produce a hard bodily aesthetic that greatly differed from the soft masculinity that Miller encountered in male aesthetic salons targeting heterosexual men in the late 1990s and early 2000s. Japan's gay culture privileges instead a physicality linked to hegemonic understandings of masculinity as strong and active, which Miller suggests had become less prominent in mainstream Japanese culture, particularly among young people.[10]

On occasion, as we discussed their attitudes and understandings of desirable masculinity, I also asked the young gay men I met in Ni-chōme's bars and clubs to reflect on their conceptualizations of the salaryman. I did so as I was curious to learn about these men's opinions about a figure that remains central to the academic literature on masculinity in contemporary Japan (see introduction). I especially wished to see whether the salaryman image played a role in contouring conceptualizations of gender in Japan's gay culture, as there had been little discussion of this seminal figure in the previous literature. I found that opinions of the salaryman tended to be evenly split between those who viewed it positively as an index of hard masculinity and those who rejected it as an outmoded symbol tied to their parents' generation and lacking aesthetic appeal. This split in attitudes toward the salaryman image, I discovered, was often grounded in whether the man with whom I was speaking privileged "hardness" in personality traits or bodily aesthetics. Those holding this opinion were more likely to evaluate the salaryman positively.

For example, one young man who viewed the salaryman positively indicated that while the salaryman may not necessarily be hard in terms of their physical appearance (that is, they may not have a gym-sculpted body), they certainly embodied the hard-working ethos grounded in Japan's traditional corporate culture that informs mainstream conceptualizations of masculinity.[11] Furthermore, for this man and others like him, the salaryman was desirably "hard" since it embodied a gendered identity that was the supposed opposite of womanhood. In holding such beliefs, these men drew upon the logics of the hetero system to conceptualize masculinity as active and productive and femininity as passive and weak. The fact that the salaryman goes to work every day, commits to difficult overtime, and sacrifices himself for his family was viewed by these men as integral to hard masculinity and was a desirable trait they aspired to possess themselves. That is, the salaryman continued to represent an aspirational symbol tied to these men's desire to eventually become "full members of society" (*ichininmae no shakaijin*).[12] On the other hand, other young men rejected the idea that the salaryman was desirable, instead suggesting that such masculinity was linked to an "uncool" (*dasai*) generation that lacked bodily and aesthetic discipline. Junho and Yōichi, who were both among the youngest men I interviewed, shared this opinion. Yōichi particularly argued that salarymen were more likely to be "drunken old men" than possessors of a hard masculinity that he found attractive. In making this claim, Yōichi admitted that he was reflecting on his father, a "typical salaryman" who had eventually deserted his family (thus "failing" as a man) and who Yōichi consistently explained was a "useless alcoholic," as stated in the previous chapter.

## Soft Masculinity: Rejecting Effeminacy and Problematizing Cuteness

While differing in their opinions about whether the salaryman represents an example of desirable hard masculinity, all the men with whom I spoke appeared to believe that hardness was what separated desirable masculinity from undesirable effeminacy. As the above discussion makes clear, Nichōme's gay bar culture continues to deploy the logics of the hetero system explored in the introduction to promote a system of gender/sexual duality whereby masculinity and femininity are viewed as mutually opposing concepts. If masculinity was conceptualized as hard, the young gay men I interviewed in the bars and streets of Ni-chōme consistently positioned femininity as soft. Likewise, if hardness was considered desirable, then the logics of the hetero system inculcated in young Japanese gay men the belief that softness was somehow less desirable or even undesirable. Even men who admitted to finding softness desirable, or who possessed a "softer" identity themselves such as Haruma, were aware of the rejection of softness within Ni-chōme and believed that this rejection was typical of Japan's gay culture more broadly. The hetero system thus operated as a regime of desire, contouring how young gay men understood the desirability of masculinity and locking gay men into heteronormative logics that foreclosed the possibility for performances of masculinity that deviate from the societal privileging of hardness to be considered desirable.

The supposed perils of softness as a kind of effeminacy became especially obvious to me during conversations concerning the ambivalent desirability of cuteness (*kawaii*). As I explored briefly in chapter 1, while spaces that valorize cute men do exist in Ni-chōme, these bars and clubs tend to be positioned outside of the district's central areas, where the "hard" *gatai* bodies of the *ikanimo-kei* dominated advertising. Whether cuteness was considered desirable within Ni-chōme was thus unclear. On the one hand, the existence of spaces privileging cuteness indicated to me a modicum of acceptance for the potential desirability of a softer masculinity, tied to the *kawaii-kei*. On the other hand, the location of these bars and clubs on the edges of the neighborhood and their lack of central prominence suggested that desires for cuteness were likewise peripheral or marginalized. As I strolled through the neighborhood, early in my fieldwork, with groups of young Japanese gay men to learn about the social organization of the space, my interlocutors certainly justified the peripheral location of these bars as indicative of the uncertain place that cuteness holds in Japan's gay culture. As we strolled past a prominent bar for admirers of the *kawaii-kei* located on the edge of Ni-chōme, one young man put it this way: the links that many believed existed between cuteness and femininity made it "inappropriate" for such bars to be in the center of Ni-chōme, a space set aside for what this man termed the "worship of masculinity."

During my visits to Ni-chōme, the young gay men I interviewed would often position cuteness as somehow suspect because of these links between cuteness and femininity. For instance, a young man whom I met in 2015 and who very firmly identified with the *ikanimo-kei* identity explained to me that "he had nothing against *kawaii-kei*" but that "people who like these kinds of effeminate (*memeshii*) men aren't really that gay." When I asked him to elaborate on this somewhat confusing statement, he laughed and explained that since gay men are attracted to other men, "Attraction to cuteness is a contradiction . . . How can a gay man like someone who is like a woman (*onnappoi*)? They might as well be straight!" While most men I met in Ni-chōme did not take such an extreme position regarding cuteness (and this man's statement was definitely expressed somewhat idiosyncratically), this narrative demonstrates the clear influence of the hetero system and the regimes of desire that inculcate desires for hardness as an index for normative masculinity among young gay men in Ni-chōme. For this man and the many others I met who possessed less extreme versions of his opinions, softness as linked to the notion of cuteness is so strongly tied to the feminine that any gay man who is attracted to cuteness is in truth actually desiring femininity. Cuteness is thus representative of the "female role" within the hetero system, and men such as this informant believe that gay desire logically represents attraction to the "male role." That is, men who desire cuteness are somehow not "fully" same-sex attracted because of their supposed interest in femininity. Overall, cuteness and softness were consistently linked to femininity in my interlocutors' narratives, and many men explained to me that it was therefore "common sense" (*jōshiki*) for gay men to prefer hardness and masculinity over cuteness.

Of course, not all young gay men whom I met over the years I visited Ni-chōme personally identified with hard masculinity, and many believed that their identities were softer and cuter than the Types privileged in both Ni-chōme and the Japanese gay media landscape. Further, I naturally met some men—although they appeared to be a minority—who did indeed find cuteness desirable and who saw softness as a legitimate expression of desirable masculinity. But one common topic of conversation that I had with such men concerned their recognition that their beliefs were neither dominant in Ni-chōme nor accepted by those possessing the desirable hard masculinity privileged in Japanese gay media. This was a source of frustration for many of these men, since the broader rejection of cuteness in Ni-chōme often stymied their attempts to enter into sexual or romantic relationships with other men. One such man was my key informant Haruma who, as revealed in the previous chapter, strongly identified with the "herbivorous boy" subculture and viewed himself as cute. In the following extended extract from an interview in October 2013, Haruma details his own understandings of cuteness. I share this extended extract as it provides a representative example of the dilemma faced by those men I met during fieldwork who wish to be recognized for their cuteness but who are also aware that such gender performances are viewed with suspicion by most men active in Ni-chōme.

> HARUMA: Being asked to define cuteness, I mean it's not something that I can define very easily. Maybe that is the definition, "something which is difficult to define." [laughs] But I can tell you what other [gay men] think about cuteness. They will tell you that being cute is effeminate, that it's being like a woman or that it's not manly. Others will define it as the opposite to the *ikanimo-kei*, and other people will say that maybe being cute is not very straight-acting . . . Maybe someone will say that it's androgynous, and others might even say, "Oh, that's someone who is a bottom" or something like that—
> THOMAS: [interjects]—and what about the media?
> HARUMA: [pauses] . . . Um yes, media . . . I think these [ideas] are the kinds of responses that gay media program [into men]. But still, this doesn't give you too much of an idea about what cuteness actually is, it just tells you what people expect cuteness to be. I think that being cute is a very personal experience. It's certainly true that as someone who feels cute I have a "salty face" [*shiogao*][13] . . . As they used to say a few years ago [laughs]. But cute is a style which emphasizes softness . . . Maybe gay guys don't think cute is manly because they feel it feeds into the common-sense idea that all gay guys are camp . . . Most [gay men] would say that being cute and manly are mutually exclusive. In the end, being cute is just how you feel, but that feeling is influenced by the media we read and that media doesn't share my opinion! So yes . . . that's what cute means to me! [laughs]

In the above extract, Haruma clearly struggles to define cuteness, suggesting that while most Japanese gay men draw upon tropes relating to femininity to make sense of it, he instead understands cuteness as a feeling or affect that is highly personal. Indeed, within the emerging field of "cute studies," there is a growing recognition that cuteness is predominantly an affective phenomenon based in expectations surrounding lovability, care, and winsomeness.[14] Haruma appeared to reject an understanding of cuteness based purely in a certain bodily aesthetic typified by softness. But my conversations with men in Ni-chōme uncovered that, unlike hardness which was sometimes understood in aesthetic terms and sometimes in terms of personality, most young gay men active in Ni-chōme's gay bar culture conceptualize cuteness in purely aesthetic terms. That is, cuteness was understood by most of the men with whom I conversed as a "soft" bodily aesthetic that was evaluated negatively when compared with the desirable *gatai* body. It was only men, like Haruma, who identified with cuteness that would make a case for understanding cuteness affectively, possibly to recuperate its desirability when faced with a culture that privileges hard, heteronormative conceptualizations of masculinity.

Continuing my conversation with Haruma excerpted above, I learned that his negative experiences with his ex-boyfriend Akito had played a crucial role in his affective understanding of cuteness and softness. As recounted in the previous chapter, Haruma felt that he lost control of his "selfhood" (*shutaisei*) because of Akito's insistence on making him more "masculine." This experience produced in him a healthy skepticism of the Japanese gay media landscape's regimes of desire. For Haruma, cuteness as an affective experience fundamentally represented feelings of "difference," where one's gender performances and associated bodily aesthetics were positioned by others as contradicting or challenging the heteronormative gender norms of Japan's gay culture. Haruma's narrative makes clear his belief that media played a strong role in producing these affects at the same time as it inculcated desires for hard masculinity as normative, a topic I explore more fully in subsequent chapters. Ultimately, Haruma's experiences reveal the political economy of desire that conditions attitudes to masculinity underpinning the ideologies circulating in the Japanese gay media landscape. Femininity is problematized as part of a broader heteronormative ideology that positions hegemonic masculinity as desirable, and this means that any man whose gender performance deviates from such norms is made to feel othered and marginalized. According to Sara Ahmed's phenomenological understandings of queer experience, such men fail to be "smoothed" into heteronormativity and thus experience discomforting affects that strengthen their sense of alienation from the majority.

## *The* Bishōnen *Curse: Retreating into Fantasies of the Past to Escape the Present*

The young gay men I met over the years in Tokyo appeared to problematize cuteness because of a heteronormative logic that positions the feminine in an abject position vis-à-vis desirable masculinity in Japan's gay culture. But their concerns regarding soft masculinity were not solely confined to spaces such as Ni-chōme: a distaste for softness also colored several of these men's understandings of contemporary Japanese society more broadly. My conversations with these men revealed a pervasive belief in Ni-chōme as a bastion where masculinity is both worshiped, as one of my interlocutors put it, and protected from an increasingly "effeminate" Japanese culture "cursed" by the figure of the *bishōnen*. I now turn to consider this paradox where a community that mainstream society stigmatizes as failing to uphold hegemonic gender ideologies positions itself as the defenders of heteronormative understandings of masculinity.

During interviews with my interlocutors concerning cuteness and softness, quite a number expressed a belief that Ni-chōme was increasingly becoming a space where "true masculinity" (*hontō na otokorashisa*) was found, whereas broader society represented a site within which this masculinity was becoming corrupted and weakened. When I asked these men to clarify what kinds of gender performances constituted true masculinity, they would explain that the hard masculinity valorized in Ni-chōme represented the "true" expression of masculinity in Japan. One young man suggested over drinks at a bar in 2015 that the fact that a gay town such as Ni-chōme now represented the site of traditional masculinity demonstrated just how "weakened" Japanese masculinity had become in recent years. This young man found the situation ironic since the space mainstream society viewed as gender-suspect was the only place where people understood what he termed "real" masculinity. Yōichi was another strong and vocal proponent of this position, despite his initial concerns over the relationship between his same-sex attraction and his identity as a man. As we conversed in 2013, Yōichi explained that the idea of Ni-chōme as a space where traditional masculine ideals and aesthetics were celebrated was central to the practices of *hayatteru ikemen* such as himself. "The rest of Japan has succumbed to beautiful boys," he stated, further arguing that the *hayatteru ikemen* celebrated hard masculinity in order to resist the growing "weakness" sweeping across Japan. In Yōichi's narrative, the privileging of hard masculinity, at the heart of the heteronormative regimes of desire circulating in Ni-chōme, is thus a defensive reaction against the destabilization of "true" masculinity in the rest of the country. Interestingly, many men described this destabilization as a "weakening" of culture, suggesting that masculine identities such as the *bishōnen* were somehow damaging to Japan.

When asked to reflect on his understandings of contemporary Japanese masculinity more broadly, one young man explained to me his disappointment in soft masculinity's rise in mainstream popular culture. This young man, whom I met at a Korean pop music–themed club event in Ni-chōme, argued that Japan was suffering from what he termed a "curse of the beautiful boy" because of the dominance of young women's desires for "male actors with feminine faces" (*onnagao haiyū*). Interestingly, many men I met during fieldwork used the metaphor of a curse to explain the *bishōnen*'s rise in Japan, and this phrase was particularly common in bars catering to the normatively desirable *ikanimo-kei*. For many of the men that I met in Ni-chōme's gay bars and clubs, young women's texts had come to dominate contemporary Japanese popular culture and to strongly influence ideals of masculinity. *Shōjo* manga (girls' comics) and the "trendy dramas" that became popular in the 1990s were singled out as representative of this trend. For many of the men with whom I spoke, Japanese masculinity was becoming soft; they saw an increasing focus away from hard masculinity since such gendered performances were supposedly no longer popular among young women. That is, the shifts that Miller identified in her ethnography of Japan's aesthetic salon industry were viewed as a curse that was somehow weakening or diluting contemporary Japanese masculinity. Most of my interlocutors viewed the *bishōnen*'s rise in Japan negatively and positioned Ni-chōme as an important space of resistance where hard masculinity remained prominent and respected.

There was one group of *bishōnen* that my interlocutors viewed especially negatively: the male idols managed by the talent agency Johnny's and Associates. "Johnny's idols" were variously described as "too cute," "too androgynous," or "effeminate" during interviews, and young gay men employed the vocabulary tied to undesirable femininity in Ni-chōme to make sense of these popular performers who are often positioned as "national" idols in Japan's mainstream media.[15] The principal reason these men disliked Johnny's idols was because they lacked the *gatai* physicality privileged in Japanese gay media, and many men I interviewed expressed a related dissatisfaction with the so-called *hoso macho* (thin but muscular) bodily aesthetics that these idols supposedly possessed. Yōichi, an avid gym enthusiast with a hard *gatai* body, singled out *hoso macho* as a weakened form of masculine bodily aesthetics that apparently pandered to what he termed "young women's desires for emasculated men." Although some gay men I met in Ni-chōme did not necessarily view Johnny's idols negatively and even idealized the *janīzu-kei* (Johnny's Type), my impression from fieldwork was that Johnny's idols were considered problematic in Ni-chōme because of their association with young women's popular culture. Nowhere was this clearer than in a regular annual feature in *Bádi* titled "Ranking of Celebrities Who Gay Men Love and Hate" (*Gei ga suki kirai geinōjin rankingu*). Between 2011 and 2015, Kimura Takuya—the Johnny's idol that Miller identified as representative of the new soft masculine aesthetic that emerged in 21st-century Japan[16]—was selected as the celebrity gay men hated the most. Interviews with some of my informants revealed that Kimura was particularly unpopular because of his central role in promulgating soft masculinity in contemporary Japan, and some young men I met in bars and clubs especially blamed Johnny's idols and their obsessive female fans for "weakening" Japanese masculinity.

In their discussions with me, young gay men seemed to be unconsciously drawing upon a common sentiment that emerged in Japan after the collapse of the bubble economy and the subsequent neoliberalization of society that criticizes the supposed feminization of contemporary Japanese culture.[17] As anthropologist Jennifer Prough insightfully notes in her ethnography of the *shōjo* manga industry in the early 2000s, young women emerged as the drivers of the Japanese economy by the late 1990s, and cultural production therefore increasingly targeted these consumers, producing new mainstream discourses of gender, such as the soft masculine *bishōnen* that appealed to this demographic.[18] As consumer culture shifted to cater to the desires of young women, traditional ideologies concerning sex and gender were explicitly challenged through the centering of women's sexual agency, partly unsettling Japan's patriarchal expectations concerning the role of women in society.[19] Young Japanese women's desires were now not only recognized and celebrated but they were almost considered more "active" than those of men, strongly influencing ideologies of masculinity and the growing rejection of hegemonic, hard masculinity in mainstream society.[20]

Naturally, the rise of young women's consumer culture and its subversion of traditional gender norms have been met with considerable conservative backlash, particularly within male-dominated industries such as anime and manga.[21] Most notably, the alternative right-wing social media users known collectively as *netouyo* have often mobilized around criticisms of young women's consumer culture as a site to express their ultranationalist dissatisfaction with mainstream Japanese culture.[22] My interlocutors' distaste for *bishōnen* must be understood as one manifestation of this conservatism. When young Japanese gay men idealized Ni-chōme as a bastion for true, traditional hard masculinity, this represented an almost patriarchal reaction against the subversion of gender norms by young women's popular culture. This is a clear instance where the regimes of desire that contour understandings of gender in Japan's gay culture fail to queer or subvert the status quo, leading young gay men to retreat into fantasies of a lost masculine past via their resuscitation of heteronormative gender norms. Changes in society engendered by rising precariousness therefore appear to be pushing Japan's gay culture in more conservative directions than young women's culture. Whereas Prough and Miller both argue that changes to the Japanese economy have ultimately (and perhaps unintentionally) challenged some heteronormative logics of sex and gender, my ethnography of Ni-chōme highlights how these same processes have instead resuscitated traditional forms of masculinity and created significant criticism of young women's popular culture among some young gay men.

A skepticism of femininity and a fear of the implicit links between the feminine and male same-sex desire has a long history in Japan, and my interlocutors' distaste for the rise of the *bishōnen* in mainstream society must also be understood within this broader historical context. As discussed in the introduction, the postwar period saw the emergence of an increasingly "transgendered" understanding of same-sex desiring men tied to the figure of the *gei bōi*, cross-dressing performers who embraced soft aesthetics similar to that of the *bishōnen*.[23] The *homo* subculture that developed in the 1970s and found expression in magazines such as *Adon*, *Barazoku*, and *Sabu* explicitly reacted against these mainstream depictions of effeminate gay men, borrowing from American aesthetics culture to valorize heavily muscular bodies and rough masculinity.[24] Indeed, the 1970s saw softness positioned as undesirable because of its links with femininity, a view that my informants echoed in their reported opinions. Magazines such as *Sabu* even explicitly valorized Japan's martial past and romanticized the figure of the samurai and the ethics of bushido,[25] demonstrating that contemporary young gay men's retreat into fantasies of a lost masculine past is a common trope in Japan's postwar gay culture.

Going further back into Japan's past, we can see that in many ways my interlocutors' discourses also echoed the sentiments of noted "homosocialist"[26] author and right-wing admirer of Japan's imperial past Mishima Yukio, who called for a return to a hard and military style masculinity as a way to revitalize a weakened postwar Japanese nation. Mishima, who many have speculated was a homosexual man and whose novels *Confes-*

*sions of a Mask* (1949) and *Forbidden Colors* (1951) were highly influential in Japan's postwar *homo* culture,[27] argued that both Japanese literature and culture were inherently founded in a "rough masculinity" based in what he called the "hard faction" (*kō-ha*),[28] a term with homoerotic overtones. As discussed in the introduction, *kō-ha* emerged in the late 19th century, during Japan's modernization, to refer to premodern homoerotic practices.[29] According to Mishima, modern Japan had devolved into a weakened state as a result of its "shameful" loss of empire and its adoption of "decadent Western" cultural forms. Mishima links this devolution to the *nanpa,* or "soft faction," of aesthetes and *bishōnen* who indulged in heterosexual relationships with women and "capitulated" to Western notions of romance. Like many of the young gay men I met in Ni-chōme at the end of the Heisei period, Mishima longed for a past where Japanese "men were real men," and he found expression for this in a narrative that privileged the rough masculinity of Japan's colonial period and that feminized contemporary Japanese culture through implicit criticisms of "womanly" romance.[30]

In his novel-length autobiographical essay *Sun and Steel,* Mishima develops a "colonial nostalgic" logic of strong and rough masculinity by evoking the strength of Japanese imperial masculinity via the metaphor of the sun during wartime. By colonial nostalgia, I refer to more than just a desire to reverse the "decline of national grandeur and the international power politics connected to political . . . hegemony" engendered by the loss of empire, but instead a desire for "the colonial lifestyle" and a return to the sociocultural hierarchies that dominated colonial governance and everyday life.[31] Thinking back to his youth during World War II, when he was particularly "weak" and "feeble," Mishima explains that his first taste of true "power" was imbued within him by the brilliance of the sun.[32] Mishima argues that the power of the wartime sun derived in part from its "pervasive corruption and destruction," and he suggests that truly powerful individuals—all described as men possessing muscular bodies and rough temperament, a description apparently analogous to the contemporary *gatai* aesthetic—faded from Japanese society as Western modernity swept across the nation after Japan's defeat by the Allied powers.[33] Once again, Mishima specifically singles out the supposedly Western notions of sentimentality and romance as driving this degeneration. In other words, Mishima believed that Japan's defeat and subsequent occupation by the US-led Allies engendered an emasculation that had disastrous effects on Japan's culture. According to Fushimi Noriaki's memoirs, Mishima's philosophies concerning the gendered nature of Japan's defeat gained currency in the 1970s among some same-sex desiring men as a way to both understand and criticize mainstream society's "transgendered" conceptualization of male same-sex desire.[34]

After discussing the sun as a corrupting and primal masculine force, Mishima then explains his own turn toward bodybuilding, boxing, and Japanese fencing (*kendo*) and his desire to recuperate this rough masculinity and "power over death" through training in the traditional arts of Japan's "masculine past."[35] Turning his attention to discussions of steel, it is at this moment in this autobiographical essay when colonial nostalgia becomes most apparent in Mishima's narrative: he states that "[this] manliness was no longer of any practical use in society, it was scarcely distinguishable from art that depended on imagination."[36] Although this novelistic essay does not necessarily evoke homoeroticism explicitly in quite the same way as his earlier writing on the "hard and masculine" basis of Japanese literature, throughout *Sun and Steel*, Mishima writes about Japan's traditional martial past in an elegiac tone that clearly demonstrates an almost erotic longing for rough masculinity. I share this narrative because, like Mishima, my own interlocutors also sought to retreat into fantasies of a more masculine past when faced with precarious social change. This tendency to retreat into heteronormative formulations of masculinity thus has a long history in Japan, and it is unsurprising that young men living at the end of the precarious Heisei period would therefore seek to position a site like Ni-chōme as a space within which "true" masculinity is protected.

As Bernstein Sycamore insightfully notes, a stigma against femininity is common within the neoliberalized and globalized gay culture that has swept across the globe, and thus once again, it is evident that Ni-chōme is responding to broader homonormative trends that valorize heteronormative understandings of masculinity around the world.[37] When young gay men complain about the "curse of the beautiful boy" and argue that Japan's gay culture represents a bastion of hard masculinity within a world weakened by the rise of young women's popular culture, they demonstrate how the neoliberalization of Ni-chōme has produced particular negative affects. Japanese gay men possess considerable anxieties surrounding their gendered performances, and these anxieties have a long history resulting from the intense societal discrimination against same-sex attracted men that has developed in the postwar era. The Japanese gay media landscape, in selling fantasies of hard masculinity that ultimately affirm the masculinity of same-sex desiring men, thus plays upon these fears in order to produce profit. That is, the neoliberal regimes of desire that inculcate these fantasies for hardness deliberately subvert the queer potentials of soft masculinity, identified by scholars such as Laura Miller; they repurpose softness as a threat to Japan's gay culture rather than a site where heteronormativity can be deconstructed and alternative futures can be imagined. My interlocutors' attitudes to soft masculinity and their desires for a lost past thus explicate how Ni-chōme ultimately privileges heteronormativity through the regimes of desire circulating in the Japanese gay media landscape.

## Boys Love Manga: Debating the Feminization of Gay Men in Young Women's Popular Culture

During my interviews with young gay men, one site where debates over the curse of softness sweeping Japan emerged was during conversations concerning Boys Love manga and *geikomi*, two popular culture forms that formed part of my four key interlocutors' patterns of gay media consumption (see chapter 2). Boys Love (or BL) is an umbrella term that emerged in the 1990s to refer to a genre of manga and other related products depicting romantic and sexual relationships between *bishōnen* and produced primarily for heterosexual female consumers.[38] *Geikomi* refers to a diverse range of manga produced for and by male homosexuals.[39] All four principal informants reported consuming both BL and *geikomi*, and Shōtarō and Haruma identified as fans of these manga. Junho and Yōichi, on the other hand, read them both less frequently and in a more casual manner. Shōtarō, echoing the other three key informants, linked BL and *geikomi* as "gay manga" when asked to talk about his understandings of the manga he consumed. But such an opinion is somewhat controversial in Japan's gay culture, and very few men I met in Ni-chōme considered BL as "gay" media and rather believed in its links to the soft masculinity privileged in young women's popular culture.

Given the separate developmental histories of BL and *geikomi*, the term "gay manga" today usually refers specifically to *geikomi* as manga produced for and by gay men, distinguishing it both stylistically and theoretically from BL.[40] But Junho, Yōichi, Haruma, and Shōtarō used the term "gay manga" as a kind of meta-generic label to organize their discussions of BL and *geikomi*, without any prompting from me as the interviewer. The four men often explicitly resisted my attempts to separate the two genres during our interviews, arguing that it is not possible to do so since both media contain representations of men they understood as "gay." Influenced by their understanding of the term "gay" as an identity category explicitly tied to their experiences of same-sex attraction, these four men understood BL and *geikomi* as interconnected. They all variously argued that both BL and *geikomi* represent equally valid yet fantastic depictions of "gay identity" (*gei aidentitī*). For this reason, the four men saw no need to sharply disassociate BL from *geikomi* when discussing their consumption of gay media. Yōichi, whose consumption of both BL and *geikomi* is highly casual, explained that to conceptually separate the two genres made little sense; he stated, "They are both manga, two sides of the same coin . . . They have gay guys in them, even if they look different . . . so they're gay manga." This admission was despite the fact that Yōichi was a firm believer in the primacy of hardness and despite his denigration of soft masculinity. Upon further prompting, Yōichi admitted that he occasionally viewed BL with suspicion and would consume BL works only when he was "desperate" for something quick to masturbate over. He also noted that he would consume only BL content that "looked like" *geikomi*, noting that recent years had seen the emergence of BL with hard aesthetics and highly pornographic scenes.

It should be mentioned, however, that the majority of men I met during fieldwork expressed little interest in discussing manga; thus, the four principal informants' interest in BL and *geikomi* might be atypical of young Japanese gay men. In fact, it is unsurprising that a number of the young gay men with whom I conversed in Ni-chōme's bars possessed a particularly negative attitude toward BL since they saw it as an example of the young women's popular culture that had cursed contemporary Japan with soft masculinity. Whereas regular BL consumers, such as fans like Haruma and Shōtarō, were willing to accept BL as a form of gay media because of their affective attachment to the genre, young gay men who admitted during interviews that they did not engage with BL tended to dismiss it as inauthentic given its status as young women's media. Of particular concern to these men was their belief that BL reinforced Japanese society's tendency to view same-sex attracted men as effeminate. One young man explained to me that "BL is a nonsense created from prejudice read by silly school girls."

Stylistically, BL and *geikomi* differ greatly, although it is important to note that both BL and *geikomi* are not monolithic and contain great stylistic variation across artists working in either genre.[41] During interviews, my four key informants raised particular stylistic differences between BL and *geikomi* essential to their understanding of both genres. For Junho, Yōichi, Haruma, and Shōtarō, BL was typified by its depiction of its characters, such as the *bishōnen*, that are viewed as problematic in Ni-chōme and by its focus on romantic escapism. A focus on *bishōnen* is typical of BL, Mark McLelland argues, because the beautiful boy image has been argued to represent a "softer" masculinity that is "safer" for female consumption.[42] On the other hand, the four principal informants understood *geikomi* to depict gay men as possessing wild, rough, and uncontrollable urges. Previous scholarship suggests that this depiction may be due to *geikomi*'s emergence from 1970s *homo* magazines, such as *Sabu*, which promoted hypermasculine visions of gay desire.[43] Throughout interviews, Junho, Yōichi, Haruma, and Shōtarō argued that the depictions of masculinity in *geikomi* were "extreme" (*kageki*) and further understood this extremeness as highly desirable. This was an opinion shared by other young gay men I met during fieldwork: they viewed *geikomi* positively (even if they did not necessarily consume it) because it conformed to their preconceived notion that desirable gay masculinity is both "hard" and "violent," as discussed earlier in this chapter. Interestingly, my four key interlocutors drew upon Typing to further articulate the differences between the two genres. BL was positioned as containing predominantly *kawaii-kei* characters and *geikomi* as containing either *ikanimo-kei* or *gaten-kei* characters who possess *gatai* or *gachimuchi* bodies respectively.

It is thus clear that for fans and nonconsumers alike, BL and *geikomi* are evaluated from the perspective of the political economy of desire that conditions knowledge about masculinity in Ni-chōme. Both groups of young gay men agreed that *geikomi* represented a desirable hard gay masculinity, but fannish consumers were more likely to "forgive" BL for its focus on soft masculinity than nonfans, who tended instead to problematize BL texts' representational and aesthetic strategies. Shōtarō, who consumed BL well before engaging with other forms of gay media, highlighted that his specific history of fandom was the reason he did not view BL as problematic, suggesting that if—like other gay men—he lacked a history of engagement, he would likely reject the genre because of its focus on *bishōnen*. That is, Shōtarō argued that his affective attachment to BL ameliorated its potentially problematic representational politics. Haruma also explained that his personal history and issues with his ex-boyfriend Akito should have "logically" led him to dislike *geikomi* because of its focus on hardness. Yet Haruma reported that because of his fannish history, he found himself "unable" to abandon the media even though he had stopped reading magazines such as *Bádi* within which *geikomi* are abundant. Within these two men's narratives can be seen a sort of fannish agency that provided them the ability to reject the regimes of desire that inculcate a suspicion of BL among young gay men.

Another important distinction between the two genres, which Junho, Yōichi, Haruma, and Shōtarō did not mention but which did seem important to other men with whom I spoke, is that there is a tendency in most BL texts for the characters to identify not as homosexual but rather as heterosexual men who are somehow attracted to other men.[44] That is, the characters' identities are not presented as linked to an inherent and unchanging same-sex desire but rather represent a contextualized attraction to a specific individual who just happens to be of the same sex.[45] This is in distinction to *geikomi*, where at least one of the characters is often explicitly identified as either *homo* (during the 1970s) or gay (since the 1990s),[46] although it is not uncommon for one partner to be a fetishized heterosexual man (who is often a victim of rape).[47] The fact that my four key informants discounted such a crucial generic distinction between BL and *geikomi* is firmly rooted in their understandings of gay desire as fundamentally attached to an individual's subjectivity, but this also speaks to their affective attachments to the genre. To my mind, it was almost as if these four men were seeking to justify or excuse their fandom within a broader social context that problematizes softness and views women's popular culture with hostility. That is, knowing about Japanese gay culture's broader negative attitudes toward young women's texts, Junho, Yōichi, Haruma, and Shōtarō strategically neglected to mention a point commonly drawn upon by others as a criticism of BL. At best, because of these prevailing attitudes, BL represents a genre of media that is ambiguously "gay," and only those with significant affective attachments are willing to afford the genre a modicum of acceptance.

Since BL contains representational practices that privilege softness and often does not contain explicit gay characters, a debate emerged in the 1990s concerning whether BL can be viewed as "authentically" gay. These debates became known as the *yaoi ronsō* (*yaoi* dispute). *Yaoi* refers to BL texts produced at an amateur level by fans and which were dominant in the 1980s through to the early 1990s.[48] Writing in the feminist coterie magazine *Choisir*, self-professed gay man and activist Satō Masaki argued that the depictions of gay men found in BL were "effeminate," linking this to the discriminatory tendency in Japanese society to understand male homosexuality as transgendered (see introduction).[49] Satō claimed that such representations differed greatly to gay men's lived experience and ultimately reinforced harmful mainstream ideas about gay life in Japan. Satō's position was echoed by the prominent *geikomi* artist Tagame Gengoroh, who argued that *geikomi* represents a more "realistic" example of what he termed "gay erotic art," which focuses on the hypermasculine and rough nature of gay men's desires and thus challenges normative understandings of gay men as transgendered.[50] In many ways, Tagame's argument is emblematic of the normative equation of heteronormative masculinity and gay desire in Japan's gay culture, and it certainly reflected the attitudes of the men I met in Ni-chōme concerning BL. Indeed, my interviews with young gay men who did not consume BL revealed that the *yaoi* dispute remains very much alive in the present day, even if young gay fans of BL do not believe consuming such texts was problematic.

In response to these gay men's arguments, female authors and BL fans such as Fujimoto Yukari and Mizuma Midory emphasized that BL instead functioned as a "fantasy" that allowed young women to explore their own sexuality in a nonthreatening manner.[51] Crucial to their argument was the fact that the men depicted in BL were not traditionally expected to be understood as "gay." For these authors, whether or not BL accurately reflected the lived experience of gay men was immaterial. Fujimoto and Mizuma both argued that because BL texts were essentially women's texts, all that was important was the fact that BL provided women with the sexual agency to explore their identities and desires. Such arguments, sociologist Ishida Hitoshi suggests, can be summed up as centering on women readers' use of gay men as surrogates for their own sexual selves, a practice that he terms "the appropriation of representation (*hyōshō no ōdatsu*)."[52] For the young gay men I met in Ni-chōme, it was this appropriation that was particularly problematic, and they saw the further conflation of gay men and the soft *bishōnen* in these women's texts as contributing to the weakening of Japan's culture of masculinity, as discussed above.

For my four key informants, both BL and *geikomi* are equally fantastic, and they viewed claims that one is more authentic or real than the other with derision. They each stated that they believed BL and *geikomi* depict two different yet ultimately fantastic and complementary discourses of gay desire and identity. Their stylistic differences were reported as presenting two equally valid depictions of this "gay" subjectivity, and the regimes of desire that the informants encountered in the Japanese gay media landscape influenced the four men to approach BL as depicting "another kind of gay" linked to *kawaii-kei* ideals. In the words of Junho, "Gay manga . . . that is BL and *geikomi* . . . show the two sides inherent to gay men." Explaining further, Junho suggested that BL demonstrated gay men's need for and investment in romantic relationships, whereas *geikomi* depicted the "carnal" nature of gay desire. For these four men, it did not matter that BL was written by women. The author's gender was not an important factor in how the four men consumed and understood BL and/or *geikomi*. Rather, it was the media's content and their belief in the fundamentality of male same-sex attraction to a gay subjectivity that informed their conceptualization of the meta-genre of "gay manga."

## Conclusion

This chapter has revealed that many young gay men in Ni-chōme have retreated into fantasies of a supposed hard masculine past in response to widespread gender anxieties that sit at the heart of the historical experiences of same-sex attracted men. At the same time as figures such as the *ikanimo-kei* are valorized because of their hard bodily aesthetics, personalities, and behaviors, mainstream society appears to be turning to alternative forms of soft masculinity deriving from young women's popular media. Ni-chōme's gay culture has thus responded to precariousness and the neoliberalization of the media market in the opposite manner to young women's texts, and this chapter nuances previous discussions within the literature of masculinity in Japan by suggesting that hard masculinity remains hegemonic. In fact, as I interacted with men in Ni-chōme's bars, I came to understand that the Japanese gay media landscape produces a gendered political economy strongly tied to heteronormative and conservative conceptualizations of sex and gender. This in turn produces a regime of desire that resuscitated hardness and produces a hostile attitude toward soft masculinity and the *bishōnen* figure.

For the young gay men whose ideas form the backdrop of this and subsequent chapters, the *bishōnen* was viewed with particular disdain because of its apparent weakening of contemporary masculinity. Drawing upon a long history of skepticism toward young women's popular culture and often employing patriarchal narratives, young gay men presented Ni-chōme as the last bastion of true, hard masculinity within a society that has been cursed by young women's desires for cute and emasculated men. Nowhere was this hostility more visible, and perhaps misdirected, than the distaste directed toward BL media by those young men who had very little experience of consuming it. Overall, the gendered ideologies explored in this chapter speak to the broader homonormativity that has swept through Ni-chōme, producing fears of softness throughout the Japanese gay media landscape that are deployed by media producers to increase consumption of the hard masculinity promoted as desirable in gay media. In the following chapters, I turn to in-depth analyses of specific media content to chart how Junho, Yōichi, Haruma, and Shōtarō came to understand hard masculinity as the only legitimate expression of a desirable gay masculinity. I trace the heteronormative logics that circulate in Japan's gay media through the system of Typing used to catalogue and express desire in the bars and shops of Ni-chōme.

# FOUR

# Japanese Gay Pornography

## *Typing and the Fetishization of Heterosexuality*

As the first explicitly gay media that all the young men I met in Ni-chōme typically consumed, pornography is central to how they conceptualize their same-sex attraction. In this chapter, I attend to the ideologies of masculinity and desire appearing in a corpus of Japanese gay pornographic videos—also known as GV (gay video), *gei* AV, or *gei bideo*—and investigate how young Japanese gay men understand these discourses through a case study of my four key informants' histories of pornographic consumption. I first explore how these men's methods of accessing GV online via tube sites and physically in Ni-chōme's *gei shoppu* represented their first encounter with the socio-semiotic system of Typing that is central to the Japanese gay media landscape. Typing, I then reveal, plays a crucial role in providing the young men who frequent Ni-chōme with a vocabulary to make sense of their desires as a system of categorization based on bodily aesthetics and instills certain tastes that privilege hard masculinity. Following this, I discuss the representations of masculinity appearing in GV, teasing out how desire for heteronormative masculinity is fetishized through the figure of the *nonke* (heterosexual or straight man) at the same time that a muscular gym-trained bodily aesthetics is promoted as normatively desirable. Throughout, I investigate how consuming pornography has inculcated desires for the hard masculinity explored in the previous chapter through the production of fantasies of straight, hegemonic masculinity. This chapter's broad aim is to therefore uncover how pornography consumption has influenced Junho's, Yōichi's, Haruma's, and Shōtarō's conceptualizations of their desires, charting how these four men's growing awareness of the privileging of heteronormative masculinity impact their evolving sense of self.

In today's world, where access to pornography has been facilitated by the popularization of the internet, young people increasingly view pornography as an important pedagogical resource to learn about sexuality.[1] Despite this, serious investigation of the impacts of pornographic consumption has emerged only in recent years, typically centering the industries of North America and Europe as representative of broader global trends.[2] Previous research into human sexuality has tended to disregard individuals' pornographic consumption as uncritical and lacking reflexivity since watching porn is often viewed as a highly ephemeral practice.[3] But my discussions with young gay men in Tokyo between 2013 and 2015 revealed the opposite to be true, with most men demonstrating high critical reflexivity about the porn they watch and their motivations for watching. Within the emerging field of porn studies, a recognition has developed that pornographic films represent important cultural products that inform individuals about social norms and sexual ideologies, either challenging dominant conceptualizations of sex and gender or reinforcing them.[4] My conversations not only with my four principal informants but also with other young men suggest that those who frequent Ni-chōme's bars and clubs are particularly savvy porn consumers, which is unsurprising given the centrality of GV to this space.

Media scholar Katrien Jacobs, in discussing the potential of internationalized porn studies in the Asian region, has noted that Asian porn consumers do in fact critically engage with, and wish to discuss, their pornographic consumption. Of interest to Jacobs was the fact that many of her informants in Mainland China and Hong Kong did not "easily endorse [the] western ideologies or bodily aesthetics" that have become central to porn studies research.[5] Studies of North American pornography, whether it be gay or straight, have revealed that the bodily aesthetics that dominate representations of masculinity are highly patriarchal and heteronormative, tied to heavily muscular bodies and often violent and aggressive sexual practices.[6] Through interviews with heterosexual and same-sex desiring individuals in both Mainland China and Hong Kong, Jacobs argues that rather than these images of extremely muscular and well-endowed men, Asian consumers of pornography prefer the slender, "soft" bodies of the so-called *bishōnen* explored in the previous chapter.[7] Yet, as I reveal below, the young gay men I interviewed in Ni-chōme do in fact endorse the focus on hard masculinity typical of North American pornography as well as this industry's privileging of straight-acting performers. This speaks to the broader homonormativity of global gay culture, critiqued by such theorists as Lisa Duggan and Jasbir Puar, where gay media industries fail to challenge heteronormativity and instead sustain its ideological hegemony.[8] That being said, this endorsement of hardness must also be understood as emerging out of the cultural politics of sites such as Ni-chōme, a truly pornographified space, as discussed in previous chapters.

Within studies of North America's gay porn industry, there has been much discussion about how Asian men are represented. Porn studies scholar Nguyen Tan Hoang reveals through careful visual and historical analysis that most gay pornographic media produced in North America present Asian men as more "effeminate" than White men via their positioning as supposedly "natural bottoms" that take the passive role in hardcore sex.[9] My discussions with informants very rarely touched on this broader representational debate, however, since almost all the young gay men I met preferred consuming pornographic films produced in Japan rather than those produced in America and thus lacked the cultural literacies related to films such as those analyzed by Nguyen. During interviews, when I raised these concerns and asked for informants' opinions, only the five men identifying as *gai-sen* (foreigner specialists) found this debate meaningful, as many had directly experienced sexual racism from the White men they had met in Ni-chōme or overseas. Most men to whom I spoke about porn consumption simply dismissed the feminization of Asian bodies as a practice that sits outside the cultural realm of GV, a medium within which interracial coupling is exceptionally rare and that whose focus, I reveal below, is instead on the gendered performances of models. While it is important that the study of Japanese gay pornography respond to these broader debates in future scholarship, my research design unfortunately failed to elicit data relating to young Japanese gay men's opinions of the racial politics of gay pornography. I thus restrict my analysis in this chapter to discussions of the political and affective economies of the gendered representations in GV and its impacts on consumers I encountered in Ni-chōme during fieldwork.

## A Brief Introduction to Japanese Gay Pornographic Films

As I strolled along Ni-chōme's central thoroughfare, together with gay men I met there, I was overwhelmed by the prevalent use of pornographic imagery to advertise the district's bars and adult stores, which these men pointed out to me. It was common to see GV playing on prominently placed TVs in these neighborhood bars, and posters advertising the newest releases from various GV companies were often plastered on the walls. According to Fushimi Noriaki, GV has permeated the majority of Japan's gay media (including gay magazines, news websites, and online dating sites) because of the increasing economic ties between GV production companies and other gay businesses.[10] These economic ties between pornography producers and sex entertainment businesses have a long history in Japan, and Kawamoto notes in his history of Japanese erotic magazines that such business relationships emerged in the late 1960s as a result of the Anti-Prostitution Law of 1958.[11] Further, it is these relationships between businesses in Ni-chōme, pornography producers, and other gay media companies that have produced the pornographification of both the neighborhood and the broader Japanese gay media landscape explored in chapter 1.

Japan's pornography industry is one of the largest in the world, with sales of both heterosexually orientated AV (adult videos) and GV reaching trillions of yen in the early 2000s.[12] Historically speaking, both AV and GV emerged out of a genre of experimental soft-core erotica known as "pink films" (*pinku eiga*) that were popular in the late 1960s.[13] While sex in traditional pink films was usually simulated, the 1980s saw the emergence of hard-core films containing actual sex acts, including anal, oral, and vaginal penetration. The first commercially released homoerotic film depicting nonsimulated sex between men was a pink film titled *The Constellation of Roses* (*Bara no seiza*) released by Toei Central Film (TCN) in 1982.[14] Concurrently, Nikkatsu also launched a subsidiary production company called ENK Promotions to produce homoerotic pink films, screened in venues known as "*homo* cinemas" to compete with TCN.[15] As home cinema technology, such as the video cassette player, became increasingly affordable in the 1990s, however, production of pink films decreased as they became less profitable.[16] Soon, GV was consumed primarily in the private domain of the home via VCR and then DVD[17] and were produced by smaller specialized pornographic companies drawing upon business practices that emerged in North America's porn industries. Nowadays, with the advent of the internet, GV is primarily distributed and consumed online, usually via dedicated streaming services (many of which are owned and managed by GV production companies).[18] In many ways, the historical development of Japan's GV mirrors that of American gay pornography, where cinema-based "stag films" popular in the 1960s led to a gay porn studio system that eventually migrated online in the late 1990s and early 2000s.[19]

Because of strict censorship laws in Japan, where Article 17 of the Penal Code prescribes petty fines or jail time for "a person who distributes, sells, or displays in public an obscene document, drawing, or other objects,"[20] AV and GV producers are required to pixelate the sexual organs through a process known as mosaicking. This has led to many GV films focusing less on the act of penetration than on shots of facial expressions and performers' techniques and positions. Porn with sadomasochistic themes have also flourished in Japan as a method to titillate viewers without focusing on the sexual organs obscured by mosaicking. As these so-called obscenity laws also technically prohibit the depiction of the "money shot,"[21] both AV and GV films tend to have models give each other "facials," involving one performer ejaculating onto another model's face so that their cum may be visible to the viewer.[22] One distinctive feature of GV when compared to Western gay pornography is the presence of a "goggleman" (*gōguruman*), staff members who "break in" virgin models, taking either an active/penetrating (*tachi*) or passive/penetrated (*neko* or *uke*) role in oral and anal sex. The gogglemen are so named because of the distinctive black sunglasses or swimming goggles they wear while performing. Wearing the goggles not only maintains the gogglemen's anonymity but also deindividualizes them so that the viewer's gaze is directed towards the scene's main model. Most GV films represent *tantai* (single-person) films that begin with an interview conducted by the goggleman or an off-screen voice discussing the model's personal and sexual history before proceeding to hard-core sex.

Further, GV companies typically rely on amateur performers, advertising for models and staff online and recruiting talent from the streets by approaching men in entertainment districts via a practice known as *nanpa* (scouting).[23] These amateur recruits, however, can eventually become pornstars, whose business is to perform in GV. The famous and influential Koh Masaki represents the most prominent example of such a performer. This trajectory was not particularly common during the period I conducted fieldwork in Ni-chōme, and most models tended to appear in only a few scenes before leaving the business. Although films with gogglemen are common, films containing only models are becoming increasingly popular, as are *kikaku*, or "planned films," featuring limited plots and erotic scenarios. Further, in the years after my first research trip to Tokyo in 2013, GV actors have become increasingly visible online, promoting not only their work but also their lifestyles via social media. Like many spaces around the world, Japan has seen a shift from studio-based pornographic production to more DIY and amateur production in which performers directly manage production and distribution through social media services such as Twitter.[24] The analysis within this chapter, however, focuses specifically on pornography produced by GV studios, as these were the films my four principal informants discussed with me during our interviews.

### *Typing as Categorization: Gay Tube Sites and Bodily Aesthetics in GV*

Patterns of pornography consumption were a common topic of conversation with the many young gay men I interviewed in Ni-chōme, and I rarely met men who were too shy to share details about their porn viewing habits. Indeed, I received the impression that casually chatting about porn was a common form of socialization among young gay men in the neighborhood. Conversations with these men revealed that they typically consumed pornography online via dedicated streaming sites, either on their smartphones or on their computers. Others streamed videos shared on Twitter among friends. During our interviews, Junho, Yōichi, Haruma, and Shōtarō also identified two main distribution methods through which they accessed gay pornographic videos: official and unofficial gay tube sites accessed online and Ni-chōme's *gei shoppu*, where they would browse through the DVDs. The four men never purchased the DVDs from *gei shoppu*, however, and instead browsed the stores to find movies they could later watch on tube sites. For many men with whom I conversed, including the four principal informants, the tube sites represented their first engagement with Typing, and they started coming to Ni-chōme to visit the bars and *gei shoppu* only after having become adept users of these sites.

Despite small superficial differences, gay tube sites typically share a similar navigational structure, normally a navigation bar listing preset categories of films hosted on the site. The top of most pages usually also contain a search bar where users can input a custom search. Clicking on one of the predetermined categories opens up a second navigation page listing a number of films "tagged" with that category. Japanese gay tube sites also organize their videos by categorizing them with a Type drawn from the socio-semiotic system circulating in the wider Japanese gay media landscape. Shōtarō explained, however, that when he first encountered Typing on a gay tube site, he understood it to be "just a method of categorization" used to navigate the site; at that time, he was not yet aware that the vocabulary on these sites had a wider use in the context of the Japanese gay media landscape. Likewise, Junho suggested that Typing initially only appeared to him as a method of grouping videos, which contained similar content, and thus he did not ascribe any particular meaning to it. Haruma had encountered similar methods of organization on AV tube sites, but he highlighted the fact that on such sites, they were usually called "categories" (*kategorī*) and not "Types" (*taipu*). This suggested to Haruma that Typing might have been a "unique characteristic of GV," but he did also note that the word's use was common in other contexts in Japan.

Reflecting on their first impressions of Typing, my four key interlocutors all explained that they did not initially conceive of Types as identities and instead viewed them as "descriptions" of bodily aesthetics. Importantly, they explained that they initially viewed Types as "impersonal" categories that could be attached to an "other" but not to the "self." Haruma went as far as suggesting that he felt the Types as they appeared on gay tube sites lacked "emotional depth," echoing the critical views of Typing held by young gay men who reject the pornographification of the Japanese gay media landscape. It was only after coming to Ni-chōme and engaging with its gay bar culture, as well as beginning to read gay magazines and utilize dating sites, that these four men changed their view of Typing. My four key interlocutors also explained that they did not initially view the Types found on tube sites as identities because, unlike the Types such as the *ikanimo-kei* and the *kawaii-kei* that also refer to lifestyles, the Types found on Japanese gay tube sites represent only simple descriptions of physical characteristics or items of clothing. Representative examples of such Types include "slim" (*surimu*), "lean and muscular" (*sujikin*), "big dick" (*kyokon*), "gym-trained body" (*tai'ikukai*, literally "gym"), "chubby and muscular" (*gatchiri*), "[school] uniform" (*seifuku*), "sport uniform" (*supoyuni*), and "swimming trunks" (*kyōpan*). As I interviewed other young gay men over the years, it became apparent that viewing Typing as categorization was common for those who first encountered it in GV before visiting Ni-chōme. For these young men, Types found on tube sites represented physical descriptions applied to others' bodies. Shōtarō, reflecting on the descriptive and impersonal nature of Typing, referred to the system as found on tube sites in particular, and in relation to pornographic videos more generally, as "Typing as categorization" (*shurui toshite no taipu*). He contrasted this with "Typing as identity," (*aidentitī toshite no taipu*), which is found in other Japanese gay media.

To navigate tube sites and find videos that satisfied their desires, the men needed to become highly familiar with the vocabulary of Typing, as it appeared not only within the predetermined Types attached to videos but also attached as custom tags by uploaders and other users/viewers. Doing so formed part of a broader socialization process of learning how to express one's desires, which these four men positioned as representative of not only Ni-chōme but also Japan's gay culture more broadly. While exploring tube sites and engaging with Typing, Junho, Yōichi, Haruma, and Shōtarō began to identify the physical traits to which they were particularly attracted, and all four used the reflexive term *akogare* to make sense of this process. As a discursive system, Typing provided these men with a vocabulary they could use to express their desires, allowing them to identify ideal desired others based on specific bodily aesthetics. Yōichi explained that becoming familiar with vocabulary items such as *kyokon* (big dick) and *supoyuni* (sports uniform) helped him to explore his "fetishes" and taught him how his desires were focused on specific body types such as masculine (*otokorashii*), *tai'ikukai-kei*. Junho also mentioned that "Typing as categorization" was a useful system for identifying the physical characteristics that he particularly desired in men and that often these physical ideals were matched with ideal personalities, making links between muscular bodies and masculinity (*otokorashisa*) that were similar to Yōichi's views. Through these linkages, Yōichi and Junho's initial engagement with Typing via GV represents an early instance of these men's realization of how the Japanese gay media landscape valorizes hard masculinity, as explored in the previous chapter.

The system of Typing also came to dominate how the four men classified other men in real-life situations. Junho lamented that after years of engagement with the vocabulary of Typing, he had lost the ability to think about his desires for other men without relying on Typing as a sociosemiotic framework. This was an experience common to many gay men I met in Ni-chōme, as discussed in chapter 1. By engaging with GV on tube sites, Junho, Yōichi, Haruma, and Shōtarō increasingly became coopted into the ideological regimes of desire that circulate in the Japanese gay media landscape and which orientates desires towards heteronormative fantasies of hard masculinity. As previously discussed, this process leads young gay men to gradually lose the ability to express their desires without explicitly drawing upon Typing. Shōtarō explained that even if he consciously tried to verbally express himself without using the vocabulary of Typing—such as during an interview when I specifically requested he try to discuss his desires without using Typing to do so—his internal monologue still "unconsciously" used Typing to make sense of what he was saying. I often conducted similar thought experiments with other gay men I met in Ni-chōme, who also failed to vocalize their desires because of their reliance on Typing, revealing how this socio-semiotic system had ultimately limited their sexual agency.

## Gei Shoppu *and Encountering Ni-chōme's Regimes of Desire*

As discussed in chapter 1, Ni-chōme's *gei shoppu* represent important nodes in the Japanese gay media landscape for the distribution of gay magazines and pornographic DVDs. Visiting these shops to browse their merchandise, especially the GV DVDs prominently displayed throughout, was a common practice among the men I met during fieldwork, and the four principal informants were no exception. Observing these stores, I often saw men examining the covers of the DVDs, and through interviews, I learned that these men were determining whether the models starring in the films appealed to them. After selecting films of interest based on their covers, young men including my four key interlocutors would then return home without making purchases to view the films online. To help them classify which films contained Types that they found attractive, visitors to the stores draw upon their familiarity with the system of Typing from tube sites. This was necessary as the DVDs on display in *gei shoppu* are not arranged by Type. The *gei shoppu* represent the space where Junho, Yōichi, Haruma, and Shōtarō first became aware which films were popular and which targeted what Shōtarō termed "niche" audiences, educating them about which of their desires were considered "normal." Engaging with *gei shoppu* thus represented an important instance in which these four men directly encountered the regimes of desire that resuscitate hegemonic masculinity and produce heteronormative conceptualizations of gender and sexuality.

The *gei shoppu* do not organize their DVD merchandise by Type, and it is incredibly rare to see signage in stores using Typing as labels. This contrasts directly with tube sites, where each film is explicitly tagged with at least one Type. Instead, the stores organize their shelves by GV production company, with more recent films placed prominently on the top of shelves and second-hand back issues placed on a lower shelf. This method of displaying merchandise is common throughout Japan, where bookstores and music stores alike group products via publisher rather than by author or title. Shōtarō explained that when he first visited a *gei shoppu*, he had low familiarity with GV companies, and the large number of films organized according to an unfamiliar system disorientated him. Without knowledge of the implicit system of Typing circulating throughout the Japanese gay media landscape, the four men explained that they felt bewildered and were unable to process the vast amounts of pornographic information that *gei shoppu* presented them. The men did, however, eventually begin to browse through the DVD merchandise on their second or third visits and hence became familiar with the GV production companies operating in Japan. In fact, as a result of experiencing confusion and disorientation during their first visits, Junho, Yōichi, and Shōtarō explained that they researched GV companies online and then returned to the *gei shoppu* armed with the knowledge required to understand how the stores were organized.

Learning how to navigate *gei shoppu* introduced the men to the idea that GV companies themselves—and not just the models they employ—can be categorized by the system of Typing. This is another example of the complicated nature of Typing introduced in chapter 1, whereby a film or an entire production company can be ascribed a *kei* Type. Yōichi explained that although the *gei shoppu* did not explicitly organize their DVD merchandise using Typing, they did so implicitly because each GV company typically uses models of a certain Type in their films to strategically target audiences who desire specific physical traits and gendered performances. A representative example is COAT Corporation, whose website claims that their films specialize in "young, straight, hunky athletes" (*wakai nonke ikemen asurīto*).[25] Yōichi further suggested that his experiences with tube sites allowed him to "categorize" the men he saw on the covers of DVDs according to their physical traits. All four men came to recognize that Typing was much more complex than simply representing a marker of an individual's bodily aesthetic. This paved the way for these men to eventually view it as an indicator of lifestyle as they continued to visit Ni-chōme and its businesses (as I explore more fully in the following chapter). Haruma highlighted, however, that Typing was often an implicit form of characterization and suggested that only those who had become familiar with the physical tropes related to each Type through the use of tube sites or some other gay media would be able to read the displays in the *gei shoppu* in this way. That is, Typing employs tropes of physicality drawn from the Japanese gay media landscape that GV producers assume their audiences will implicitly understand. I myself only learned how to "read" media in such a way through my 2013 strolling interviews, during which my interlocutors gradually taught me how to recognize particular physical traits as indexes for specific Types. I thus underwent an apprenticeship in reading Typing along with my informants through my ethnographic practice.

An important consequence of my four key interlocutors' engagement with implicit Typing in *gei shoppu* was their growing realization that certain Types are considered more attractive than others, as indicated by the prominence and apparent popularity of certain GV companies over others. That is, visiting *gei shoppu* introduced these four men to the political economy underlying Typing that privileges hard masculinity and hegemonic fantasies grounded in heteronormative conceptualizations of sexuality and gender. Shōtarō explained that visiting *gei shoppu* revealed to him how the majority of GV companies only included models with the hard *gatai* bodies developed through intense gym training discussed in chapter 1. Indeed, advertising for films containing these Types literally covered the walls of most *gei shoppu* I visited. These models are commonly referred to as *tai'ikukai-kei* on the covers of GV films, and my conversations with various young gay men in Ni-chōme's bars and *gei shoppu* revealed that this term was viewed as a synonym for the heteronormative *ikanimo-kei*. Films that depicted models which Shōtarō and others termed cute, on the other hand, were not always as easily visible as *tai'ikukai-kei*. Browsing the DVD shelves revealed to Yōichi that most films depicted "lean and muscular" men with "beards and huge dicks," such as the famous gay pornstar Koh Masaki, who was valorized as representative of the *ikanimo-kei* Type privileged as normatively desirable in Ni-chōme's gay bar culture. The promotion of films depicting men who conformed to hard masculinity— including fetishized images of the hegemonic salarymen—represents an example of how the heteronormative regimes of desire that circulate throughout the Japanese gay media landscape influence how *gei shoppu* arrange their stock.

From my own observations during fieldwork in Ni-chōme's *gei shoppu*, I discovered that films depicting Types other than the *tai'ikukai-kei* were usually placed in less prominent positions and that they were consistently fewer in number than the films of GV companies specializing in *tai'ikukai-kei* films. *Gei shoppu* are typically arranged so that *tai'ikukai-kei* films are immediately visible upon entry and are often closest to the cash register. *Kawaii-kei* films, which are the second most prominent, are usually located to the periphery of the *tai'ikukai-kei* films. Interestingly, *debu-kei* films are often sold in *gei shoppu*, but they are placed in small corners and clearly represent a niche market. In a few of the shops that I visited, *debu-kei* films were even covered in dust, suggesting that they were browsed infrequently. According to the store clerks of the *gei shoppu* that I visited both in 2013 and 2015, including Lumière and Check, it was indeed true that *tai'ikukai-kei* films were in high demand, and these films typically drove their profits. Further evidence for the popularity of *tai'ikukai-kei* films among consumers in Japan can be seen on various online stores specializing in the sale of Japanese gay pornographic films on DVD, which often provide lists of each month's and each year's highest-selling releases. One such website is Rainbow Shoppers (www.rainbow-shoppers.com), one of the largest online GV retailers, used by both Japanese and foreign customers. Rainbow Shoppers interestingly has both a Japanese- and an English-language interface and sells films from approximately 50 GV companies. Much like gay tube sites, Rainbow Shoppers also tags the films it sells by Type, and *tai'ikukai-kei* is one of many such tags. An examination of the bestsellers for each month in 2013 through 2015, as well as each year's top sellers (a total of 39 films), makes clear that *tai'ikukai-kei* films dominated the market, as 84.6 percent of the top-selling films (33/39) were explicitly labeled as such.

For Junho, Yōichi, Haruma, and Shōtarō, the realization that *tai'ikukai-kei* films were most popular was unsurprising. Junho and Yōichi indicated that they were attracted to this Type, and Yōichi stated that he strived to attain a similarly "hard" and gym-sculpted body through his own exercise regimes. Although Junho sought out videos containing this Type on tube sites, he explained that it was only when he visited the *gei shoppu* in Ni-chōme that he understood that the *tai'ikukai-kei* was the dominant depiction of desirable masculinity in Japanese gay culture. Junho argued that tube sites gave a "false impression" that all Types are equal since the organization of the Types on tube sites appears arbitrary, and there are usually equal numbers of films for each Type. Shōtarō also expressed that he was mostly attracted to *tai'ikukai-kei*, but he rejected the idea that this Type was inherently better or more "normal" than other Types. Demonstrating a high level of critical reflexivity, Shōtarō indicated that this fact instead reveals advertising's important influence on people's perceptions of what is attractive and how GV companies collaborate with *gei shoppu* to sell desires. As Haruma believed his alignment with the herbivorous boy subculture made him attracted to "feminine" men such as himself, he found it difficult when he first became aware that *kawaii-kei* models appeared to be less popular than *tai'ikukai-kei* models. Haruma became concerned that, on account of his "feminine features," he did not meet the ideals promoted through GV, and these concerns were deepened by his ex-boyfriend Akito's insistence that Haruma become more masculine.

It was engagement with GV in *gei shoppu*, where the stratification of Types is highly visible, that represented my four key interlocutors' first explicit interaction with the regimes of desire that produce and contour knowledge of desirability in the Japanese gay media landscape. Unlike on gay tube sites, where the broader political economy of Typing is hidden underneath a purported democratized desire, as critiqued by Junho, the privileging of hard masculinity is literally on display in Ni-chōme's *gei shoppu* through the prominence of the *tai'ikukai-kei*. As the four men continued to engage with GV after visiting Ni-chōme, their consumption of pornography on tube sites evolved as they became increasingly aware of the promotion of the *tai'ikukai-kei* as the most attractive Type. This awareness validated Junho's and Yōichi's sense of the naturalness of their desires, and they thus internalized the hierarchies underpinning these regimes of desire. On the other hand, explicitly coming into contact with these ideologies for the first time caused Shōtarō to become concerned over the manipulation of his desires by a GV market and negatively impacted Haruma's sense of self as a self-proclaimed herbivorous boy. In fact, the anxieties these two men experienced after coming into contact with the valorization of hard masculinity reveal the affective as well as political economy of both Typing and the regimes of desire that resuscitate heteronormative conceptualizations of masculinity. Haruma's and Shōtarō's anxieties reflect Sara Ahmed's phenomenological theory of queerness whereby deviation from straightness can be destabilizing, producing intensities of discomfort, fear, and rejection.[26] On the other hand, Yōichi's and Junho's acceptance of the primacy of hard masculinity represents an alignment with heteronormativity, and the "smoothing" of their queerness thus produces positive intensities of acceptance and release.

## Typing within GV: Valorizing "Hard" Gym-Trained Bodies

Conversations with young gay men in Ni-chōme consistently revealed a preference for hard masculinity and muscular bodies, as has been well established in previous chapters. Many men pointed to the prevalence of this bodily aesthetics in GV as one reason that this hard masculinity was particularly privileged in Japan's gay culture more broadly, suggesting that its status in Ni-chōme was representative of a broader national trend. This led me to wonder about the empirical truth of these men's belief: How prevalent was the *tai'ikukai-kei* within Japanese gay pornographic videos? To investigate which Types are mostly commonly featured in GV films, I collected a sample of 810 DVD covers from eight of the most popular GV companies for analysis over a period of two and a half years starting in January 2011. I analyzed DVD covers rather than the films themselves since the covers are specifically designed to promote the films. They therefore include highly strategic depictions of the models' Types through text and imagery, which I could "read" for the purposes of analysis. The eight companies chosen for analysis were KO-Company, COAT Corporation, Get Film (MediaWave), G@MES, ACCEED, Cheeks, OSUINRA, and Justice. I selected films from these production companies because they were the most popular GV companies in Japan during my fieldwork in 2013 and their films were consistently advertised in gay magazines, on various Japanese gay websites, and in *gei shoppu* and bars in Ni-chōme. Furthermore, interviews with *gei shoppu* clerks revealed that these eight companies produced the highest-selling films, with KO-Company and COAT Corporation in particular dominating the market. Importantly, the young men I met in Ni-chōme were all familiar with these companies. Although, out of my four key interlocutors, only Junho and Yōichi indicated that they had watched films from all of them. Table 4 presents a summary of the corpus.

As is evident from the table, the companies in the corpus differ significantly in the number of films produced each year, a reflection of their respective corporate models. KO-Company and COAT Corporation, Japan's largest producers of GV at the time of my initial fieldwork, are

Table 4. Corpus of Japanese gay video DVD covers

| COMPANY | No. of DVD covers | Percentage of corpus | Average no. DVDs released a year |
|---|---|---|---|
| 1. KO-Company | 309 | 38.1 | 124 |
| 2. COAT Corporation | 226 | 27.9 | 90 |
| 3. Get Film (MediaWave) | 84 | 10.4 | 34 |
| 4. G@MES | 79 | 9.8 | 32 |
| 5. ACCEED | 50 | 6.2 | 20 |
| 6. Cheeks | 24 | 2.9 | 10 |
| 7. OSUINRA | 20 | 2.5 | 8 |
| 8. Justice | 18 | 2.2 | 7 |
| TOTAL | 810 | 100.0 | 5 |

conglomerations of semiautonomous GV studios called "labels"; they produce films with different themes and featuring models of a specific Type. KO-Company has 21 labels, whereas COAT Corporation has four. KO-Company and COAT Corporation produce a large volume of content and thus dominated the GV market. Get Film (MediaWave), G@MES, and ACCEED are medium-sized firms that produce a number of series that, similar to the labels, are themed or focus on models of a certain Type. They differ, however, as the series are all produced by the same studio. Cheeks, OSUINRA, and Justice are relatively smaller GV companies that focus on producing a limited catalogue of similarly themed films. They explicitly provide niche content, such as SM films (Cheeks) or condom-free, "bareback" films (Justice). Importantly, KO-Company and ACCEED differ from the other companies in that, as well as running GV studios, they also run sex-on-premises venues and gay saunas throughout Japan, from which they sometimes draw their talent. KO-Company and COAT Corporation also run their own gay tube sites, where members can watch films produced by their labels after paying a fixed price per film.

To determine the particular model Types each company commonly utilized, I examined the text on the DVD covers for explicit references to Typing, confirming my classification with my four key interlocutors. As the DVD covers almost always contained depictions of the naked male body, I compared the text on the DVDs with the physical appearance of the film's models to ascertain how various male physiques are utilized as markers for specific Types. Much like the Typing found on gay tube sites, it is unsurprising that the DVDs employed "Typing as categorization," and almost all DVD covers explicitly labeled the Types of their models, although often only in small print on the scene descriptions found on back covers. In order to cross-reference for consistency, I compared the data on the covers with each GV company's webpage, where the films are also commonly categorized by Type, and with the categories attached to their reviews in the gay magazine *Bádi* and on the online GV store Rainbow Shoppers. I utilized these particular resources for cross-referencing as my conversations with young gay men in Ni-chōme revealed that they commonly draw upon such resources when researching GV films for their own consumption. In fact, I also occasionally checked the Typing of specific films with the many young men I met in *gei shoppu* and with whom I conversed about their GV preferences and their porn viewing habits. In all instances, the sources I drew upon to classify the Typing in films correlated, demonstrating both the pervasiveness of Typing in the Japanese gay media landscape and the interconnectedness of these various media. Overall, I uncovered only five Types in the corpus: *tai'ikukai-kei* (Gym Type), *kawaii-kei* (Cute Type), *debu-kei* (Chubby Type), *josō-kei* (Cross-Dressing Type), and *gaijin* (foreigners; White or Black men).[27] Whereas *josō-kei* and *gaijin* reference sartorial practice and ethnicity, respectively, the first three Types are based in bodily aesthetics.

Table 5 presents the percentage of DVDs devoted to these five Types in the corpus and the average percentage of films in the corpus devoted to each specific Type. The majority of films in the corpus are *tai'ikukai-kei* films, with *kawaii-kei* films representing the second-most common Type, followed by *debu-kei*, *josō-kei*, and *gaijin* films. Through our discussions, I learned that my four principal informants believed Types other than *tai'ikukai-kei* and *kawaii-kei* represented niche markets. The corpus appears to justify this, as these two Types together account for 97.5 percent of the films produced between January 2011 and July 2013. The eight GV companies in the corpus clearly prioritize the market that desires *tai'ikukai-kei*: approximately two-thirds of films produced by these companies cater to this audience. The greater representation of *tai'ikukai-kei* films compared with *kawaii-kei* films further demonstrates that the muscular, gym-trained *gatai* body is considered normatively desirable in Japan's gay culture. In fact, the overwhelming focus on this Type led both Junho and Yōichi to describe the typical GV performer as possessing "an explosion of muscle" (*kinniku bakuhatsu*). Even ACCEED, which produces a majority of *kawaii-kei* content, appears to produce *tai'ikukai-kei* films in order to tap into this mainstream market. The models in most ACCEED films typically lack *gatai* aesthetics and are instead described as *chūseiteki* (androgynous) by many young gay men I met in Ni-chōme. Overall, the corpus clearly confirms that the eight most popular GV production companies in Japan contributed to the regimes of desire that construct hard gym-trained bodies as normatively desirable. This suggests, once again, that some of the trends I encountered in Ni-chōme were representative of broader national trends.

For the many young gay men I met in Ni-chōme between 2013 and 2015, the famous pornstar Koh Masaki—who headlined 39 of the films in this corpus—was the perfect representative of the *tai'ikukai-kei* aesthetic. All four of my key interlocutors knew of Koh and admired him to different degrees: Yōichi was a passionate fan, whereas Haruma felt somewhat ambivalent. As Shōtarō expressed to me during our initial discussion about Typing, presented in the introduction, it was Koh's highly

Table 5. Typing in the DVD corpus

| TYPE | GV COMPANIES | | | | | | | | | |
|---|---|---|---|---|---|---|---|---|---|---|
| | KO-Company | COAT Corporation | Get Film (Media Wave) | G@mes | ACCEED | Cheeks | OSUINRA | Justice | AVERAGE | TOTAL |
| *Tai'ikukai* | 64.1 (198) | 73.5 (166) | 58.3 (49) | 96.2 (76) | 26 (13) | 58.3 (14) | 100 (20) | 66.7 (12) | 67.8 (68.5) | 67.7 (548) |
| *Kawaii* | 29.8 (92) | 26.5 (60) | 40.5 (34) | 3.8 (3) | 72 (36) | 41.7 (10) | 0 (0) | 33.3 (6) | 31.0 (30.1) | 29.8 (241) |
| *Debu* | 3.2 (10) | 0 (0) | 0 (0) | 0 (0) | 0 (0) | 0 (0) | 0 (0) | 0 (0) | 0.4 (1.3) | 1.2 (10) |
| *Josō* | 2.3 (7) | 0 (0) | 1.5 (1) | 0 (0) | 1 (2) | 0 (0) | 0 (0) | 0 (0) | 0.6 (11.0) | 1.1 (9) |
| *Gaijin* | 0.6 (2) | 0 (0) | 0 (0) | 0 (0) | 0 (0) | 0 (0) | 0 (0) | 0 (0) | 0.07 (0.3) | 0.2 (2) |
| TOTAL | 100.0 (309) | 100.0 (226) | 100.0 (84) | 100.0 (79) | 100.0 (50) | 100.0 (24) | 100.0 (20) | 100.0 (18) | | 100.0 (810) |

*Note.* Figures in parentheses represent the number of DVDs produced. The percentages, the top figure in each cell, in all but the Total and Average columns represent the percentage of films out of the total produced by that company. The Average column provides the mean for each row and the Total column provides the sum, expressed first as a percentage of the corpus and then the number of films.

muscular body, his height, and his short hair and beard that marked him as both masculine and desirable to GV consumers. Koh's physical traits, which were strategically deployed by GV companies to boost his popularity and sell movies, became situated within the Japanese gay media landscape as the normative construction of ideal masculinity. The development of Koh's personal aesthetic into the current standard of masculine gay desirability, however, is more complicated than a mere appropriation of physical traits circulating in the Japanese mainstream media. After all, as can be seen in figure 5, Koh's bodily aesthetic drastically deviates from the softer masculinity of the boyish young idols, actors, and models who have become popular in contemporary Japanese media, as discussed in the previous chapter. Rather, it is Koh's deployment of a hard *gatai* body in conjunction with a public display of his same-sex attraction as an out and proud gay man that led many of the men with whom I spoke to view Koh as what Yōichi termed the embodiment of the "Japanese gay culture's ideal Type" (*Nihon gei karuchā no risō na taipu*). Further, it was via discussions about Koh with young gay men in both gay bars and *gei shoppu* that I became aware of how the *tai'ikukai-kei*, which for all intents and purposes appeared to describe a certain bodily aesthetic, was tied to the *ikanimo-kei* privileged in Ni-chōme as an ideal identity and lifestyle.

Throughout his career, Koh actively positioned himself as representative of a new kind of GV star who was interested in not only promoting an explicitly gay identity but also presenting a new form of "gay masculinity" (*gei otokorashisa*) through his pornographic work. Indeed, in many of his interviews—including a July 2011 feature article in *Bádi*—Koh specifically referred to himself as "the gay porn star who represents Japan" (*Nihon o daihyō suru gei porunosutā*), presenting himself as a national symbol for Japan's gay culture. Koh's rugged masculine physique and his forceful performances, I learned in my interviews, represented an explicitly "Japanese" form of masculinity tied to the hard and rough ideals that had emerged from the Japanese gay media landscape. Some men even linked Koh's somewhat rough style of sex and his exclusive performance as a "top" to broader stereotypes of the "kinky" nature of Japanese pornography, arguing that his performance style represented the violent nature of traditional Japanese masculinity. This kind of narrative evokes the links made between tradition and hard masculinity discussed in the previous chapter. In the figure of Koh, then, can be seen an attempt by consumers of his films to lay claim to a specifically Japanese gay subject position that is ideologically tied to the regimes of desire circulating both in the bars

Figure 5. Koh Masaki, Japan's first openly gay pornstar.

and clubs of Ni-chōme and in Japan's gay media. When Shōtarō described Koh as "the most handsome gay man in Japan" during our conversation at Lumière, which opened this book, he was doing more than simply describing Koh's desirability. Like many of the men I met in Ni-chōme, Shōtarō was (perhaps unconsciously) using Koh to make broader claims concerning what it means to be a gay man in Japan. Through Koh, the hard masculine figure of the *ikanimo-kei* was thus positioned as representative of Japanese gay culture itself.

For Yōichi, who initially had trouble reconciling his same sex attraction with his ideas concerning appropriate masculinity, Koh Masaki represented a role model who embodied his belief that to be gay did not compromise his sense of what it means to be a man. Seeing Koh's appeal in Thailand during his travels there, Yōichi strategically began to mold his own physical appearance to mirror Koh's bodily aesthetic so as to become popular himself; and it was through this process that Yōichi became a *hay-atteru ikemen* like Koh when he returned to Japan. Junho and Shōtarō mentioned that they also found Koh highly attractive and agreed that he represented an ideal masculinity that they understood as the embodiment of the "perfect" *ikanimo-kei*. By contrast, Haruma, who had developed a negative attitude to the *ikanimo-kei* discourse after his experiences with Akito, found Koh to be a problematic figure. Haruma argued that Koh and other popular figures like him were doing more harm than good: in their explicit performance of heteronormative masculinity, they implicitly positioned as somehow problematic any men, such as Haruma himself, who failed to live up to their gym-trained bodily aesthetics and ideal of a harder masculinity. Ultimately, however, for most young gay men to whom I spoke, Koh represented an example where "Typing as categorization" as embodied in discourses of the *tai'ikukai-kei* moved toward "Typing as identity" as indexed by the *ikanimo-kei*. The tying together of these two Types is a topic I explore in more detail in the following chapter.

Browsing DVD covers in *gei shoppu*, Junho, Yōichi, Haruma, and Shōtarō explained that they implicitly understood that the *tai'ikukai-kei* body that Koh typified was more masculine than the *kawaii-kei* body. This was a view that was shared even by Junho, Shōtarō, and Haruma, who lacked *gatai* bodies and perceived that their own physicality was more closely aligned to the aesthetics of the *kawaii-kei*. All four men viewed the *tai'ikukai-kei* and *kawaii-kei* to represent a complementary dyad, with the *tai'ikukai-kei* understood as masculine and the *kawaii-kei* as somewhat effeminate. In many ways, these two Types thus match the broader heteronormative logics of the Japanese gay media landscape and respond to the binary between hard and soft masculinity explored in the previous chapter. During interviews, when I asked Junho, Yōichi, and Shōtarō to further explain why they understood the *tai'ikukai-kei* as masculine and the *kawaii-kei* as feminine, they all explicitly drew upon Japanese society's heteronormative tendency to equate "failed" men with women and effeminacy. Since *kawaii-kei* models are believed to have failed to achieve hard muscular bodies, the men I met in Ni-chōme positioned them as representative of what Fushimi Noriaki terms the "female role" within the hetero system governing knowledge about sexuality and gender in Japan.[28] These men's reading of Types, however, did not derive from the texts appearing on the DVD covers, which only very rarely explicitly mentioned effeminacy. Instead, their gendered reading of these Types derives from their internalization of the heteronormative discourses of gender that pervade Japan in general and the Japanese gay media landscape specifically. Thus, it was not the case that GV inculcated in the four men an understanding that *kawaii-kei* are effeminate. It was rather that since *tai'ikukai-kei* explicitly drew upon tropes of masculinity already promoted as normatively masculine by mainstream society, the four men came to understand *kawaii-kei* as effeminate because of its supposed "failure" to live up to these ideals. This is an important instance of the four men's interpretation of gay media being influenced by the heteronormative regimes of desire that construct the *gatai* body as always already indexing desirable hard masculinity.

My four key interlocutors' opinions of GV, as well as the prevalence of certain Types in the corpus, reveal much about the regimes of desire that structure the Japanese gay media landscape. If *tai'ikukai-kei* films are understood as normatively masculine and all other films are understood as focusing on less desirable Types that have somehow "failed" in terms of their gendered performances (especially in the cases of the *kawaii-kei* or *josō-kei*), this is because heteronormativity remains a pervasive ideology even within Japan's gay culture. In the previous section, I intimated that the *tai'ikukai-kei* films also often fetishized such hegemonic images of Japanese manhood as the salaryman. Indeed, within the corpus, approximately 30.7 percent (249/810) of the films had covers with a model explicitly performing the role of a salaryman, often marked by the salaryman uniform of a black suit, white shirt, and tie. In fact, promotional images in which salarymen are depicted ripping open their suits to reveal heavily muscular torsos are common within *gei shoppu* and are also a common trope on the covers of gay porn DVDs. It was exceptionally rare for films focusing on a model Type other than *tai'ikukai-kei* to contain scenes with salaryman characters: only two *kawaii-kei* films did so. This suggests that, to a certain extent, GV promotes the discourses underlying the salaryman image, as "successful" and hard-working men, which are integral to mainstream media ideologies of manhood. Even if GV does not produce the demand for *tai'ikukai-kei* content itself and is merely responding to a pre-existing desire, GV and its use of Typing still reinforces heteronormative discourses of masculinity, inculcating in its consumers the desirability of hegemonic masculinity through the fetishistic depictions of mainstream masculine symbols such as the salaryman.

Indeed, this is also a case where the *gatai* and *ikanimo-kei/tai'ikukai-kei* can be viewed as acting as a hegemonic form of masculinity in Japan's gay culture. As revealed in the above discussion, the men I met in Ni-chōme—including Junho, Yōichi, Haruma, and Shōtarō—judged the desirability and masculinity of the *kawaii-kei* and other Types with reference to the *tai'ikukai-kei*. In so doing, they deployed the heteronormative logics of the hetero system to produce knowledge concerning desirability. This is a clear example of the hegemony possessed by this Type, revealing the ways desire and masculinity are hierarchized within the Japanese gay media landscape. What is most important here is how the specifics of Typing as it has emerged from the Japanese gay media landscape and a concomitant desire for a hard bodily aesthetic are married to broader sociocultural norms of masculinity. The dyad produced between the *tai'ikukai-kei* and the *kawaii-kei*, where the former is understood as strongly linked to the hegemonic ideology of *otokorashisa* ("masculinity," or perhaps more accurately in this instance, "male nature"), dramatizes the tensions between hardness and softness discussed in the previous chapter. The *tai'ikukai-kei* has thus come to inhabit the "male role" within the hetero system and becomes privileged by its hegemonic power over the *kawaii-kei*, which is, in turn, positioned as representative of the "female role." The political economy of Typing thus resuscitates heteronormativity and produces homonormative affects. This shows how the Japanese gay media landscape differs dramatically from contemporary women's media and certain young male subcultures such as the herbivorous boys. Rather than challenging hegemonic forms of masculinity through new desires for softness, GV instead promotes hardness as desirable, and this has strongly impacted how consumers conceptualize their own desires and gendered experiences. GV ultimately plays an extremely important role in educating young men to accept hard masculinity as normatively desirable, thus producing regimes of desire that fail to challenge hegemonic masculinity within broader Japanese society.

*Fetishizing the Straight Man:*
*An Analysis of Japanese Gay Porn DVD Covers*

In interviews with men in Ni-chōme—including with Junho, Yōichi, Haruma, and Shōtarō—I uncovered that most young gay men understood the gym-trained and highly muscular body of the *tai'ikukai-kei* to be linked to the image of the straight man or *nonke* as a fetishized trope of desirable masculinity. Through a close reading of the DVD covers in my corpus, it became apparent that GV companies were even deliberately advertising their films as containing *nonke* models to create a discourse wherein straight men were presented as objects of desire. The slang term *nonke* itself is of particular interest, since it literally means "men who have no Type." The fact that straight men are fetishized in GV and are ascribed Types when they are ostensibly "outside Typing" has interesting ramifications for the regimes of desire outlined in this book, complicating GV's promotion of heteronormative masculinity as normatively desirable because of its inherent "straightness."

All the GV companies in the corpus explicitly advertise, both on their webpage and on the text of their films' DVD covers, that the models performing in the majority of their films are *nonke*. Many of the films include *nonke* in their titles, including in series such as *Diary of Eating Straight Men* (*Nonke-gui nikki*), *We'll Show You Straight Men's Real SEX* (*Nonke no maji SEX misechaimasu*), and *Straight Cruising Paradise* (*Nonke nanpa paradaisu*). Within the majority of these films, the *nonke* performers appear together with the GV companies' gogglemen staff, who are described as gay men by all the men who spoke to me about their GV viewing habits. In my corpus, the models were not advertised as *nonke* in two instances: when the films featured Koh Masaki, who was well known for his explicit identification as an out and proud gay man, and when the company was strategically utilizing "gay" models as a means of titillating the audience in a cultural medium where *nonke* are the norm. Out of the DVD corpus, 95.5 percent of the films (767/810) featured only models labeled as *nonke*, whereas 4.5 percent (43/810) featured models explicitly presented as gay men; but sometimes even these models performed together with *nonke* as was common in Koh Masaki's films. Indeed, a fetishistic focus on straight men is also common in North American gay pornography, emerging out of the economic necessity to employ straight-identified performers because public stigma made it initially difficult to recruit same-sex desiring men.[29] Similar economic pressures are likely common in Japan's gay porn industry.

As most companies utilize *nonke* models, the use of a gay model is presented with much fanfare. Often there is an emphasis placed on how the sex depicted in these films is more "real" or authentic than that conducted with *nonke*, as can be seen in the ad copy for a film by Justice:

*Horarete tobideru!!! Odoroku hodo 18-sai no honma no gei seiyoku!*
*Jasutisu shijō sho!!! Maji kappuru no nama SEX!!!*

Being fucked causes cum to fly everywhere!!! The surprising sexual
desires of a real 18-year-old gay! A first in the history of Justice!!!
The raw SEX of a real [gay] couple!

The fact that the depiction of a gay model is so heralded indexes them as
exceptional. In this example, the exceptionality is strongly implied by the
fact that this film, featuring a "real gay couple," is the first in the company's
history. That this particular DVD uses emphatic adjectives such as *honma*
and *maji*—both slang terms meaning "real"—to describe the nature of the
models' relationship, however, may also suggest that it is the depiction
of romantic couples that is not normative in GV. Nevertheless, throughout the corpus, adjectives such as *genjitsu no, riaru na, honma/hontō*, and
*maji* (all roughly translating as "real" or "true") that index the reality and
authenticity of the sex between gay men are utilized to explicitly market
films containing gay models. Indeed, 86 percent of the films featuring gay
models (37/43 films) utilized at least two of the aforementioned adjectives
to describe the model's sexual prowess. If, then, GV presents sex between
gay men as authentic, there is a need to determine how the prevalence of
*nonke* is justified in the majority of Japanese gay pornographic films.

Through a close reading of the DVD corpus, I investigated how the
*nonke* models' participation in the films was justified by GV companies. Obviously, the companies are not motivated to discuss the financial motives for their casting as this would ruin the fantasies underlying
the films. My analysis uncovered three discourses commonly employed
both to justify why *nonke* would engage in sex with other men and to
create a sense of fantasy and titillation for audiences: (a) to emphasize
the *nonke* model's gay sex act as his "first time" to create a sense of adven-
ture, (b) to present the sex act as "forced" upon the *nonke* (often evoking
images of rape and pain), and (c) to focus upon the "surprise" of a *nonke's*
unexpected ability to enjoy sex with men. Interestingly, each discourse
accounted for approximately one-third of the explicitly *nonke* films in the
corpus and was equally likely to be applied to any film Type. Thus, *kawaii-
kei* films were just as likely as *tai'ikukai-kei* films to deploy one of these
three discourses. Examples of each discourse drawn from the corpus are
presented in table 6.

Importantly, these discourses present no discussion of reality or

Table 6. *Nonke* discourses in the DVD corpus

| DISCOURSE | EXAMPLES |
|---|---|
| First time | *Fumiya, anaru nama kaikin* <br> Fumiya lifts the ban on fucking his ass raw <br> *Otoko hatsutaiken de ikinari gekihori monzetsu* <br> During his first time with a man, he's suddenly and painfully fucked deeply <br> *Hatsutaiken no danshi ga shosatsuei de ikinari sutaffu ni nama hori sare zekku!* <br> During his first shoot, this newbie is lost for words as he is suddenly fucked raw by our staff! |
| Forced/rape | *Shojo anaru ni kyokon ni buchikomare zekkyō! Nakisakebō yōsha naku horareru!* <br> Screaming from having his virgin ass filled with huge dick! Crying out from being screwed without mercy! <br> *Onna dewa ajiwatta koto no nai kaikan ni shōten suru!! Onna to yarimak-utta nikutai o kamera no mae de bakuhatsu saseru!!* <br> Killed by a pleasure [he] hasn't tasted from a woman!! We make bodies that have only ever fucked women explode on camera! <br> *Jisatsu kōi!! Saitei de saiaku no nama SEX!! Shinu hodo suriru ni michita torokeru yō na gokujō no kaikan! Ōru shinsaku! "Mō shindemo kamawanai!!"* <br> An act of suicide!! The absolute worst raw SEX!! Enchanted by the ulti-mate release, he's thrilled to death! All new scenes! "I don't give a fuck, even if I die!!" |
| Surprise | *Onna no kōbi shika dekinai no ni, dōshite otoko no ana no naka de itte shimatta no darō!?* <br> Even though he can only fuck women, why is it that he came in a man's ass!? <br> *Daininki no Yamato-kun ga, tachi ni uke ni daikōfun! Yappa otoko no etchi wa kimochiissu!* <br> The super popular Yamato gets excited either topping or bottoming! Fuck-ing men feels good after all! <br> *Kanojo gomen nasai! Daiji na kareshi o konna sugata ni . . . ikatsui danshi mo otoko ni koko made kanjiru!* <br> We're so sorry, girlfriends! To find your precious boyfriends in such a position . . . even reticent guys can be made to feel [good] by men! |

authenticity nor do they attempt to legitimize the *nonke*'s enjoyment of sex between men. The discourses found on the covers often take an almost perverse pleasure in accentuating the physical and emotional pain inflicted on the *nonke* models, drawing upon highly explicit language that frames the *nonke* as mere objects for pornographic consumption. In the major-ity of the texts analyzed, passive sentences are utilized to construct dis-courses concerning the *nonke* models, as can be seen in the table. This was particularly true of the "first time" and "forced/rape" discourses, which emphasize the pain inflicted upon *nonke* models, whether it is the physical pain derived from rough sex or the psychological pain or guilt from enjoyment. This is even true in the discourse of "surprise" where subtexts of betraying girlfriends and discourses of shame constructed through passive expressions and the use of the totalizing verb *shimau* remind consumers of the GV films that the *nonke* is not necessarily fully enjoying his experiences.[30] According to many men I spoke to about their GV consumption, including Junho, Yōichi, Haruma, and Shōtarō, the fact that the *nonke* is passively "being fucked" (*horareteiru*, literally "being plowed") reinforces their straightness. This is in direct contrast to heteronormative Japanese understandings of sexuality in which passivity is conflated with the feminine and hence is understood as indexing homosexuality in men, as discussed in the introduction.

For Junho, Yōichi, Haruma, and Shōtarō, the fact that the *nonke* models were "being fucked" did not compromise their normative masculinity. According to the four men, it repurposed the *nonke* as a "gay fantasy" where the *nonke*'s masculinity could be consumed and enjoyed. This is an explicit instance where heteronormative masculinity, which GV consumers viewed as tied to the *nonke* figure, is rendered an explicit fantasy in the Japanese gay media landscape. The passivity of the *nonke* bodies in GV also rendered them commodities, with heterosexuality becoming a symbolic object for gay male consumption. The explicit fetishization of salarymen, athletes, construction workers, policemen, and delinquent high school boys—figures that the young gay men I interviewed in Ni-chōme considered representative of broader masculine ideals—sublimates hegemonic expressions of Japanese masculinity for gay men's pleasure. The representational politics of *nonke* in GV thus represents a further example of the commodification of desire that typifies the hyperconsumerist Japanese gay media landscape, where male heterosexuality becomes objectified in GV through the erasure of the *nonke*'s agency. In turn, this renders hegemonic images of Japanese masculinity passive through the consumption of this media. This objectification had the surprising secondary effect of affirming the masculinity of gay men, since it constructed gay men as active consumers with access to normative masculinity through consumption. In fact, since *nonke* were rendered objects, gay men gained the sexual agency often denied them in wider society. To a certain extent, then, consuming GV affirms the masculinity of Japanese gay men via the reappropriation of the "active" nature of heteronormative masculinity. This affirmation is

Japanese Gay Pornography 141

constructed, however, in a context where *nonke* are rendered objects upon which pain is inflicted. The *nonke's* passive construction in GV thus also echoes the problematic objectification of women in pornographic videos worldwide,[31] and Japan in particular.[32]

My four key interlocutors, as well as other men I met in Ni-chōme over the years, explained that watching films depicting straight men "being fucked" represented an important fetish in Japan's gay culture. In so doing, the men I interviewed once again positioned their experiences in Ni-chōme as representative of a broader national gay culture. Indeed, the *nonke* fetish appears to have a long history in Japan. Historian Jonathan Mackintosh argues in his history of 1970s *homo* magazines that *nonke* consistently represented the reference point for desirable masculinity in *Barazoku*, Japan's first mainstream magazine for same-sex desiring men.[33] Junho, Yōichi, Shōtarō, and even Haruma explained that they had developed a desire to experience sex with a *nonke* at least once in their lives through their consumption of GV, although Haruma was quick to mention that he felt a sense of shame over this fantasy. Shōtarō even blamed his consumption of GV for his unfortunate tendency to develop crushes on heterosexual men, such as his senior in high school. This is despite the fact that he claimed to have experienced this crush—his *hatsukoi*—well before engaging with GV. This is an interesting example of how one's later engagement with media can encourage one to forget or reinterpret the past, a process previously explored in chapter 2. The other informants suggested that the development of their desire to have sex with a *nonke* was indeed influenced by their consumption of GV later in their lives, although Haruma argued that his desire to sleep with a *nonke* was not indicative of an acceptance of heteronormative masculinity as such but was rather due to "natural curiosity." In the interviews I conducted in Ni-chōme, many other men with whom I conversed about their GV consumption expressed desires similar to my four key interlocutors, revealing that the desire to sleep with *nonke* may be common to the young gay men who gather in the district's bars.

The overwhelming presence of *nonke* models in GV has strongly influenced how young gay Japanese men understand their desires, inculcating in many the belief that the *nonke* represents an ideal sexual partner. This is despite the fact that sex with *nonke* is not usually depicted as "authentic" or "real" in GV. Young gay men's belief in the *nonke* as an ideal sexual partner, however, has driven many of the men with whom I spoke to seek out sexual and romantic partners whom they described as upholding "straight male characteristics" (*nonke no tokuchō*). These supposed characteristics, I learned through my conversations in Ni-chōme, included the hard bodily aesthetics particularly valorized in the Japanese gay media landscape. In particular, most young gay men—including Junho, Yōichi, and Shōtarō—expressed a desire to find partners who possessed a *gatai* body, which they viewed as a supposed *nonke* characteristic. For young gay men in Ni-chōme, this ideal "*nonke* body" was the physicality attached to the *ikanimo-kei*, as discussed in chapter 1. Their belief that an ideal *nonke* would have a gym-trained, muscular *gatai* body derived from the heteronormative regimes of desire circulating in the Japanese gay media landscape, and it was these regimes that led many informants to conflate the *tai'ikukai-kei* they viewed in GV with the "straight-acting" (*nonkerashii*) *ikanimo-kei* they encountered in Ni-chōme. This was a mostly unconscious process, and when I highlighted during interviews that, in my analysis, GV covers never explicitly linked *tai'ikukai-kei* with *ikanimo-kei*, the men would often express surprise that this was the case. For most informants, including Junho and Yōichi, the fact that the *tai'ikukai-kei* found in GV was the same Type as the *ikanimo-kei* was common sense. Typing as a classificatory system for bodily aesthetics was thus linked to lifestyle through young gay men's desires for ideal partners who would be both masculine and straight-acting.

*Conclusion*

This chapter has revealed that young Japanese gay men's consumption of GV has led them to conceptualize a desire for a masculinity based upon *nonke* tropes as normative in the Japanese gay media landscape. The fetishization of the *nonke* has reinforced in GV consumers a normative understanding of the desirability of hegemonic forms of masculinity as rough, active, and heterosexual. But this is only part of the story. Interviews with young gay men in Ni-chōme, including my four principal interlocutors, indicated that their consumption of heterosexual men as objects who passively "get fucked" allowed them to challenge wider heteronormative understandings of same-sex desire that position gay men as passive objects. In some ways, one could argue that their consumption of GV thus queered normative gender roles, allowing them to view themselves as men whose desire was active and masculine rather than passive and effeminate. While the broader positioning of *nonke* in GV is problematic given its reliance on discourses of pain and unwillingness, consumption of these pornographic texts appeared to give limited agency to consumers. Men with whom I conversed ultimately felt that they could challenge Japanese society's positioning of *nonke* as the symbol of hegemonic masculinity by reappropriating heterosexual men's agency through their consumption of GV. Objectifying straight men gave members of Japan's precarious and marginalized gay community a certain sense of hope, but access to this hopeful discourse was predicated on an acceptance of a highly specific bodily aesthetic and concomitant ideologies of hardness explored in the previous chapter. GV drew upon discourses of masculinity to affirm the authenticity of sex between gay men but, in so doing, excluded those men who choose not to identify with hegemonic masculinity. This is a point to which I return in more depth in the conclusion to this book.

Consuming GV thus educated Junho, Yōichi, Haruma, and Shōtarō that Typing represented a system of categorization based in physical appearance and gendered performance. Through their engagement with GV on both tube sites and in Ni-chōme's *gei shoppu*, these four men came to understand that heteronormative masculinity as embodied by the *tai'ikukai-kei* was privileged in the Japanese gay media landscape as normatively desirable. They subsequently internalized this discourse, linking the figure of the *tai'ikukai-kei* to a fetishized image of the straight male. This feeds into the political economy of Typing, whereby hardness is privileged as normatively desirable because of its links to heteronormativity and softness, embodied by the *kawaii-kei*, is viewed as only ambiguously desirable. For many men reflecting on the positioning of the famous gay pornstar Koh Masaki, this hardness was also conceptualized as a distinctive feature of an explicitly "Japanese" gay masculinity, and their investment into this cultural stereotype provided strong justification for accepting heteronormative understandings of gender and sexuality. That being said, this chapter has also revealed that the initial encounter with Typing via GV led the four key informants to consider "Typing as categorization" as something applied to another person and never to the self. In the following chapter, I explore how engaging with the Japanese gay magazine *Bádi* introduced the four young men to the notion that Typing had something to say about one's subjective experiences and personal identities and how this process led the men to further internalize the logics of GV that promote desires for masculine and straight-acting men as normative in Ni-chōme.

# FIVE

## Gay Magazines

*Typing, Lifestyles, and Gay Identity*

One of the most surprising observations from my fieldwork was that print media, especially gay magazines, remained an important source of information for young gay men seeking to learn not only about Ni-chōme but also about their same-sex attraction more broadly. This is despite the fact that circulation and readership figures collected by the Japanese Research Institute for Publications have consistently demonstrated that magazine readership in 21st-century Japan starkly declined.[1] As discussed in previous chapters, I often observed young men in Ni-chōme consuming gay magazines in spaces such as *gei shoppu*, gay bars, and specialized libraries such as the one found in CoCoLo Café in the center of the neighborhood. It was certainly the case that Junho, Yōichi, Shōtarō, and even Haruma to a certain extent would often quickly read through gay magazines as a prelude to other later online media consumption or social engagements in Ni-chōme. Although the impressions I gathered during visits to Ni-chōme in both 2015 and 2017 suggest that young gay men may no longer regularly buy magazines, I reveal in this chapter that in 2013 these print media still played a crucial role in circulating knowledge about Japan's gay culture generally—and gay desire specifically—via the trope of "lifestyle." In fact, through a careful examination of how my four key interlocutors consumed *Bádi*, this chapter reveals the importance of this popular Japanese gay magazine to the production of a homonormative and neoliberal gay culture that restricts gay identity to a particular Type, the *ikanimo-kei*.

Anthropologist Laura Miller argues that the ethnographic study of Japanese magazines provides important "insights into culture, society, and language."[2] Miller notes that, despite falling sales figures in contemporary Japan, it is problematic for scholars to discount the study of Japanese magazines, particularly since "a magazine contains many voices and images, some opposing others"; further, this multiplicity of voices "may either buttress or challenge prevailing social norms."[3] The study of magazines, especially when coupled with the ethnographic study of magazine reading practices and audience reception, thus provides access to the views and values of a community.[4] Writing in an earlier, pre-internet context, John Clammer notes that Japanese magazines have always represented important guides for consumption and maintain a privileged position within Japan's hyperconsumerist culture.[5] In fact, Marilyn Ivy has revealed through a careful study of magazines in recessionary Japan that throughout the late 1980s and early 1990s, magazines were strategically deployed to segment the population via consumer practices, creating "micromasses" that identified around particular consumer lifestyles.[6] Clammer's and Ivy's arguments are echoed in Gabriella Lukács's study of 1990s television production. She suggests that contemporary TV culture in Japan has taken cues from the magazine publishing industry to reconfigure televisual entertainment as "a catalogue for designers, a shopping guide wed to the culture of celebrity."[7] Clammer argues that studying magazines may provide access to the discourses that broadly structure Japanese mediascapes, also noting that the study of magazines is particularly useful for understanding contemporary Japanese gender ideologies.[8] Indeed, both Masafumi Monden's study of men's fashion magazines and Alexandra Hambleton's analysis of the women's magazine *anan* demonstrate that magazines continue to play a crucial role in reinforcing the heteronormative ideologies that contour knowledge about sexuality and gender expression in Japan among heterosexual consumers.[9] The aim of this chapter is to thus reveal how the consumerism promoted in a Japanese gay magazine likewise produces heteronormative logics via neoliberal frameworks.

## Bádi *Magazine: Diverse Content, Selective Reading*

*Bádi* specifically targets an audience of young gay men, positioning itself via its catchphrase as "spreading a happy gay life" (*happī gei raifu o hirogaru*) throughout Japan. Beginning publication in 1994, *Bádi* quickly became Japan's most popular monthly magazine targeting the gay community, displacing *Barazoku* after the older influential magazine ceased publication in 2004. During my fieldwork, *Bádi* had the highest circulation of any gay magazine in Japan, roughly 80,000 issues a month nationwide. Whenever I visited the various *gei shoppu* in Ni-chōme, I always noticed many gay men—both young and old—standing in the aisles flipping through issues of *Bádi* and my conversations with these men indeed revealed that *Bádi* was consistently more popular than its nearest competitor, *G-Men*. Despite *Bádi*'s evident popularity when I visited Tokyo for fieldwork, it greatly declined in later years, and *Bádi* eventually folded in early 2019 after releasing a special issue celebrating its 25th anniversary. The magazine's demise was met with considerable surprise by online commentators, and many prominent gay activists, artists, and writers took to social media to eulogize what they considered to be a major loss to Japan's gay culture.

Despite *Bádi*'s wide readership and influence, there has been a paucity of scholarly attention paid to the magazine. One exception is sociologist Moriyama Noritaka's content analyses of the articles appearing in *Bádi* in 2005, which demonstrated the magazine was instrumental to developing a sense of gay communal identity in 21st-century Japan.[10] Another exception is linguist Hideko Abe's investigation of *Bádi*'s advice columns, which specifically focused upon how authority is managed through the manipulation of polite language.[11] Neither of these studies, however, explicitly investigated how gay men consume and interact with the magazine and did not reflect on audience reception. Furthermore, *Bádi* had changed since Moriyama and Abe conducted their research in the early 2000s. In 2010, there was a drastic reduction in the number of pages per issue (from 600 to 250 pages), and the bulk of the pre-2010 content—including articles, manga, and erotic stories—moved online, where it could be accessed only after inputting a code found in the physical magazine. These editorial strategies were most likely adopted to attract readers who were increasingly turning to the internet for news, current affairs, and fashion advice. Indeed, many men suggested to me during fieldwork that they would access *Bádi*'s online content (although not always frequently). That being said, the magazine's eventual collapse in 2019 reveals that these editorial strategies were ultimately ineffective.

My analysis of *Bádi* presents an updated investigation of the magazine based on a close reading of 48 issues from 2010 to 2013 (12 issues per year). These four years of data collection allowed me to develop an overall impression of the magazine's content and facilitated analysis of any content changes over the years. Consistent with the broader "ethnoliterary" focus of *Regimes of Desire*, however, my analysis of *Bádi*'s content focuses specifically on the sections that my four principal informants reported they consistently consumed. More than any other section of this book, this chapter focuses on the highly personal act of magazine reading, and it is thus appropriate that my analysis centers on individual case studies, which can be explored in depth, rather than attempting to generalize based on the reported recollections of men met during fieldwork. Of particular interest to me was how my four key interlocutors' understandings of *Bádi*'s content was contoured by their situated consumption of the magazine within Ni-chōme. I was also interested in their reading of the lifestyle presented in the magazine as *ikanimo-kei* as representing a particular kind of creative reading born out of their experiences in the neighborhood's gay bars and clubs. As I reveal through this chapter, the four men's reading of *Bádi* was highly selective and, in some ways, strategically linked to their visits to Ni-chōme.

An Overview of a Typical Issue of *Bádi*

*Bádi*'s content is highly diverse, as can be seen by the average page space afforded each section of the magazine, depicted in table 7. This diversity of content is a common feature of Japanese magazines, which Clammer argues are typified by a "mixture of genres, with text, advertisements, visuals and comics all in the same publication."[12] Clammer further suggests that Japanese magazines are designed as "commodities with a short shelf-life which mostly demand only a very short attention span" and are "generally looked at and browsed rather than read like a novel might be."[13] This implies that *Bádi* is not designed to be read in depth, which is further evidenced by the prioritizing of large images with very little text in most sections of the magazine. Only the articles, editorials, erotic stories, and letters to the editor can be considered text-heavy, although even the articles tend to be accompanied by titillating images of handsome young men in salacious poses, exposing their taught *gatai* bodies. In discussing Japanese women's magazines, Brian Moeran highlights similar editorial practices, with priority given to images rather than text.[14] Magazines in Japan can thus be considered image-heavy media.

The topics of the articles appearing in *Bádi* are likewise quite diverse. Figure 6 presents the number of pages afforded to various article topics in an average issue. Political articles, which I define here as articles that explicitly engage with social issues facing gay men in contemporary Japan, represented only 23 percent (6/26) of the page space afforded articles in an average issue. These political articles included discussions of gay mar-

Table 7. Average page space for each section of *Bádi*, 2010–2013

| CONTENT | No. OF PAGES | PERCENTAGE |
|---|---|---|
| Advertisements | 121 | 43.5 |
| Manga (*geikomi*) | 60 | 21.6 |
| Porn reviews | 27 | 9.7 |
| Articles | 26 | 9.4 |
| Gravure images | 16 | 5.8 |
| Erotic stories | 11 | 3.9 |
| Letters to the editor | 6 | 2.2 |
| Fashion features | 4 | 1.4 |
| Event listings | 4 | 1.4 |
| Editorials | 2 | 0.7 |
| Health | 1 | 0.4 |
| TOTAL | 278 | 100 |

riage (*dōseikon*), LGBT activism in Japan and overseas (with a surprising focus on international rather than domestic news), and LGBT film festivals. It is important to note that these political articles were the only spaces in *Bádi* to mention lesbian and transgender issues, often via the umbrella terms "LGBT" or "sexual minority community" (*seiteki shōsūsha komyuniti*), and that the magazine was avowedly male-centric in its discussions of sexual minority culture both in Japan and abroad. That being said, I noticed through casual reading of *Bádi* after the LGBT boom of 2015 that a broader focus on issues facing same-sex desiring and gender nonnormative men and women had emerged in response to this seminal moment in Japanese society when LGBT rights discourse gained mainstream media attention. Between 2010 and 2013, however, the number of political articles was significantly fewer than event reports (38.5 percent) and slightly greater than advisory articles addressing aspects of Japan's gay culture (19.2 percent), including articles exploring how to have good sex, how to navigate gay bars, and how to find a boyfriend or sex friend.

Except for articles addressing ostensibly political themes, the majority of *Bádi*'s content was designed to promote the consumption of various products and services tailored to the Japanese gay community. Often, these articles tied discussions of products and services to GV, representing another instance in which the Japanese gay media landscape had become pornographied as discussed in chapter 1. Structurally, the political articles tended to be printed in black and white rather than glossy color and were situated toward the middle of a typical issue, along with the editorials and letters. Other sections of the magazine printed in black and white

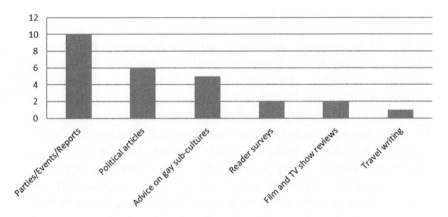

Figure 6. Average page space afforded each kind of article in *Bádi*.

on cheaper paper included manga, erotic stories, and the vast majority of the advertisements collected toward the end of a typical issue. Conversely, porn reviews, and all other kinds of articles, were typically in glossy full color and situated at the front of the magazine, as were fashion and shopping features, soft pornographic centerfolds known as "gravure" imagery, and some prominently placed promotional material for gay parties and club events.

Overall, the focus on lifestyle rather than politics in *Bádi* suggests that sociologist Mark McLelland's claim that 1990s gay magazines prioritize apolitical consumption grounded in notions of "play" (*asobi*) continues to be true of contemporary gay magazines, at least in some respects.[15] In fact, in her overview of *Bádi*'s content, Hideko Abe has also argued that *Bádi* is best considered a "pornographic lifestyle magazine" in comparison to the more politically driven activist magazines such as *Queer Japan* and *Queer Japan Returns*, which were published in the late 1990s and early 2000s.[16] Citing an interview with Ogura Yō, one of *Bádi*'s early supervising editors, Abe notes that most Japanese gay magazines are ultimately "designed to help readers understand, interpret, appreciate, and enjoy sex."[17] Finally, nearly half of a typical issue of *Bádi* contained advertising for pornographic videos, "host clubs" (in this context, a euphemism for spaces where one can hire sex workers), various sex toys, and gay circuit parties and night club events. Overall, like most Japanese magazines, *Bádi* aimed to promote consumption, and it did so through implicitly privileging the lifestyle of the *ikanimo-kei*, an argument I elaborate below.

## Informants' Selective Reading of *Bádi*

Junho, Yōichi, Haruma, and Shōtarō all read *Bádi* to varying degrees. This is not to say, however, that they read all of the magazine's content. Instead, their reading of *Bádi* was highly selective, and each explained to me that they would read only the content they felt relevant either to their visits to Ni-chōme or to satisfying their sexual desires through masturbation, demonstrating how Abe's positioning of *Bádi* as a chiefly pornographic magazine is partly true. Table 8 summarizes the content each informant reported reading and how often. As Haruma's consumption of *Bádi* changed after his breakup with Akito, his consumption both pre- and post-breakup is presented in the table. Only that content which the informants mentioned consuming is included in the table and, as is clearly evident, this does not represent the majority of the magazine's content.

The four principal informants frequently read the event listings, and conversations in 2013 with other young gay men in Ni-chōme indicated that this section was very popular among those searching for recommendations about what to do in the district on a night out. Indeed, many men I observed in *gei shoppu* would quickly flip through *Bádi*'s event listings while standing in the aisles, and after gathering the information they sought, they would return the magazine without purchasing it. This seemed to be a practice that store clerks tacitly approved, as I rarely encountered people being confronted for not purchasing the magazines. Junho, Yōichi, Haruma, and Shōtarō used event listings to determine what was going on each month in Ni-chōme. Junho noted in 2013 that the print-based listings were often more useful than event notices on social media, which did not necessarily allow one to plan one's month in advance. Each issue of *Bádi* contained four black-and-white pages of event listings, organized in the form of a calendar, with the advertising for many of these

Table 8. Informants' consumption of content in *Bádi*, 2010–2013

| Informants | Event listings | Porn reviews | Gravure images | Manga | Articles |
|---|---|---|---|---|---|
| Junho | Very frequent | Very frequent | Frequent | Rare | Occasional |
| Yōichi | Very frequent | Very frequent | Frequent | Rare | Occasional |
| Haruma (with Akito) | Frequent | Frequent | Occasional | Occasional | Rare |
| Haruma (after Akito) | Rare | Never | Rare | Occasional | Never |
| Shōtarō | Frequent | Frequent | Rare | Very frequent | Rare |

events depicting sexy models with the hard *gatai* bodies representative of the *ikanimo-kei* ideal. Events from all over Japan were typically listed in *Bádi*, although events in Tokyo, Osaka, and Nagoya tended to dominate. The most commonly advertised events were circuit parties or theme nights at bars; advertisements for roundtables and activist events were quite rare. The focus appeared to be on promoting patterns of consumption that are typical features of the *ikanimo-kei* lifestyle; namely, attending large dance parties at certain well-known gay venues.

The second-most frequently read content was the glossy color reviews of pornographic videos. For Junho, Yōichi, and Shōtarō, reading these reviews helped them to determine which GV films to next view online. Junho and Yōichi, in the privacy of their own homes, also used the reviews as masturbatory aids since they often purchased copies of the magazine. The majority of reviews focused on films depicting *tai'ikukai-kei* models, which is consistent with the broader trends in GV discussed in the previous chapter. Haruma and Akito used to read these reviews as a prelude to their sexual intercourse, and Haruma explained to me that they would often attempt to mimic the positions they had seen in the photographs, which is an interesting—if atypical—example of how magazine consumption can influence sexual behavior. Haruma stopped reading the reviews after his breakup with Akito, however, and mentioned to me that their previous sexual practices with the magazine had always "made him feel uncomfortable."

Closely related to these pornographic reviews are the gravure center-folds, which these four men also reported consuming. Gravure imagery is a genre of soft-core erotic photography designed to sexually excite the reader, but which never displays the sex act itself. The models depicted in these gravure images almost all overwhelmingly conform to the hard bodily aesthetics of the *ikanimo-kei*, and it was exceedingly rare for any of the models depicted in the magazine to express a physicality that deviated from this normatively desirable Type. Yōichi reported that he drew upon the gravure imagery as inspiration for his life as a *hayatteru ikemen*, recreating photographs with his own body and distributing them to his fans via LINE and Twitter. In fact, before his death, Koh Masaki was often featured in both the gravure imagery and porn reviews, and Yōichi used *Bádi* as an important resource to mimic the pornstar's style and cultivate his own personal aesthetics based in the hard and rough "Japanese" masculinity that Koh embodied as the "gay porn star who represents Japan." Indeed, *Bádi* often contained interviews with Koh, and he was even given a regular column in 2012. It was in these spaces that Koh developed his arguments concerning a "Japanese" gay masculine aesthetic.

Shōtarō and Haruma primarily consumed *Bádi* for the *geikomi*, which accounted for approximately 21.6 percent of an average issue's pages. Most *geikomi* in the magazine typically contained explicit and pornographic depictions of sex designed to excite the reader, hence adding to the magazine's pornographic focus.[18] In order to read *geikomi*, Shōtarō would first preview the comics, quickly flipping through pages of the magazines while visiting Ni-chōme's *gei shoppu*. He would then return home, where he would find unofficial online copies of the specific *geikomi* he had enjoyed in the store and would then use them as a masturbatory aid. Likewise, Junho and Yōichi, who consumed *geikomi* casually, typically did so as a masturbatory aid. Haruma continued to consume the manga in *Bádi* after his separation from Akito, usually during his renewed visits to Ni-chōme. When I expressed surprise that he would continue to read the magazine, Haruma explained that it was "like an addiction." Haruma was well aware that his continued fandom for *geikomi* in *Bádi* contradicted some of his arguments concerning the Japanese gay media landscape being filled with "poison," and he used the discourse of addiction to rationalize his continued consumption of a media form that he understood as somewhat problematic.

Only Junho and Yōichi mentioned reading the magazine's articles in 2013. They reported reading only the regular reports of gay parties and events and avoided articles that they found overly political. It is unsurprising that these two men would mention political articles, considering they often bought copies of the magazine and had issues at home, unlike Haruma and Shōtarō who did not purchase copies. Yōichi viewed the political articles in *Bádi* as "uninteresting" and said he had "no need for them," particularly as he viewed articles that explicitly engaged with lesbian or transgender issues as irrelevant to his life as a gay man. Yōichi's strongly negative opinion of political articles did, however, appear to be gradually changing when I lost contact with him at the end of my initial fieldwork period. Junho claimed that he preferred to read about political issues online, listing Twitter as his primary source for this kind of news. He viewed *Bádi* as a magazine for fun, not politics, which is reinforced by the lack of page space afforded in an average issue to discussions of politics. Interestingly, Shōtarō and Haruma also claimed that they did not read the articles in *Bádi* for reasons similar to Junho's. Shōtarō further explained that *Bádi*'s take on political issues was "too simplistic" given the magazine's focus on "play" (*asobi*). Other young gay men I met in Ni-chōme similarly stated that they did not view *Bádi* as a political or activist resource, and the magazine's positioning as something lighthearted and fun seemed to be fairly common to most men I met in the district. Junho, Yōichi, Haruma, and Shōtarō primarily viewed *Bádi* as a magazine for general entertainment or as a masturbatory aid rather than an appropriate venue for reading about gay news, even though the magazine did contain such articles. My four key interlocutors' selective reading of *Bádi* ultimately privileged information about gay lifestyles, and it is their understanding of *Bádi* as "lifestyle media" that has most influenced how they conceptualize their gay desires.

### Promoting the Ikanimo-kei *Lifestyle: Typing as Identity and Lifestyle in* Bádi

In contrast to the other gay media examined in this book, Typing rarely appears explicitly in the pages of *Bádi*, usually appearing only as a way to organize the information presented in event listings and porn reviews. Occasionally, Typing is referred to in event reports when the events in question specifically target niche Types, such as the single report for a *debu-kei* event appearing within my corpus of 48 issues published between 2010 and 2013. Use of Typing was especially uncommon in the vast majority of reports and articles promoting events, and many young gay men I surveyed about the magazine's content believed these events targeted an ideal *ikanimo-kei* audience. Similar to GV, *Bádi* thus ostensibly draws upon "Typing as categorization." Reflecting on how they consumed *Bádi*, however, the young gay men I met in Ni-chōme in 2013—including my four key interlocutors—surprisingly viewed the use of Typing in *Bádi* differently from how Typing appears in GV. Many of these men explained that Typing within *Bádi* is best understood as a form of identity management rather than a simple socio-semiotic system of classifying bodily aesthetics. Indeed, young gay men argued that *Bádi* could be strategically used as a resource to situate oneself within particular communities of men identifying with a specific *kei* Type, especially the mainstream *ikanimo-kei* community that gathers in Ni-chōme. Junho, Yōichi, Haruma, and Shōtarō ultimately indicated that *Bádi* promoted the idea that Typing may be utilized to describe one's "subjectivity" (*shutaisei*) or "identity" (*aidentitī*), although Haruma explained that he did not identify with or support the identity politics presented in the magazine. It appeared that my four principal interlocutors' selective reading of *Bádi*'s content, influenced by the situatedness of this consumption within Ni-chōme, led them to creatively read Typing in *Bádi* in ways that emphasized the trope of "lifestyle."

Indeed, viewing *Bádi* as a guide to living a "gay lifestyle" (*gei raifu-sutairu* or sometimes just *gei raifu*) was a common theme in many of my conversations with Junho, Yōichi, Haruma, and Shōtarō. That this trope was often employed during interviews is unsurprising given that the magazine explicitly and visibly flags its intent to "spread a happy gay life." In his daily life, Yōichi used *Bádi* as a style guide to develop a "manly" attractive appearance. Shōtarō particularly drew upon *Bádi*'s manga as a resource both to understand how to engage with the gay scene in Ni-chōme and to understand his desires. Each of the four principal informants explained to me that *Bádi* promoted an *ikanimo-kei* lifestyle. Junho and Yōichi stressed the importance of the magazine to their current understandings of this Type's normative desirability. Junho argued that the magazine's purpose was to teach young gay men how to enjoy their lives as gay men; he highlighted that the magazine revealed to him that an *ikanimo-kei* lifestyle was "the most exciting" given its focus on partying at the fashionable clubs featured in its pages. Yōichi claimed that *Bádi*'s focus on the *ikanimo-kei* demonstrated that it was "normal" for gay men in Japan to be masculine, citing as evidence for this view the large number of models with *gatai* bodies in this nationally circulating magazine. For Yōichi, who used *Bádi* as a personal style guide, the magazine was an important resource that justified the necessity of his intense gym training and attention to his physical appearance. Haruma explained that Akito also introduced the magazine to him first as a "guidebook on how to live as a gay man" and that the magazine played a crucial role in Akito's attempts to teach Haruma how to behave in a manner he deemed as appropriately masculine.

During interviews, it became apparent that all four of my key interlocutors tended to conflate "living a gay life" with "living an *ikanimo-kei* lifestyle." Even Haruma, who ultimately rejected the masculinist focus of the *ikanimo-kei* image, made this unconscious connection on occasion, and this was why he had ultimately come to reject the magazine's identity politics and read it only because of his fandom for *geikomi*. What particularly interested me was the fact that my extensive reading of the magazine revealed that *Bádi* only rarely made explicit mention of *ikanimo-kei* and, like the GV discussed in the previous chapter, would instead discuss *tai'ikukai-kei* in porn reviews and event listings. The informants would subsequently creatively read this as referring to the *ikanimo-kei*, a practice influenced by their experiences in Ni-chōme's gay bars, where use of the term *ikanimo-kei* was fairly prevalent. It is important to remember here that the four men's readings of *Bádi* emerged out of their contact with Ni-chōme and their prior consumption of GV, a medium they had come to view as tying together the *tai'ikukai-kei* and the *ikanimo-kei* via the fetishization of straight men. This demonstrates that *Bádi*'s situatedness within the overall Japanese gay media landscape plays an important role in influencing how the informants understood the magazine's contents. In fact, the Japanese gay media landscape's regimes of desire appear to have conditioned Junho, Yōichi, Haruma, and Shōtarō to experience and understand particular lifestyles as implicitly linked to the image of the *ikanimo-kei*, even if the text that they are reading does not explicitly do so. These four men thus extrapolate a particular narrative contained in certain sections of the magazine as representative of the magazine as a whole, creatively reading into the magazine the ideologies of Typing that circulate in Ni-chōme. This is a clear example of Stuart Hall's seminal argument that consumers of media commonly deploy their own personal experiences and knowledge when interpreting media rather than the ideologies included in the media themselves by their producers.[19]

Lifestyle is an important trope when considering the content of *Bádi*, since the magazine relies upon the notion of the "gay life" to educate men about Japan's gay culture rather than explicitly using the framework of Typing. When asked why magazines such as *Bádi* tended to avoid Typing, many of the men I met in Ni-chōme explained that because Typing is "common sense" to young gay men in Japan, *Bádi* did not need to explicitly explore it in its articles. That is, these men believed *Bádi* did not need to explicitly include Typing: given their experiences in Ni-chōme's gay bar culture, readers already possessed the sociocultural knowledge required to read the system into the magazine, thus making "lifestyle" a more important and relevant trope. A representative example of the usage of the discursive trope of the "gay life" can be seen in a March 2012 article reporting on a reader's poll on grooming and personal styling:

> In this month's issue, we are focusing on all of our reader's lifework
> (*raifuwāku*) . . . so, from questions that uniquely concern the gay
> life (*gei raifu*) to questions about trivial aspects of your lifework, we
> conducted an extensive survey.[20]

Throughout the article from which this quote is excerpted, "gay life" is juxtaposed with the idea of "lifework," the process of bettering oneself through the consumption of specific beauty treatments, regular exercise, correct diet, and the purchasing of specialist goods, which is a common trope in young women's and men's fashion magazines in Japan.[21] Lifework, then, represents a conscious utopian project of seeking to improve one's life via consumer practices; it evokes aesthetic discipline and the strategic management of the body as a method of similarly managing identity and gendered performance. The article also juxtaposes "lifework" with "body-work" (bodīwāku), the process by which the physical body is modified through aesthetic discipline and training in order to present particular gendered and other identities.[22] Interestingly, in this article and much of Bádi, a "gay life" is consistently presented as resulting from the consumption of very specific products and services and from the participation in specific body management regimes that ultimately produce the hard masculinity valorized in both Ni-chōme and the Japanese gay media landscape. In fact, this focus on lifework explicitly evokes the aesthetic discipline inherent to the gatai body, representing an example of Bádi's promotion of the ikanimo-kei—for whom the gatai body represents an essential identity marker—as normatively desirable. As is clear, the body-work that Bádi promotes differs greatly from the softer and "elegant" masculine ideals found in fashion magazines and style guides for heterosexual men,[23] once again demonstrating how Japan's gay media were resisting broader trends in mainstream women's media that ostensibly challenge the primacy of hegemonic modes of masculinity based in activeness and hardness.

The trope of the gay life was also explicitly mentioned in a small feature published on the inside front cover of each issue of Bádi titled "VOICE x GAYLIFE: the gay life which [we] walk together with you" (VOICE x GAYLIFE: anata to issho ni ayumu gei raifu). This feature presented a short interview with the issue's cover model about what living as a gay man means for them. The aim of this feature, I argue, was to encourage readers not only to consume the models as objects of desire but also to understand them as individuals with an explicit gay identity and hence to legitimize the model's inclusion in the magazine. This initial section of the magazine thus overtly mobilized gay identity politics, tying the discussion of lifestyle found throughout the magazine to a broader discourse that centers same-sex attraction as the foundation for a personal and communal identity. "VOICE x GAYLIFE" typically discussed the model's recollections of coming out, what being gay means to them and their preferences in a partner, and unsurprisingly, these preferences matched the characteristics of the *ikanimo-kei* that these models themselves typified. Consistent with the rest of *Bádi*, Typing was never explicitly utilized in this section, but my conversations with both my four key interlocutors and other young men who regularly consumed *Bádi* revealed that most readers understood the models featured in these magazines as *ikanimo-kei* since most possessed *gatai* bodies. The activities that many of these models discussed in their interviews, including working out at the gym and attending large gay night club events (where many work as erotic go-go dancers), were also understood as indexing the models' status as *ikanimo-kei*. Indeed, conversations with young gay men in Ni-chōme revealed that these models' explicit promotion of such activities played an important role in reinforcing the idea that participation in such events formed part of a normatively desirable gay lifestyle.

As mentioned in the introduction, Japan's media landscape has become increasingly neoliberalized as a response to the collapse of the bubble economy in the late 1980s and the ongoing recession. Lukács cogently demonstrates that, as part of this process of neoliberalization, Japanese magazines and TV serials have consistently deployed the trope of "lifestyle" (*ikikata sutairu* or *raifusutairu*) as a marketing tool. Focusing particularly on the emergence of "love dramas" in the late 1990s to early 2000s, Lukács argues that lifestyle "is an appealing tool for marketers because it suggests to consumers that they can freely choose their social selves" via their consumption practices.[24] Furthermore, Lukács notes that the trope of lifestyle "simplifies the problematic of identity" and is thus deployed within Japan's neoliberal media landscape to "provide a sense of belonging to a community."[25] As Wendy Brown notes within her conceptualization of the fundamentally exploitative nature of neoliberalism, lifestyle is mobilized to create fantasies of expanded choice that instead act to narrow consumption into highly rigid patterns that fuel capitalist accumulation.[26] Ultimately, Lukács argues that lifestyle media provides consumers in Japan with the ability to "reinforce and cultivate their individuality via taste preferences" but that these preferences are often constrained by the logics of the neoliberal market.[27] *Bádi* magazine, in promoting the consumerist lifestyle of the *ikanimo-kei* as "normal" for young gay men, thus appears representative of broader trends in Japan's hyperconsumerist society, in which identity politics are becoming increasingly mobilized for commercial means.

The gay lifestyle promoted in *Bádi* represents a particular identity based in normative consumer behaviors anchored to the *ikanimo-kei*. This use of "lifestyle" is not particular to *Bádi*. Globally circulating gay magazines such as the UK's *Attitude* and the US's *Out* engage in similar discursive practices.[28] A focus on lifestyle also represents an important part of the depoliticized homonormative gay culture criticized by Lisa Duggan.[29] *Bádi*, despite superficial coverage of political issues, serves merely to drive Japanese gay men to consume and thus fails to critique the capitalist structures that have historically disadvantaged same-sex desiring men and women around the globe. The homonormative nature of this consumer culture is especially clear when one considers that the lifestyle promoted by this magazine is based in a recuperation of hegemonic hard masculinity, as has been explicated in previous chapters. It is through linkages between lifestyle and patterns of normative consumption that *Bádi* implicitly engages with the system of Typing. As Moriyama has argued, *Bádi* privileges a youth lifestyle grounded in the consumption of beauty products, participation in the gay club scene, gym training to sculpt a *gatai* body, and the fetishization of, and identification with, straight men.[30] In other words, *Bádi* promotes the *ikanimo-kei* as the "normal" gay identity by normalizing its consumer practices and bodily aesthetics as key to living a "happy gay life." This conflation of the gay life and the *ikanimo-kei* lifestyle reinforces the Japanese gay media landscape's regimes of desire through the production of a desirable lifestyle that magazine consumers are encouraged to emulate. As mentioned above, my four principal interlocutors' creative reading of *Bádi* demonstrates the influence of these regimes of desire on interpreting the lifestyle promoted in the magazine. That is, the four men's embeddedness within Ni-chōme's particular cultural context has led them to read *Bádi* in ways that justify the ideologies with which they engage when participating in the district's gay bar culture.

As I visited Ni-chōme's *gei shoppu* and bars and spoke with the men I met about their attitudes toward Japanese gay media, I learned that reading *Bádi* was viewed as an in-group marker among men, such as Yōichi, who identified as *ikanimo-kei*. That is, the act of regularly reading the magazine was viewed as an important index for this particular identity. But this does not necessarily suggest that all readers of *Bádi* identify as *ikanimo-kei*. Junho, like many other men I met in Ni-chōme, regularly reads *Bádi* not because he wanted to become an *ikanimo-kei* but rather because he identifies as an admirer of this privileged Type. Junho, and others like him, read the magazine to learn about and share in the experiences of men they admire and sexually desire without necessarily seeking to emulate such a lifestyle. In a parallel example, sociologist Ellen McCracken has highlighted that the majority of *US Vogue* readers are typically of a lower socioeconomic class than that of the opulent upper-class lifestyle depicted in the magazine's glossy pages, and they typically consume *Vogue* to escape into a fantasy life that is fulfilling to them.[31] Magazine readers are thus involved in a utopian and escapist project in which the magazine allows a certain level of access to a desirable community. Theorist Peter Corrigan terms this process "aspirational reading."[32] Lukács similarly argues that such reading practices are particularly important in Japan's neoliberalized consumer culture as a way for consumers to construct a virtual sense of community via their aspirational consumption practices.[33] Junho and readers like him engage in aspirational reading as it allowed them to virtually join the *ikanimo-kei* communities they admire and hence vicariously participate in the community of attractive young gay men that the Japanese gay media landscape constructs as representative of an ideal "happy gay life."

When I asked young gay men I met in *gei shoppu* about their primary reason for reading *Bádi*, the vast majority expressed sentiments that demonstrated the aspirational nature of their reading. Once again, the familiar trope of *akogare*, or longing, was employed within these men's narratives to articulate their strong yearning for the "happy gay life" embodied by the *ikanimo-kei* men depicted in the magazine. For most, this "happy gay life" was tied to the broader desires for hard masculinity, discussed previously in chapter 3, and this led me to think very carefully about what the young consumers of *Bádi* aspired to become. Fundamentally, I believe that these consumers' aspirational readings for a happy life tied to a Type that resuscitates hegemonic masculinity is driven by their recognition of their abject positioning in society as supposedly failed men. After all, when I first visited a *gei shoppu* with Shōtarō early in my fieldwork, it was his yearning for Koh Masaki and his hard masculinity via *Bádi* that best encapsulated his broader anxieties about his gendered identity. Unlike heterosexual young men in Japan, who Justin Charlebois argues are increasingly and strategically embracing the soft masculinity depicted in young women's popular culture as a strategy to contest hegemonic forms of masculinity tied to the salaryman ideal,[34] the young gay men I interviewed are instead turning to the opposite end of the gender spectrum to escape from the precariousness of contemporary Japan. The lifestyle politics of *Bádi* therefore strongly inculcates in young Japanese gay men the desire for hard masculinity as a form of escapist fantasy, which may normalize same-sex attraction and hence provide affirming discourses, but only by resuscitating heteronormative conceptualizations of sexuality and gender. To paraphrase Fushimi Noriaki,[35] the lifestyle promoted in *Bádi* thus represents the male role within the gender binary at the heart of the hetero system that conditions knowledge concerning sexuality in Japan. Young gay men's aspirational readings of *Bádi* therefore merely uphold the status quo while producing a fantasy of queer liberation. Such escapist fantasies via consumer lifestyle are central to the homonormative and neoliberal politics that Lisa Duggan argues uphold the social systems that have historically disadvantaged same-sex desiring communities around the world.[36]

## *Event Listings, Typing, and Privileging the* Ikanimo-kei *Lifestyle*

It is interesting that the content that the four principal informants most frequently consumed in *Bádi*—the event listings and porn reviews—were the only sections of the magazine where Typing, not lifestyle, was commonly utilized as a discursive trope. Although the four informants reported that they rarely read articles, they did indicate that the discourse of a gay lifestyle promoted by the magazine's articles and editorials affected their understanding of the use of Typing in the event listings, leading them to view the event listings not as "Typing as categorization" but "Typing as identity." I would argue that the magazine's overall discursive tone has influenced the four men's interpretation of the use of Typing in the event listings so that they began to see it as part of the greater discourse of "gay lifestyle." Furthermore, the event listings played an important role in consolidating these four men's belief in the innateness of their gay desires, as discussed in chapter 2. Coupled with their experiences in Ni-chōme, reading *Bádi* led Junho, Yōichi, Haruma, and Shōtarō to directly identify with their gay desires as a fundamental aspect of their subjectivity.

Every issue of *Bádi* within the corpus that I collected contained a four-page, black-and-white section titled "GAY NIGHT SCHEDULE." Located near the middle of the issue (just before the advertisements), it profiled the month's upcoming events. The number of events per issue varied from 50 to 100, with an average issue containing approximately 79 upcoming event profiles. Interestingly, despite the magazine's national circulation, the majority of events listed in an average issue were in Tokyo, most often in Ni-chōme, which points once again to the Tokyo-centric nature of the

Japanese gay media landscape. Between 2010 and 2013, there were slight changes to the presentation of the listings (the amount of text in a typical listing decreased as images and links to websites and Twitter accounts increased), but the overall content and format remained unchanged. *Bádi* published two categories of events: "gay nights" (text originally in English)—referring to club events, circuit parties, and live performances such as drag shows and DJ performances—and "social clubs, noticeboards, and workshops, etc." (*sākuru/keiji/wākushoppu, hoka*). On average, the majority of events featured each month are gay nights, representing 97.5 percent (77/79) of an average issue's advertised events. The fact that *Bádi* privileges gay nights over miscellaneous discussion events is unsurprising, given that the magazine's articles tend to focus on lifestyle rather than politics, and this is consistent with the homonormative nature of the Japanese gay media landscape. The event listings ultimately privilege the promotion of what Yōichi termed the *ikanimo-kei*'s "party boy lifestyle," further demonstrating how *Bádi* ultimately promoted consumerism and failed to question capitalist systems that have historically excluded same-sex desiring men from normative conceptualizations of masculinity.

Each advertisement provides details such as time and location, the cover charge (if applicable), featured performers (including DJs and go-go boy erotic dancers), and often a sentence or two regarding dress code and special prices. It is common for images to be presented within a listing, with 64.6 percent of advertised events (51/79) in an average issue using illustrations, photos, or graphics. It is important to note, however, that only gay night events utilize images, as the depicted men convey the event's Type; social events typically use text only. This mirrors the magazine's overall editorial strategies, whereby images are more likely to accompany non-political articles. The title of the event listing, as well as the few sentences produced at the end of a listing, is where Typing is explicitly mentioned. Although the event listings represent one of the magazine's sections where Typing is commonly deployed, this does not mean that the majority of the advertisements in an issue's listings explicitly mention Types in their text. Indeed, only 36.7 percent of events (29/79) in an average issue explicitly reference Typing. Instead, I learned through my conversations with regular readers of *Bádi* that Typing is often implied through images of men whom consumers understood as possessing the physical characteristics representative of certain Types. This is also a common feature of event pamphlets and signage in Ni-chōme that draw upon the "common-sense" notion, reported by many informants and discussed in chapter 1, that all young gay men who frequent the neighborhood's bars are able to read such bodily semiotics as "codes" for specific Types. The final important feature is the use of nine special stickers (*shīru*), icons located in the bottom right-hand corner of each event listing to indicate the kind of event being offered. The categories include, in the order presented on the explanation panel, "men only" (*men onrī*), "mixed genders" (*mikkusu*), "related to social clubs" (*sākuru kanren*), "related to art" (*āto kanren*), "DJ performance" (*DJ purei*), "lounge style [a casual event]" (*raunji sutairu*), "show time [a dance party]" (*shōtaimu*), "live music" (*raibu*), and "singles night" (*neruton*).

The emphasis placed on partying and casual relationship-building in the event listings fits with the overall gay lifestyle that *Bádi* promotes as normative. Indeed, 49.4 percent of the events advertised in an average issue appeared to target *ikanimo-kei*. Table 9 presents the average number of ads for events targeting this and other Types. In determining for the purposes of this analysis the Type each event targeted, I often had to make educated guesses based on an event's associated image and text, which I subsequently cross-referenced whenever possible with the event's various online profiles. I concede here that the phrase *ikanimo-kei* was never explicitly mentioned, but I have chosen to group events marked as *tai'ikukai-kei* or events advertised with models possessing *gatai* under this umbrella term. Conversations with young gay men in Ni-chōme vindicated my decision to do so, since my classification of events reflected their own broader understandings of the event listings and its breakdown by Type. There were also a number of event listings for which I was unable determine a targeted Type because there was no explicit mention or a readily identifiable image of a specific Type.

For those events where I was able to identify a Type, *onē* events and *kawaii-kei* events followed *ikanimo-kei* events as the second and third most

Table 9. Average number of events targeting specific Types in *Bádi*, 2010–2013

| TYPE | Number of ads | Percentage |
| --- | --- | --- |
| *Ikanimo-kei* | 39 | 49.4 |
| *Onē* | 10 | 12.7 |
| *Kawaii-kei* | 8 | 10.1 |
| *Gaten-kei* | 5 | 6.3 |
| *Gaijin/Gai-sen* | 1 | 1.3 |
| *Debu-kei* | 1 | 1.3 |
| *Not enough information to discern Type* | 15 | 18.9 |
| **TOTAL** | 79 | 100 |

frequently advertised events in an average issue's listings. It was somewhat surprising that *kawaii-kei* events were quite frequently advertised, given the hostility I had observed toward this Type among men in Ni-chōme; but Junho explained to me that since the *kawaii-kei* aesthetic can also be linked to youth, it makes sense that a magazine targeting young gay men would include this Type in its event listings. Further, the high number of *onē* events advertised, Haruma explained, was because they represent the only kind of event that truly welcomes all Types, although I was not able to verify this fact during my fieldwork since I did not visit any *onē* bars or shows. Events with no discernible Type may also fall into the category of welcoming many different Types, but some young men with whom I spoke believed that there was also a high likelihood that such events would also target *ikanimo-kei* as this was "common sense" in Ni-chōme. Importantly, the low frequency of *gaten-kei* and *debu-kei* events further suggests the process of "niching" these desires that was discussed in chapter 1. For Haruma, who had expressed concerns about the niching of *kawaii-kei* through his experiences with GV, the event listings further inculcated the belief that those with "slim bodies" and "effeminate personalities" such as himself were not necessarily considered desirable in Ni-chōme's gay bar culture. Overall, the event listings ultimately conform to the regimes of desire that privilege hard masculinity via the *ikanimo-kei*, demonstrating *Bádi*'s explicit role in bolstering and promoting ideologies that revive and resuscitate heteronormative conceptualizations of sexuality and gender within Japan's gay culture.

## Bádi, *Ni-chōme, and the Fundamentality of Gay Desire to Young Men's Subjectivities*

When Junho, Yōichi, Haruma, and Shōtarō first started consuming *Bádi*'s event listings—usually reading them while standing in gay bars or *gei shoppu* during their first exploratory sojourns in Ni-chōme—they had comparatively little knowledge of how the district's bars deployed Typing as an organizing principal. In Yōichi's words, they were "beginners" (*shoshinsha*) who had not yet been introduced to Ni-chōme and hence had not been socialized into the neighborhood's community of young gay men who viewed Typing as common sense. This is true even of Haruma, who explained that Akito never sat down and specifically discussed Typing with him when they read *Bádi* together. My four key interlocutors explained that they were able to occasionally classify the models appearing in the event listing images by Type, drawing upon their experiences with "Typing as categorization" and GV. They were unable, however, to extrapolate this categorization to the events themselves, initially viewing Typing solely as a method of classifying the bodily aesthetics of the models depicted in the event listings' photography. More salient to their use of the listings were the nine categories attached via the "stickers" explained above, which are more noticeable than the occasional reference to Typing in the event listing text. This reflects these four men's highly instrumental and superficial engagement with the event listings; at first, they viewed them only as a collection of advertisements and nothing more.

As the four men began visiting the bars of Ni-chōme and learned about each bar's target clientele, however, they came to understand both Typing and same-sex attraction itself as a locus for identity formation and expression. This process occurred concurrent to their engagement with the idea of a "gay lifestyle" via their consumption of *Bádi* in general and the event listings in particular. In the four men's experience, learning a bar's Type involved learning to evaluate the clientele of a bar using the same semiotic cues such as bodily aesthetics, hair style, and clothing utilized to read the Type of GV models. They also reported the importance of reading the ambience of a bar. My conversations with young gay men in Ni-chōme revealed that this learning process, which forms part of the broader education about desire through Typing, discussed in chapter 1, was necessary since the name of a bar is often an ineffective way to determine the Type of its clientele. Indeed, many bar owners explained during interviews that the names of their bars were often arbitrary, chosen for aesthetic reasons rather than as a means to convey information concerning Type.[37] Instead, lighting, music, and décor were all semiotic tools that young gay men read as indexing particular Types and that bar owners strategically deployed to attract specific clientele. For example, the groups of young men with whom I strolled through Ni-chōme in July 2013 explained that electronic dance music and strobe lights were common in bars targeting *ikanimo-kei*, whereas bars with a traditional *izakaya,* or "Japanese pub," aesthetic commonly targeted the more working class *gaten-kei*. Further, the language on signage was important. Bars with English names almost overwhelmingly targeted *ikanimo-kei*, with English conceptually linked to the status of this Type as a supposed "cosmopolitan" and "worldly" gay identity.[38] By learning these semiotic codes, many young gay men in Tokyo quickly become socialized into Ni-chōme's bar culture and begin to participate in a community for whom this semiotic knowledge is not only common sense but also a marker of one's status as a knowledgeable gay man.

Junho, Yōichi, Haruma, and Shōtarō explained that they quickly learned that other men in bars would ascribe them Types based on their physical appearances and that if they were judged a mismatch for the physical ideals of the bar's Type, they would be made unwelcome by both customers and staff. By visiting the bars and being ascribed a Type by others, these four men learned that they would also be expected to behave in certain ways and perform particular gendered identities. Once again, this was a socialization process that many of the men I met in Ni-chōme mentioned when I interviewed them about Typing in the district. For Junho and Yōichi, this process of being ascribed a Type presented no problems, as the gendered identities and personalities associated with the Types assigned to them by others matched their own conceptualizations of their identity. Yōichi quickly came to identify as an *ikanimo-kei* and Junho, as a *kawaii-kei*. Importantly, this led Junho and Yōichi to draw upon *Bádi*'s gravure imagery as a model of a desirable style and physique, encouraging Yōichi in particular to continue with his fitness regime to develop a *gatai* body that matched his identification as an *ikanimo-kei* and appealed to others through his desirable hard masculinity. Junho, who adopted a *kawaii-kei* personality and physical appearance while expressing interest in the *ikanimo-kei* lifestyle of partying, was able to be accepted into *ikanimo-kei* communities. He explained that he ultimately situated himself "between *ikanimo-kei* and *kawaii-kei*," always recognizing and privileging the normative desirability of the "manly" *ikanimo-kei* over his "slightly effeminate" *kawaii-kei* physicality. As was often the case, both Junho and Yōichi were thus "smoothed" into the heteronormative logics of Japan's gay culture, producing positive affects that translated into acceptance within the broader community.[39]

On the other hand, being ascribed a Type was a more problematic experience for Haruma and Shōtarō. They both separately explained that because of their slim bodies, lack of facial hair, and relatively short stature, they were quickly assessed by other men in Ni-chōme as *kawaii-kei*. Although Haruma accepted this given his prior identification as an herbivorous boy, his ex-boyfriend Akito was unhappy and tried to have Haruma gain muscle and grow facial hair so as to be considered *ikanimo-kei*. Haruma reported that he found it increasingly hard to live with the strain of having his physical appearance influenced by another and to thus lose control of his agency in matters of body-work. While Haruma's breakup with Akito was traumatic, he ultimately viewed it positively since it allowed him to explore being *kawaii-kei* and eventually led him to find alternative spaces in Ni-chōme that supported his beliefs in the acceptability of soft masculinity. Shōtarō, however, identified as normatively masculine and did not like being assumed to be effeminate based upon his slim body figure. His initial experiences of being ascribed a Type in a bar motivated him to start visiting the gym in order to build up a *gatai* physical appearance that would match the gendered identity he wished to show others; in doing so, he engaged in the kinds of body-work that *Bádi* promoted as necessary for full socialization into the "happy gay life." All four of my key interlocutors thus came to be active participants in the system of Typing, becoming adept readers of physicality as semiotic indexes for specific Types and their respective lifestyles.

Setting aside whether the process of being ascribed a Type was a positive or negative experience, the four men's experiences in the bars introduced them to the idea that Typing was viewed as an identity category by others and that physical appearance was understood to index particular identity categories and related lifestyles. This was similar to their realization via their consumption of GV that the *tai'ikukai-kei* indexed a straight-acting masculinity, discussed in the previous chapter. The four men explained that they especially noticed how communities formed around both the identification with and the desire for particular Types. In this sorting, *kei* Types indexed the identities that individuals adopted, and *sen* Types described communities of men united in their attraction, or *akogare*, for specific traits or *kei* Types. In having an identity ascribed onto their body, they could either accept or reject this identity. Junho, Yōichi, Haruma, and Shōtarō radically changed their attitudes to Typing as they became more and more cognizant of the concept of "Typing as identity." In particular, the men reported becoming aware that a Type was something that could describe not only one's physical appearance but also one's subjectivity, particularly relating to one's masculinity and its links with one's identity. They also became increasingly comfortable with the idea that a Type is something that can be attached both to an "other," in the sense of "one's preferred Type of partner," and to one's "self," in the sense of "the Type with which you personally identify." Ultimately, this idea paved the way for my four principal interlocutors to understand their gay desires as a fundamental referent for describing and understanding their selfhood.

Having acquired a new understanding of Typing through their experiences in Ni-chōme, Junho, Yōichi, Haruma, and Shōtarō all reported that they came to view the event listings in *Bádi* differently. First, having gained the ability to read the semiotic clues such as imagery and musical genre used to mark Types in the event listings, the four men became increasingly aware of the dominance in *Bádi* of events catering to *ikanimo-kei*. This normalized in all but Haruma the notion that the heteronormative masculinity tied to this Type is ultimately desirable in Ni-chōme's gay bars and clubs, representing the identity tied to the "happy gay life" promoted by the magazine. Secondly, by concurrently using the event listings and visiting various clubs and parties catering to specific Types, the four men reported that they came to view Typing as the basis for various communities in Ni-chōme. Junho and Yōichi in particular came to socialize with the same men in various clubs. They soon became aware that there was a group of young gay men who read *Bádi* frequently and identified either directly as *ikanimo-kei* or as admirers of *ikanimo-kei* and who strived to emulate at least part of this Type's lifestyle. These men that Junho and Yōichi encountered and whose community they eventually joined are the *hayatteru ikemen* discussed in chapter 1. Junho explained that having come to understand Typing as the basis for his own subjectivity, he then quickly came to also understand that Types could represent the basis for a sense of "communal identity." Haruma, who was thrust by Akito into a group of young men who identified as *ikanimo-kei*, also noticed how these men would draw upon the gay lifestyle promoted in *Bádi* as the central idea uniting them into a community. After his breakup, Haruma used the event listings in *Bádi* to find spaces where *kawaii-kei* would be welcome, eventually finding a new community that accepted him for who he was. The event listings, according to my four principal informants, provided a highly structured list of events that, when coupled with the advice published throughout the magazine, could be frequented in order to express one's belonging to the normatively desirable *ikanimo-kei* community privileged in Ni-chōme.

Ultimately, their consumption of *Bádi* presented my four key interlocutors with an understanding that "Types" and "lifestyles" were related. In fact, discussions with other young gay men in Ni-chōme concerning Typing also revealed that this linking of Typing to lifestyle was common among those who frequented the district's gay bars, demonstrating the pervasiveness of the neoliberal logics that structure not only *Bádi* but also the Japanese gay media landscape more broadly. Perhaps even more importantly, Junho, Yōichi, Haruma, and Shōtarō's consumption of *Bádi*'s event listings and their concurrent visits to Ni-chōme confirmed the four men's vague notion that heteronormative masculinity was privileged among gay men. As Lukács argues in relation to young women's consumption of love dramas in the early 2000s, Japanese lifestyle media does indeed promote a sense of group solidarity based in consumption.[40] Lukács also notes, however, that such lifestyle media erases difference and creates artificial universal categories for the purposes of economic exploitation by marketers and advertisers.[41] As a nationally circulating magazine, *Bádi* played an important role in creating a homonormative gay male culture firmly attached to the heteronormative masculinity of the *ikanimo-kei*. Within *Bádi*, the conflation of possessing same-sex attraction and the *ikanimo-kei* lifestyle also had the unexpected consequence of providing justifying discourses for the four principal informants' prior belief that their gay desires are innate and natural, as discussed in chapter 2. By engaging with "Typing as identity," these four men came to directly identify with their gay desires and hence understood their same-sex attraction as a fundamental aspect of their subjectivity.

This discussion reveals that there has been a shift in how young gay men conceptualize their identities in Japan. Previous work by both Mark McLelland and Yajima Masami conducted in the mid- to late 1990s revealed that homosexuality was often viewed in Japan as distinct from one's subjectivity, described instead as "play" (*asobi*) or as a "hobby" (*shumi*).[42] But all of the young gay men I spoke to in Ni-chōme concerning Typing strongly argued that their same-sex attraction was fundamental to their identity, particularly in relation to their gendered identities. It would be simplistic to argue that this change is due entirely to the wider visibility of North American–style queer identity politics in contemporary Japan, as has been suggested elsewhere in light of the recent LGBT boom.[43] Rather, I argue here that Typing also plays a role in this process, introducing important regimes of desire that shape consumers' knowledge concerning sexuality. For Junho, Yōichi, Haruma, and Shōtarō, *Bádi's* neoliberal lifestyle politics and concomitant privileging of the *ikanimo-kei* reinforced the idea that all expressions of male same-sex attraction represent an explicitly "gay" identity tied to the heteronormatively masculine *ikanimo-kei* lifestyle. This is because *Bádi* reduces all experiences of male same-sex attraction into a single identity category called "gay," which is in turn equated with the *ikanimo-kei* lifestyle to promote certain consumer behaviors as fundamentally attached to this identity. To live a "happy gay life" is therefore to adopt the male role in the hetero system that Fushimi argues has dominated Japan's sexual cultures.[44] Ultimately, this process produces a homonormative culture that stymies expressions deviating from heteronormative conceptualizations of gender. Living a "happy gay life" comes to represent a cycle of endless consumption and partying tied to a very narrow understanding of what it means to experience same-sex desire.

## Conclusion

Throughout this chapter, I have demonstrated that print media such as magazines remained important resources that influenced how young Japanese gay men conceptualize their desires, despite the fact that fewer men actually purchase physical copies of these magazines. Of particular interest to me as I conducted my fieldwork was the fact that the situatedness of magazine consumption within Ni-chōme strongly impacted how the content of a magazine such as *Bádi* was understood by consumers, particularly as it seems piecemeal and selective reading of magazines represented a common practice among the young gay men who frequent the district. Overall, my interviews revealed that my four principal informants read Typing into *Bádi*, conflating this magazine's focus on lifestyle politics with the tendency to deploy Typing as a method of making sense of gay desire and identity in Ni-chōme's gay bar culture. By conflating Typing and life-style politics, *Bádi* inculcated in consumers a belief that the *ikanimo-kei* represented the only expression of a "happy gay life." As an important ideological resource in the Japanese gay media landscape at the time of my initial fieldwork in 2013, *Bádi* normalized this Type's hard bodily aesthetics through the promotion of certain consumer practices that young gay men came to view as indicative of the *ikanimo-kei*'s desirable lifestyle.

In its promotion of consumerism as the foundation for both personal and communal gay identity, *Bádi* was complicit with a neoliberal politics that fails to critique capitalist structures by which same-sex desiring individuals have been excluded from full participation in public culture both in Japan and abroad. *Bádi*'s implicit promotion of the *ikanimo-kei* as the only legitimate expression of a "happy gay life" thus produces a highly homonormative culture. While the magazine affirmed same-sex desire and played an important role in justifying my key informants' belief in the innateness of these desires, the magazine was avowedly apolitical and simply sought to promote consumption among its readers. The magazine thus bolstered the Japanese gay media landscape's heteronormative regimes of desire, suggesting that consumerism tied to a heteronormative masculinity such as the *ikanimo-kei*'s represents the only fulfilling expression of gay desire and identity. Although Haruma's experiences with his ex-boyfriend Akito instilled a healthy skepticism of such ideologies, my impression from fieldwork was that most young gay men simply bought into *Bádi*'s neoliberal logics because of their desire for an affirming representation of same-sex attraction. Typing emerged as a locus for identity formation but did so in ways that disenfranchised identity categories deviating from *ikanimo-kei* norms. These tensions are explored in more depth in the following chapter through an investigation of online dating services.

SIX

## Online Dating Services
### *Strategic Typing and the Limits of Agency*

Dating sites and location-based dating apps play a crucial role in Ni-chōme, assisting the development of sexual, romantic, and other forms of intimate relationships between men. Use of online dating services, especially location-based dating apps such as Grindr, Jack'd, and 9monsters, has led to new and innovative patterns of socialization that have revitalized Ni-chōme. Online dating services have thus become an integral part of the Japanese gay media landscape and it was certainly the case that Junho, Yōichi, Haruma, Shōtarō, and many other young men I met during my fieldwork viewed them as essential to their lives as gay men. As a part of the Japanese gay media landscape, dating sites and location-based dating apps are heavily influenced by—and implicated in circulating— the regimes of desire that privilege heteronormativity in Ni-chōme's bars and clubs. In fact, this chapter reveals how the widespread use of these online services ultimately normalizes desire for the straight-acting masculinity and *ikanimo-kei* lifestyle explored in the previous chapters. My interviews with the four principal informants further revealed that the strategic manipulation of Typing on online dating services to produce desirable representations of their "selves" became extremely crucial to their lives. Toward the end of my fieldwork in 2013, my discussions with Junho, Yōichi, Haruma, and Shōtarō suggested that online dating services had caused these four young men more anxiety and indecision over their identities and the appropriateness of their desires than had any other gay media with which they engaged.

Monica Whitty, an influential theorist of the psychology underlying the use of online dating services, has persuasively argued that such services represent "marketplaces of desire" where individuals strategically manipulate language to present themselves in ways that conform to socially constructed modes of desirability.[1] This is certainly the case among the young gay men I met in Ni-chōme, where online dating services perpetuate the commodification of desire via Typing found in Ni-chōme's bars and in lifestyle media such as *Bádi*. Whitty argues that as a result of the commodification of desire found on dating sites, online daters must subsequently learn to "sell their 'selves,'"[2] with their desires representing marketable objects in the sexual marketplace. Drawing upon interviews with users of heterosexual dating services, Whitty suggests that while dating services theoretically provide individuals with the potential to present only idealized portraits of themselves, most users do seek to present "as authentic an identity as possible" to successfully attract a partner.[3] Among the young gay men to whom I spoke during fieldwork, notions of authenticity were heavily influenced by the regimes of desire of the Japanese gay media landscape and were intimately tied to broader desires for hard masculinity, which have been explored in previous chapters. For my four key interlocutors, the need to "sell" their "selves" online also had a profound impact on their understandings of their gay desires and identities.

### Strategic Typing: Identity Management on a Japanese Gay Dating Site

Sociolinguistic research into the representational strategies deployed on gay dating sites in a variety of European and North American contexts has uncovered that users of such sites tend to explicitly promote heteronormative modes of gendered identity as desirable.[4] In this section, I survey how identity is typically managed on Japanese gay online dating services via a case study of a site that I call JP MEN'S CLUB and reveal that such services likewise privilege heteronormative conceptualizations of sexuality and gender. JP MEN'S CLUB is a large "mega-site" that provides a number of services catering to a gay male clientele, including a GV tube site, a news bulletin, event listings and club reports, and a dating service known as the *deai-kei* BBS, or "dating bulletin board system."[5] My conversations with various young gay men that I met in Ni-chōme during my 2013 fieldwork revealed that many did utilize JP MEN'S CLUB, but upon returning to the field in 2015, I learned that the popularity of such services had rapidly declined as use of location-based dating apps such as 9monsters and Grindr became preferred. At the time of my initial fieldwork, JP MEN'S CLUB appeared to be representative of Japanese gay dating sites as a whole.

The dating BBS on JP MEN'S CLUB is broadly divided into two sections, each with a specific purpose. The first of these sections, the Serious Forum (Majime Keijiban), represents a space where men seeking romantic, long-term, and intimate relationships post advertisements looking for partners with similar motivations. The second service, the Adult Forum (Miseinen Kinshi [18+] Keijiban, literally "forum forbidden to minors [18+]"), is designed to be utilized primarily by men seeking ephemeral hookups, but a few men appeared to use it also to seek romantic partners. Unlike large international English-language gay dating sites such as Manhunt and Gay Romeo, JP MEN'S CLUB does not allow users to include images, and thus users are required to include thick, linguistic descriptions of their physicality in their posts to sell their selves in this marketplace of desire. The Serious Forum is subdivided into regional threads, and I gathered 50 posts each from the Tokyo, Osaka, Tokushima, and Fukuoka threads to create a sample of 200 posts for analysis in July 2011 before commencing fieldwork. During fieldwork in October 2013, I collected a further smaller sample of 50 posts from the Tokyo thread to determine whether any changes had occurred since 2011. Furthermore, I collected another 50 posts from the Tokyo thread in December 2015 for further comparative analysis. These latter periods of data collection were motivated by a slight change in 2013 to the formatting of posts. From 2013 onwards, users were required to select a number of predetermined categories related to age, sexual position, height, weight, and the Type of one's desired partner to attach to their posts, whereas previously such information had to be manually included in the text.[6]

A typical post to the Serious Forum, drawn from the 2011 data, is presented in the following extract.[7] Discourse analysis of my corpus of posts from JP MEN'S CLUB highlighted that a description of a user's desired partner usually precedes a description of the user's "self." The discourse within the posts is thus centered on what sociolinguist Tommaso Milani refers to in his study of an English-language gay dating site as the "discourse of the Desired Other."[8] Users of the Serious Forum appear to mobilize desirable discourses of ideal partners as a site to develop a sense of intimacy with potential respondents. As I spoke to young men in Nichōme about their use of gay dating sites in 2013, I learned that many think strategically about how they present the discourse of their Desired Other online. Many men reported that they often invested more time and energy into strategically manipulating language in ways that will "target" very specific desired partners than they did to describe themselves and utilized Typing to do so. Haruma, who frequently used sites such as JP MEN'S CLUB in order to make new friends, argued that gay men in Japan tend to present more "general" or "descriptive" presentations of their selves online. He linked this behavior to a supposed Japanese reluctance to "brag about oneself" to strangers:

> *Ima kara atte etchi dekiru, toshiue no kata imasu ka??'*
> *Taipu wa, sawayaka majime na supōtsuman-kei no yasashii kata*
>     *desu!!*
> *Debu-kei no kata wa gomen nasai! (T^T)*
> *Jibun wa 22-sai no uke desu!*
> *Otokorashiitte yoku iwaretemasu*
> *Shumi wa eiga ya supōtsu~*
> *Messēji itadaketara ureshii desu!!*

> Are there any older guys who can meet me now for sex??
> A serious, kind and hunky Sportsman is my Type!!
> Sorry, I'm not into fatties! (T^T)
> As for me, I'm a 22 year old bottom!
> I'm often told that I am manly
> My hobbies are movies and sports~
> I'd be so happy if I received a message from you!!

The text in this extract is typical of the Serious Forum in that it also constructs a desirable self-identity through the manipulation of a number of set tropes that users of this gay dating site appear to commonly deploy. The self-identities presented in the posts in my corpus—whether produced in 2011, 2013, or 2015—tend to focus on broad descriptions of physical characteristics such as body type and hairstyle, emotional traits and personalities, hobbies and other interests, and one's Type. As can be seen in the extract, physicality, personality, and Typing also represent important tropes for discussing ideal partners. The explicit use of Typing on this online dating site was unsurprising given the importance that this socio-semiotic system plays in other contexts in Japan's gay culture. Furthermore, these communicative strategies mirror broader trends in gay cultures around the world, where stereotypical identity categories linked to specific gay slang are a shorthand or code to describe the self and the other.[9]

Analysis of the data collected in 2011 revealed that *majime-kei* (Serious Type), *supōtsuman-kei* (Sportsman Type), *rīman-kei* (Salaryman Type), *imafū-kei* (Trendy Type), *janīzu-kei* (Johnny's Type), and *amaenbō-kei* (Spoiled Type), in order of most to least frequent, were commonly utilized within the discourse of the Desired Other.[10] These Types were also applied in users' discourses of the self, where *debu-kei*, *yancha-kei* (Naughty Type), and *nenpai-kei* (Elderly Type) were also occasionally employed. As is evident, the Types utilized on JP MEN'S CLUB are all *kei* Types describing personalities or lifestyles rather than the *sen* Types that indicate a desire for particular traits. This represents another example where Typing has come to be used explicitly as a system of identity management, as discussed in the previous chapter. I note here that except for *janīzu-kei* and *debu-kei*, the Types I encountered during my analysis of the 2011 Serious Forum posts seem to be somewhat idiosyncratic when compared with the Types I typically encountered in Ni-chōme. Types such as these may thus be unique to this particular forum, although there does appear to be some resonances between the *supōtsuman-kei* and *tai'ikukai-kei* since both are linked to the gym training and athleticism that produces desirable *gatai* bodies. Furthermore, some of the most common Types I encountered during fieldwork and subsequent analysis of the Japanese gay media landscape, such as *ikanimo-kei*, *kawaii-kei*, and *gaten-kei*, were conspicuously absent from the data collected in 2011. Interviews with informants did not necessarily reveal any particular insight as to why this might have been the case. I reflected on this idiosyncratic nature of Typing on JP MEN'S CLUB with one man during an early stage of fieldwork in Ni-chōme. He suggested that the focus on *majime-kei* among Serious Forum users probably related to the forum's name (Majime Keijiban) and that this might have influenced users' word choice.

In 2013, however, users of the Serious Forum became required to select a number of predetermined categories when drafting their post; this information would then be attached within a new compulsory header that also acted as a searchable index. As well as having to mandatorily include one's age, height and weight, and preferred sexual role (which had been optional until 2013), users were now required to select from four options the Type they desired: *tai'ikukai-kei*, *kawaii-kei*, *debu-kei*, and *gachimuchi-kei*. Of interest to me was the fact that users were not presented with the option to decline to select a Type, and all users were thus required to situate their Desired Other within these narrowly determined categories. While the Serious Forum had encouraged in posts written in 2011 a certain level of creativity in the construction of the Desired Other,[11] the introduction of the preselected categories greatly reduced the posts' length and descriptiveness. Analysis of the 2013 and 2015 data revealed that the format changes led users to include less information about their Desired Other within their posts and also interestingly encouraged users to apply the four predetermined Types to describe themselves. As a result, the average length of a post decreased from 182 characters in 2011 to 57 in 2015. The extract below, written in December 2015 by a user who had selected that he was looking for a *tai'ikukai-kei* partner, is representative:

> *Dare ka inai? Amari kimatte nai nonkeppoi hito boshū! Mitame futsū nande mitame waruku iwarenai yo. Jitsu wa gachimuchi-kei da yo (wara)*

> Is there anyone here? I'm looking for a straight-acting guy who isn't really into the scene. My looks are normal, [and] I haven't been told I look bad. Actually, I am a *gachimuchi-kei* (lol)

As this brief discussion demonstrates, Typing plays a central role in the management of identities on JP MEN'S CLUB, and this holds true for other gay dating services in Japan. Typing, however, is also commonly deployed in conjunction with descriptions of the physicality of both the users and their ideal partners. In many ways, as marketplaces of desire, gay dating services mimic the gay bars discussed in chapter 1, where Typing represents an organizational system that bar owners deploy to attract specific clienteles. The 2011 data set demonstrated that Typing was often utilized quite creatively on JP MEN'S CLUB, but the introduction of preset categories in 2013 dramatically shifted the discursive production of users of the Serious Forum toward less creatively rich posts. The two extracts presented in this section also reveal how the regimes of desire promoting heteronormative masculinity are also in evidence on JP MEN'S CLUB, since there is a focus on desiring straight-acting (*nonkerashii*) men and identifying as masculine (*otokorashii*).

## Exploring Identities through Strategic Typing on Gay Dating Sites

Reflecting upon their use of sites such as JP MEN'S CLUB, Junho, Yōichi, Haruma, and Shōtarō all reported that when they first began using dating services, they viewed them as spaces where they could freely explore their identities and their desires. Important to this sense of exploration and sexual agency was the purported ability provided by dating services to creatively manipulate Typing as a method to "sell" one's self to a Desired Other. In bars, the four men were ascribed Types by others based upon the perception of their physical appearances, and any attempts to control one's identity could be rejected at the first instance. By contrast, dating profiles initially appeared to provide a space within which the men could explicitly manage their own identities. The four men did, however, quickly learn that they were required to conform to the norms of communication on the dating services they had started using, which privileged Typing. Indeed, they all became adept users of dating services as the primary method of managing their identities. According to Haruma, the most frequent user of dating sites among the four principal informants, managing his profile allowed him to "consciously" construct his identity in ways that he wished. Haruma juxtaposed this sense of agency quite explicitly with his previous situation, where his identities were "controlled" by his ex-boyfriend Akito. Importantly, both Haruma and Shōtarō suggested that dating services allowed them to challenge the identities ascribed to them by others in bars and other settings. On the other hand, using dating services reinforced both Junho's and Yōichi's positioning by others as a member of the trendy young *hayatteru ikemen* whose lifestyles and identities mirrored *ikanimo-kei* ideals. For Haruma, who used dating services to make friends rather than engage in sexual adventures, the initial agency provided by dating services ultimately led him to reject Typing entirely. As explored in the following section, however, the initial sense of agency and control that dating services seemed to provide the four key informants would prove phantasmal.

Since utilizing Typing represented a communicative norm on Japanese dating services, their use furthered the influence of Typing on the informants' broader understandings of their same-sex attraction. From their experiences participating in Ni-chōme and reading *Bádi*, Junho, Yōichi, and Shōtarō had become comfortable with the idea that Types could be utilized to express one's identities. Dating services provided them, however, with an opportunity to consciously select the Types they identified with and taught them how to utilize their identities as strategic tools in selling themselves to others as desirable commodities. In particular, using dating services such as JP MEN'S CLUB, as well as the location-based dating apps discussed later in this chapter, taught the four principal informants to employ the stereotypical semiotic cues attached to specific Types in the Japanese gay media landscape as a further tactic to manage their identities online and sell their selves to their Desired Others. Junho, for example, recounted how he began to use on dating services vocabulary learned from consuming GV on tube sites and from reading the porn reviews in *Bádi* in order to describe both himself and his ideal partner in ways that other men would find both appealing and comprehensible.

Like the other three principal informants, Haruma also reported superficially utilizing Typing in his profiles because he recognized that there was a need to do so if he wanted his posts to be easily understood by others. After all, Typing is often drawn upon as a common-sense code to communicate with other gay men quickly and in a manner recognizable in Japanese gay culture, as discussed in the previous chapter. Haruma explained that he felt using Typing to describe his desired partners was a necessary strategy that would facilitate meeting men and developing new friendships. He did not, however, employ Typing to describe his self, arguing that identity was too complex and fluid to be simplistically represented via Typing. Similar to many who appeared dissatisfied with Typing and its role in stereotyping people based on certain physical traits, Haruma decided to explicitly reject the trend of self-identifying as a Type in his dating site profiles. This decision contrasts significantly with the majority of the young gay men I met in Ni-chōme—including Junho, Yōichi, and Shōtarō—who comfortably utilized Typing to describe both their selves and their desired partners on gay dating services.

Haruma's long and painful road to understanding his same-sex attraction, marked by his loss of agency and traumatic relationship with Akito, has ultimately led him to identify as "against Typing" (*datsu taipu*). During our first interview in 2013, when Haruma graciously showed me his dating profile on a certain site, his profile text explicitly stated that he rejected Typing and other such "identity labels" (*aidentitī rēberu*). Haruma subsequently told me that he found that a number of men who had responded to his dating advertisements appreciated and agreed with his position. Unlike other gay media, which he described as fixated on Typing, Haruma believed that dating sites were empowering spaces: by allowing him to reject normative modes of communication that privilege Typing and to experiment with how he presented himself, these sites facilitated his understanding of his identities and desires. Using dating sites initially showed Haruma that it is possible to meet men for romance and sex without becoming co-opted into the paradigm of Typing, although he recognized that normative expectations concerning desirable modes of being still impacted how his profile would be read. Haruma admitted that the circle of young gay men who rejected Typing with whom he came to socialize was a minority in Japanese gay culture, and he described his philosophies as somewhat "unique." It must be noted, however, that Haruma's rejection of Typing represented more an attempt to distance himself from the normative lifestyles promoted within the Japanese gay media landscape rather than a simple rejection of Typing as a classificatory system.

During my early interviews with Shōtarō, he explained that his experiences of selling himself on dating services significantly changed his attitudes toward the prevalent hierarchy of desires. As a highly active consumer of GV and *Bádi*, Shōtarō had internalized a belief in the normative desirability of the *ikanimo-kei* and its hard masculinity. But as a man who was commonly positioned as *kawaii-kei* by those he encountered in bars, this privileging was problematic when transposed onto gay dating services. The ability to manipulate one's Type online allowed Shōtarō to feel safe rejecting the *kawaii-kei* identity ascribed him by others. He reported that when discussing his physical appearance in his dating profiles, he often "massaged the truth." He focused on his gym training and aspirations for a *gatai* body in order to position himself as someone with "the potential to become an *ikanimo-kei*" (*ikanimo-kei ni naru kanōsei*). Gay dating services thus provided Shōtarō the opportunity to present as the Type he felt most met his identity. Furthermore, Junho explained that on the dating services he utilized, many users identifying as *ikanimo-kei* (either explicitly or implicitly) presented *kawaii-kei* as their ideal partner. Junho found this highly empowering, suggesting that being ascribed a *kawaii-kei* identity might not necessarily exclude him from participating in the *ikanimo-kei* communities he desired. Indeed, Junho's experiences speak to how the *ikanimo-kei* and *kawaii-kei* sometimes operate as a complementary dyad within Japan's gay dating culture, which I explore below in another section.

Utilizing gay dating sites, however, also requires users to conform to the modes of communication that are normative throughout the Japanese gay media landscape, and this lessens one's ability to explore one's desires and identities in complex ways. When I spoke with young gay men in Ni-chōme about their use of gay dating sites, many explained that Typing represented a system that helped them to "catch out" those who misrepresented themselves. For instance, if a man claims to be an *ikanimo-kei* but does not possess the hard masculinity and *gatai* body nor participate in the party boy lifestyle representative of this Type, then that man will invariably be judged as inauthentic during offline interactions. This suggests that the initial sense of creativity and agency felt by my four key interlocutors would always be tempered by how Typing normatively functions as a disciplining system that promotes very specific understandings of identity that privilege certain bodily aesthetics and lifestyles grounded in heteronormativity as desirable.

Toward the end of my initial fieldwork in 2013, Junho, Yōichi, Haruma, and Shōtarō had begun to express doubts and anxieties over their use of gay dating services. Their initial enthusiasm for explicitly and creatively manipulating their identities online had faded as all four men reported that they were finding it increasingly difficult to meet men for romantic (rather than sexual) relationships. Even Junho and Yōichi, who had expressed much admiration for the *ikanimo-kei*, began to express dissatisfaction with gay dating services. It seemed that the agency gained by creatively manipulating and strategically managing one's identity via Typing was limited in some fundamental way. As I explore below, rather than Typing itself, it was the need to sell one's self as hunky and straight-acting on Japan's gay dating sites such that one would be deemed authentic by others during offline meetups that limited the agency that Typing superficially appeared to provide. That is, despite gay dating sites providing a sense of freedom of expression, an authentically desirable identity was still tied to the hard masculinity promoted within the Japanese gay media landscape. Ultimately, the regimes of desire that privilege heteronormativity still impacted young gay men's use of dating services. In fact, the more that Junho, Yōichi, Haruma, and Shōtarō made use of dating services, the more they realized that the agency promised by such services was illusory.

*Regimes of Desire within the Marketplace: The Pressure to be Hunky and Straight-Acting*

Throughout this book, I have revealed how the gender binary inherent to the hetero system structuring knowledge of sexuality in Japan has led to the privileging of the heteronormative *ikanimo-kei* in the Japanese gay media landscape. Whether it be GV and its fetishization of straight men or the event listings in *Bádi* magazine and their conflation of a happy gay lifestyle with the party boy consumerism of the *ikanimo-kei*, my analysis of the Japanese gay media landscape has uncovered that desirable gay masculinity is produced via the disavowal of a problematic "soft" *kawaii* other. While the majority of Japanese gay media do not position this *kawaii* other as wholly undesirable per se—as evidenced by the significant minority of GV films and events catering to *kawaii-kei* and those who desire them—*kawaii-kei* do appear to be positioned as a "failed" masculinity given its links to "the curse of the *bishōnen*" discussed in chapter 3. The hierarchical dualism between the "hard" *ikanimo-kei* and the "soft" *kawaii-kei* is particularly evident on Japanese gay dating services.

Analysis of the 2011 data set from the JP MEN'S CLUB Serious Forum demonstrated that users typically position both their own identities and the identities of their Desired Others within either a meta-discourse of hunkiness (*sawayaka*) or cuteness (*kawaii*).[12] These trends were also in evidence in the 2013 and 2015 data, although the reduction of creativity brought about by the introduction of preset categories lessened the frequency of the adjective *sawayaka* to describe users' ideal partners. Instead, use of the preset categories *tai'ikukai-kei* and *kawaii-kei* seemed to take over the role of these adjectives. *Sawayaka* and *kawaii* did, however, continue to be used in the users' discourses of the self. Within the 2011 data set, analysis uncovered that 67.5 percent of users (135/200) identified as *sawayaka* and 19 percent of users (38/200) described themselves as *kawaii*.[13] It was even more common for individuals to describe their Desired Other as *sawayaka*, with 84 percent of users (168/200) choosing to do so, with only 8 percent of users (16/200) in the 2011 data set describing their ideal partners as *kawaii*.[14] Perhaps most importantly, within all the data sets collected for analysis, there was no instance of a user either self-identifying or describing their Desired Other as both *sawayaka* and *kawaii*. *Sawayaka* and *kawaii* as utilized on JP MEN'S CLUB appeared to be mutually exclusive, and discussions with young gay men in Ni-chōme concerning the use of these adjectives on Japanese gay dating services revealed that the majority certainly viewed *sawayaka* and *kawaii* as describing opposite Types. Indeed, as I strolled the district with informants early in my fieldwork, reflecting on the term *sawayaka* prompted many young gay men to express their firm desire for hard masculinity. Furthermore, Yōichi explained that *sawayaka* could be viewed as a common code word for the *ikanimo-kei*, which he described as the "complete opposite" of the *kawaii-kei* in terms of its gendered performance and desirability. Similar ideas were voiced by other men, including Junho and Shōtarō, and many positioned *kawaii* as describing a gay masculinity that is slightly "womanly" (*onnappoi*) when compared to the *ikanimo-kei*.

The fact that the vast majority of the posts sampled for analysis in 2011 described the Desired Other as *sawayaka* indicates the normative desirability of such identities. But this quantitative analysis does not necessarily indicate why *sawayaka* identities are understood as desirable. Exploring the gendered discourses attached to the terms *sawayaka* and *kawaii* on JP MEN'S CLUB, however, revealed that the regimes of desire that contour knowledge of desirability throughout the Japanese gay media landscape had a clear influence on users' identity construction within this representative dating site. As my discursive analysis of the 2011 data set attests, *sawayaka* is commonly associated with masculine (*otokorashii*) in the Serious Forum. In fact, of the 168 users who presented their Desired Other as *sawayaka*, 51.8 percent of them (87/168) also described their ideal partners as masculine.[15] On the other hand, *kawaii* is never positioned as masculine either within the discourses of the self or the Desired Other within any of the data sets that I collected. Furthermore, it must also be noted that analysis of the 2011 data set revealed that being effeminate (*onnarashii*) was explicitly presented as problematic in 61 percent of users' posts (122/200). Many users signaled that they were "incapable" (*nigate*) of dealing with effeminacy or that it was "impossible" (*muri*) for them.[16] While I encountered only one instance of a JP MEN'S CLUB user explicitly juxtaposing cuteness with effeminacy (excerpted below), my broad discussions with young gay men in Ni-chōme revealed that many understood *kawaii* as a kind of euphemism for effeminacy, as discussed in chapter 3. A blatant example of one user's recognition of the problematic nature of his *kawaii* and androgynous appearance is presented in the extract below from the 2011 data set:[17]

> *Kareshi boshū desu! Taipu wa futsū no otokorashikute, sawayaka na rīman-kei desu. Jibun wa chotto onnarashii . . . kawaii-kei desu kedo . . .*
>
> *Anmari chūseikan toka dato ninki nai kamo shirenai kedo, kawaii kanji toka janīzu-kei ga suki na kata ireba, mēru shite kudasai ne!*

> I'm looking for a boyfriend! My Type is a normal, manly, hunky Salaryman Type. I am a little bit effeminate . . . [and] I am a Cute Type . . .
>
> Although things like androgyny might not be very popular, if there are people who like Johnny's Types or those who seem cute, please send me an email, okay!

If one reads this juxtaposition of *sawayaka* with masculinity through Fushimi Noriaki's theory of the hetero system, it is clear that hunkiness is viewed as an index for the active male role whereas *kawaii* is implicitly linked to the female role via these terms' mutually exclusive natures.

Furthermore, my discussions with young gay men about their use of gay dating sites revealed that most argued that *kawaii* identities are not often considered straight-acting. On the other hand, my analysis of the 2011 data set unsurprisingly revealed that being *sawayaka* was commonly associated with being straight-acting on JP MEN'S CLUB.[18] In fact, whereas 23 percent of the users from the 2011 data set (46/200) described their ideal partner as straight-acting, the number of users choosing to position their Desired Other as such increased after the introduction of preset categories for indicating their Desired Other as *tai'ikukai-kei, kawaii-kei, gachimuchi-kei*, or *debu-kei*. Comparing this with the Tokyo regional thread data sets reveals that only 22 percent of users (11/50) described their Desired Other as straight-acting in 2011, but 54 percent (27/50) and 62 percent (31/50) of users did so in 2013 and 2015, respectively. Discussions with young men during fieldwork in late 2015 revealed that many believed that this change resulted from the influence of location-based dating apps, where there has been a global tendency to valorize heteronormative identities as desirable.[19] In many ways, Japanese gay dating sites appear to be following transnational trends. They thus represent another instance where the homonormative culture critiqued by scholars such as Lisa Duggan simply resuscitates heteronormativity rather than challenges it.[20]

My investigation of this representative Japanese gay dating service reveals that there is a strong pressure placed on gay online daters to ascribe to heteronormative gender ideals if they wish to successfully attract a partner, with the pressure to express a hard masculinity particularly prominent. Importantly, the fact that the 2011 data set is drawn from posts produced by men throughout Japan (in Tokyo, Osaka, Tokushima, and Fukuoka) reveals that the regimes of desire that form the core focus of this book may not be exclusive to Ni-chōme. The privileging of heteronormative masculinity via the trope of the *ikanimo-kei* thus has a national resonance. The pressure to conform to such ideals on gay dating sites explicitly limits the creative potential superficially provided by Typing. Interviews with young gay men uncovered that during an offline meetup many focus less on whether an individual is "authentic" in professing a given Type and instead on whether or not the individual truly conforms to the idealized notions of *sawayaka* and *kawaii* tied to the regimes of desire of the Japanese gay media landscape. These interviews thus underscore how Japanese gay media promotes hard masculinity based in heteronormative logics that fail to critique the gender ideologies by which same-sex desiring men have been historically positioned as both perverted and dangerous because of their apparent gender inversion.

My four key interlocutors reported that the main difference between gay dating services and the other media that form part of the Japanese gay media landscape is that dating services (including location-based dating apps to be discussed below) represent the only space where the valorization of heteronormative masculinity is explicit. While my analysis in previous chapters has revealed that GV, *Bádi*, and the pamphlets and signage in Ni-chōme promote the *ikanimo-kei* as implicitly normative and desirable, it is only on gay dating sites where the normative promotion of hard masculinity becomes visibly and consciously mobilized by others as a form of marginalization or gatekeeping. During our many conversations, both Haruma and Shōtarō had many stories to tell of their failed dating adventures in Ni-chōme where the men with whom they arranged dates explicitly rejected them because they did not possess hard *gatai* bodies or because they were "too cute" (*kawaisugiru*). Even Junho and Yōichi—who had originally found that the regimes of desire promoting the *ikanimo-kei* as normatively desirable affirmed their self-identities—recounted during interviews that the pressure on Japanese gay dating services to be straight-acting and masculine had stymied their attempts at romance. In fact, as Yōichi started to transition away from searching for casual sex and focused more on seeking a long-term relationship, he began to find his previous identification as an *ikanimo-kei* detrimental, since many found it hard to disassociate him from the party boy stereotype attached to this particular Type. Overall, the four men found that the users of gay dating sites in Japan were somewhat fickle. This led Junho, Yōichi, and Shōtarō to shift their focus to location-based dating apps, which they soon learned also had many problems related to identity management.

## Normative Users and Typing on Location-Based Gay Dating Apps

Except for Haruma, who viewed location-based dating apps as problematic resources that provided access only to casual sex, my key interlocutors turned to smartphone apps such as Grindr, Jack'd, and 9monsters in an attempt to reclaim some of the agency lost by the pressure on most Japanese gay dating sites to conform to a strictly heteronormative gendered identity. During my fieldwork in Ni-chōme between 2013 and 2015, I noticed that these three apps were the most frequently used by young gay men, although the Japanese-produced 9monsters was considerably more popular than the foreign Grindr and Jack'd. To learn more about how Japanese gay men use these apps, I downloaded them myself when in Ni-chōme and surveyed the ways that men created their profiles over the years. I learned that, as with JP MEN'S CLUB, Typing represented a communicative norm on these apps, including within descriptions of users' Desired Others. Unlike dating services such as JP MEN'S CLUB, however, location-based dating apps also allowed users to upload a profile image, and exploratory analysis during fieldwork uncovered that many chose to either include a profile shot of their face or an image of their body, especially when the user possessed a conspicuously *gatai* body. Furthermore, 9monsters, Grindr, and Jack'd all require users to select a preset Type to ascribe to their self.

This contrasts significantly with JP MEN'S CLUB, where users had to describe their Desired Other (rather than their self) through the ascription of preset categories based on Typing. On Grindr, which is an "international" app developed in the US, users were required to select the "tribe" to which they belonged. The available groups were named using English-language slang terms from North American gay culture such as "jock," "twink," "otter," and "bear." Consequently, these preset categories did not necessarily match the norms of the Japanese gay culture, a point that many young men in Ni-chōme criticized during interviews about their dating app use. It should be noted that most Grindr users in Ni-chōme tended to communicate in English with fellow users—typically foreign tourists. This is because the men who usually preferred this app identified as *gai-sen*, Foreigner Specialists whose ideal partners were White men; the use of Grindr and English was thus entangled in political economies of race that I explore more thoroughly below.

As a location-based dating app developed in Japan, 9monsters conformed to the Japanese gay slang commonly used in Ni-chōme bars. Users of the app are required to select a "Type" from a list of nine "monsters" and then participate in a so-called breeding game whereby interacting with others allows one's chosen monster to level up and evolve. The rationale behind this gamified style of online dating, according to men I interviewed, is to allow one's monster to develop through creating relationships with other users (with levels giving users various perks, such as priority messaging). In so doing, 9monsters apparently facilitates the expression of

# 9 Types of Monsters

**BULKY BISON**

**WILD BEAR**

**CHUBBY** PIGGY

**MUSCLE WOLF**

**SPORTY PANTHER**

**ATHLETE** KONG

**LOVELY DOG**

**COOL MONKEY**

**SLIM CAT**

Figure 7. Typing as it appears on 9monsters in 2019.

one's identity by firmly tying users to an evolving monster archetype that can be read by others as a marker of a user's Type. Figure 7 presents these nine monsters Types, whose names are presented in English in all versions of the app. These monsters are Bulky Bison, Wild Bear, Chubby Piggy, Muscle Wolf, Sporty Panther, Athlete Kong, Lovely Dog, Cool Monkey, and Slim Cat.

The promotional material for 9monsters offers very little explanation regarding the Type to which each monster specifically refers. While it is reasonable to conclude that the Wild Bear and Muscle Wolf relate to the *kuma-kei* and *ōkami-kei*, respectively—both of which were briefly introduced in chapter 1—the other seven monsters do not appear to easily match the Types typically seen in the Japanese gay media landscape. Having observed that 9monsters appeared to be the most popular dating app during my fieldwork, I consistently asked men in Ni-chōme to explain to me which Type each monster represented. Unsurprisingly, the responses I received tended to be fairly uniform, and it appeared that app users had developed a consensus regarding the monsters' corresponding Types. According to my interviews, both the Sporty Panther and the Athlete Kong were read as representing the *ikanimo-kei*, except that the Athlete Kong was linked more to a *gachimuchi* bodily aesthetics than the panther, which was understood to have a *gatai* body. The Lovely Dog and the Slim Cat were understood, on the other hand, as referring to the *kawaii-kei*, with the Slim Cat being understood as younger, slimmer, and more camp (*onēppoi*) by some men. Users of the app also explained that the Bulky Bison represented the *gaten-kei*, and the Chubby Piggy unsurprisingly referred to the *debu-kei*. Understandings of the Cool Monkey tended to be split between those who viewed it as a catch-all category and others who viewed it as a younger version of the Athlete Kong, linked to a hip-hop street style. Despite the fact that 9monsters appeared to superficially differentiate itself from more normative Types through its use of the monsters, for the majority of the young men with whom I discussed this app, 9monsters was in fact explicitly linked to the same vocabularies used in GV, *Bádi*, and Ni-chōme's gay bars.

One last difference between the communicative norms of the location-based dating apps and the web-based dating sites used in Ni-chōme was that profiles on Grindr, Jack'd, and 9monsters tended to place a heavier emphasis on one's sexual role as an aspect of one's identity. In the vast majority of the profiles shown to me by young gay men during conversations in Ni-chōme's gay bars, as well as within profiles I observed throughout my fieldwork, users identified themselves as either *tachi* (tops), *neko* (bottoms), or *riba* ("reversible," or versatile). Upon returning to Japan to conduct further fieldwork in 2017, I noticed that some gay men were also explicitly identifying as either *seme* or *uke* in their posts, perhaps showing a shift in Japanese gay slang that is influenced by BL manga. As should be apparent in much of the discussions in this book, Japanese gay media do not typically focus on sexual position except for in BL (a media form that is ambiguously "gay," as discussed in chapter 3). Because of this general lack of explicit reference to sexual position, when Junho, Yōichi, and Shōtarō first started using dating apps, they reported that they felt uncomfortable with the need to describe their sexual role in their profiles. All three listed themselves as *riba*. Shōtarō explained that this appeared to him the most "neutral" option, and all three men explained that they had no particular preference when it came to sexual position. But conversations with other gay men I met in Ni-chōme indicated that some do place an emphasis on sexual position when using gay dating apps, but it appeared to me that Typing was viewed as more important when it came to deciding on a potential casual sex partner or lover. As Yōichi interestingly explained, he believed that one's sexual role is ultimately more negotiable than one's Type. He further reflected that he had originally presented himself as *tachi* on his dating app profile until he experienced receiving anal sex for the first time and discovered that he enjoyed it.

During interviews concerning their use of dating apps, Junho, Yōichi, and Shōtarō highlighted their belief that the selection of an app provides clues about an individual's personality traits, his Type, and the Type to which he would normally be attracted. As I conversed with young gay men using dating apps in the bars of Ni-chōme, interviewing them about their preferences for certain apps and from where these preferences derived, I learned that it was extremely common for men to believe that a man's choice of app was understood as intimately tied to his Type. Quite a few men explained to me that merely accessing and using a particular dating app ultimately positioned a user as part of a particular "tribe" (*zoku*) based in Typing. These men's use of the term *zoku* is interesting given that it is intimately tied to the neoliberal marketing strategies that have typified Japan's consumer culture since the collapse of the bubble economy.[21] These young men's reliance on this neoliberal discourse demonstrates how they ultimately viewed gay dating culture as a kind of marketplace in which one's self represents a commodity, with Typing drawn upon strategically as a way to buy and sell desires that had become fundamental to their identities. For many men, the fact that each app possessed a perceived user base led them to believe that the apps themselves possessed Types, just as GV companies were ascribed Types based on the models they employ. This is despite the fact that many of these apps superficially allow users to preselect from a large variety of Types, such as in the 9monsters example presented above (and discussed previously in chapter 1). For the young gay men with whom I spoke, one's choice of dating app, much like one's choice of bar, can convey to others one's own Type and preferences in a partner.

When reflecting on his initial experiences with location-based dating apps, Yōichi recounted how he first utilized Grindr upon returning to Japan from his travels in Southeast Asia. Yōichi reported that his overall impression of Grindr was negative since the app's user base appeared to be "full of *gai-sen* and foreigners." While he noted that many of these users possessed the hard *gatai* body and expressed the *ikanimo-kei* style in which he had become interested, his previous experience of popularity in Thailand (where he had been mistaken as porn icon Koh Masaki) had inculcated within him a preference for Japanese and other Asian men. For Yōichi, the fact that Grindr was apparently full of White foreign men and the Japanese *gai-sen* who desired them led him to view his experiences of searching for sex (and later romance) on this app as unsuccessful. Yōichi described Grindr as a "White people's app" (*hakujin no apuri*) that was not necessarily "convenient" to use in Japan unless you were searching for a relationship with White foreign men. Expressing his dissatisfaction with Grindr, Yōichi was soon informed by a friend from his favorite bar in Ni-chōme who shared his preference for Asian men that he should try Jack'd, as it was supposedly "the Asians' app" (*ajiajin no apuri*). Yet Yōichi was similarly dissatisfied with Jack'd because of his perception that the majority of its users presented themselves as soft *kawaii-kei*. Through trial and error, and by speaking to his friends in Ni-chōme, Yōichi eventually settled on 9monsters, which he explained was used predominantly by Japanese men who identified as *ikanimo-kei* such as himself. This is despite the fact that 9monsters, through monsters such as the Chubby Piggy (*debu-kei*) or Lovely Dog (*kawaii-kei*), superficially created spaces for men identifying as other Types. As this brief vignette demonstrates, the user base of the apps Yōichi utilized led him to make judgments about the apps themselves, and those judgments, in turn, reveal the influence of Typing on his understanding of gay socialization more broadly and of gay dating specifically.

Yōichi's experiences reveal that many young men active in Ni-chōme's gay bar culture understand Grindr as ideologically linked to White foreigners and those who prefer them (*gai-sen*). My fieldwork within Ni-chōme, where I myself occasionally used Grindr and other dating apps as a method of exploring the district's demographics, uncovered that this impression of Grindr may be somewhat accurate. The majority of Grindr users whom I observed between 2013 and 2015 did tend to be foreigners (mostly, but not exclusively, White men such as myself) and those who admired them; and many of the Japanese users signaled in the English-language texts of their dating profiles that they desired White men. Conversely, my exploration of Jack'd and 9monsters revealed that the majority of app users were Japanese, although East and Southeast Asian tourists to Ni-chōme also appeared to be significant users of Jack'd. This reality speaks to Ni-chōme's positioning as what I have elsewhere termed an "ethnosexual frontier" within which sexual and romantic interactions between members of various ethnic groups occur, facilitated by the neighborhood's formal split into Japanese-only establishments and *gai-sen* establishments targeting foreign, ostensibly White, visitors and the Japanese men who prefer them.[22]

Junho and Yōichi preferred not to use Grindr as they did not explicitly identify as *gai-sen*, instead choosing to use 9monsters for reasons explored more thoroughly below. Some of the men I met in Ni-chōme as I was initially learning about the space did, however, use Grindr more frequently than other apps. This was because these men identified as *gai-sen* and knew that using Grindr greatly increased their chances of meeting White foreigners visiting or living in Tokyo for either casual sex or romantic relationships. For young gay men who identified as *gai-sen*, choosing Grindr was thus strategic. In fact, many of these men made initial contact with me via Grindr as I was using it to acquaint myself with Ni-chōme's gay dating culture, and these initial conversations played an important role in providing me with the sociocultural knowledge necessary to understand Typing generally and Ni-chōme's bar culture more broadly. These young men noted during our initial conversations that most of the White men who used Grindr in Japan were well aware of the fact that the majority of its Japanese users identified as *gai-sen*, even if they were not familiar with this specific terminology. In fact, a long-term American resident in Japan who actively participated in Ni-chōme's bar culture informed me during a conversation in a *gai-sen* bar that Grindr's status as a *gai-sen* app was an open secret in Japan's gay expat community. Another young Japanese man I met at this same bar on another night also explained that his use of Grindr not only facilitated his meeting White men for sex but also consolidated his belief that he truly was attracted to foreign partners and that he identified as *gai-sen*. Using Grindr, this young man suggested, reinforced the ascription of a *gai-sen* identity by other similarly identified Japanese men he met in bars, and he internalized this identity so as to strategically sell himself online through his selection and use of Grindr.

At this point, it is instructive to think through the political economy of race that conditions knowledge about desire in Ni-chōme. While I initially met many men who identified as *gai-sen* during my early fieldwork, I quickly learned that these men represented a minority within Ni-chōme and that most Japanese gay men expressed a strong preference for Japanese partners. As I have explored in previous work, Typing does not just condition knowledge concerning gendered performance; rather, an individual's ethnic background is also considered as forming a Type in Japan's gay culture.[23] Ni-chōme's gay bars are also stratified based on ethnic desires. *Gai-sen* bars represent minority spaces where Japanese men who desire White partners congregate, whereas other bars are avowedly Japanese-only establishments. Serendipitously, while conducting fieldwork for this project, I also met Chinese and Korean gay tourists in Ni-chōme who had traveled to Japan in search of Japanese boyfriends.[24] I surprisingly uncovered that these men faced significant sexual racism both in gay bars and on dating apps, with many finding that Japanese men were uninterested in them because of their status as ethnic others. As these Chinese and Korean men were not Japanese, they were forced—given the sociocultural rules that structure Ni-chōme—to visit the *gai-sen* bars that ostensibly cater to foreigners.[25] But because these spaces actually privileged desires for Whiteness, these tourists found themselves excluded from full participation. This is just one example of how Typing operates to exclude non-Japanese men from participation in Japan's gay culture and demonstrates that young Japanese gay men in Ni-chōme often view foreigners with suspicion or hostility.

While most gay men in Japan view desire for foreigners in zero-sum terms, Shōtarō identified as neither specifically *gai-sen* nor as "not *gai-sen*" (*gai-sen janai*). His reasons for using Grindr—his preferred dating app—derived instead from his familiarity with the app, gained while studying in Australia where, in his experience, gay men commonly used Grindr. Shōtarō explained that as a result of using Grindr, he tended to go on more dates with White resident foreigners than with other Japanese men. According to Shōtarō, meeting predominantly White men did not inculcate in him a belief that he was *gai-sen* but instead suggested to him that systems of categorizing desire based in race were too simplistic; and he was also a fierce critic of the culture of sexual racism that Typing had produced within Ni-chōme. Shōtarō found that his experiences dating both Japanese and foreign men made him realize that the tendency to label oneself as either *gai-sen* or "not *gai-sen*" was reductive, particularly as the White men who used Grindr were of many different Types themselves.

In order to flag his dissatisfaction with racial Typing on Grindr, Shōtarō strategically used Japanese as well as English in his profile to convey his interest in meeting men of any racial background, and he highlighted in his profile that he did not have "a Type of man which he preferred." Further, Shōtarō's continued use of Japanese represented a strategy to mitigate the implicit marking of a Japanese user of Grindr as *gai-sen* since he believed that Japanese language text "reached out" to other Japanese men. In justifying his position, he drew on stereotypes that White foreigners are fundamentally unable to understand Japanese. On the other hand, the five young men who identified as *gai-sen* that I met during my early fieldwork used only English on their dating profiles. According to these men, this was a strategy that they adopted to explicitly index their identity as *gai-sen*, suggesting that the foreign men in whom they were interested found the Japanese language daunting. Further, one young *gai-sen* explained that use of English discouraged other Japanese men from contacting them since English was usually "read" on dating apps as indexing desires for foreign partners. Overall, English language operates as a sophisticated symbol of various ideologies in Ni-chōme, including the desirable cosmopolitanism of the *ikanimo-kei* and also *gai-sen* desires for White boyfriends.

Conversations with young gay men that occurred later in my fieldwork uncovered that the implicit Typing of users on Jack'd and 9monsters was somewhat more nuanced than on Grindr and was based more in gendered performance than racial background. The fact that these apps did not have a perceived racial user base was because they are mostly used by Japanese men and hence rather than *sen* Types based in desires for particular traits such as race, users identified as *kei* Types such as *kawaii-kei* and *ikanimo-kei* that index lifestyles. It is important to note, however, that Jack'd was sometimes understood as an app used by East and Southeast Asian men visiting Tokyo—as indicated by Yōichi's experience described above—because of the app's overall popularity in these regions. I found, however, that this perception of the app was not very common among the young men with whom I spoke and did not have the same kind of symbolic power as the links between Grindr, White men, and *gai-sen*.[26]

My conversations with young gay men who desired other Japanese men in Ni-chōme uncovered that Jack'd was primarily understood as an app used by *kawaii-kei* and those who preferred *kawaii-kei*. On the other hand, 9monsters was predominantly understood as an app for what many men termed the "*ikanimo-kei* tribe" (*ikanimo-kei zoku*), despite the fact that 9monster's advertising attempted to present a more pluralistic view of an ideal user base (as discussed in chapter 1). Yōichi primarily chose to use 9monsters given these links between the app and *ikanimo-kei* ideals. Junho, who wished to date *ikanimo-kei*, also chose 9monsters, although he also occasionally used Jack'd because he understood this app as mainly for *kawaii-kei*. Junho suggested, however, that 9monsters was particularly useful for him because the existence of the Lovely Dog monster indicated that *kawaii-kei* may be accepted as long as they were looking for *ikanimo-kei* partners. When I asked Junho which of these apps had led to success-ful meetings with other men, he explained that he was more likely to be contacted by users on Jack'd but found that the meetings he had with men he met on 9monsters were more enjoyable since he was more likely to meet the *ikanimo-kei* he desired. Ultimately, use of Jack'd and 9monsters separated these two Types from each other, and there was a broad percep-tion that individuals dated within their own Type—that is, an *ikanimo-kei* would date another *ikanimo-kei*—because of this bifurcation of Japan's gay dating culture.

Throughout this book I have focused chiefly on discussing gendered regimes of desire, but this brief segue into the role of location-based dat-ing apps in Ni-chōme also reveals that there is an important racial ele-ment to the political economy that underlies Typing. Clearly desires for White men are privileged within certain spaces in Ni-chōme, and certain apps have also become tied to these spaces. The district's split into *gai-sen* and Japanese-only spaces has also, as I revealed above, provided those foreign men who sit outside the ethnic categories of White and Japanese very little opportunity to enter into romantic or sexual relationships. The entanglement of ethnicity and Typing, where the color of one's skin or the language one speaks can be conceptualized as an index for an iden-tity, also reveals that the regimes of desire disenfranchise men who lack the "hard" masculinity privileged in the district and those ethnic groups who do not have dedicated spaces to gather. During fieldwork, I occa-sionally met South Asian and Black men, for instance, who were very much situated outside of the realms of normative desirability, speaking to a current of anti-Blackness in Ni-chōme that warrants further inves-tigation in future scholarship. Further, the fact that *kei*-based Types are only ascribed to Japanese individuals suggests that these categories are implicitly tied to Japaneseness within the conceptual worlds of my infor-mants. The *ikanimo-kei* privileged on 9monsters and across the Japanese gay media landscape is therefore an implicitly Japanese identity category, with the hard masculinity this Type embodies likewise tied to the Jap-anese gay masculinity that a figure such as Koh Masaki represents, as discussed in chapter 4. There is a strong need for the racialized politics of Japanese gay dating to be investigated in much more depth than my ethnographic study of Ni-chōme has allowed.

## Interpellation via Online Dating in the Japanese Gay Media Landscape

In chapter 1, I revealed that an advertising billboard for 9monsters located in the center of Ni-chōme during my fieldwork in 2013 was broadly representative of the tendency for the Japanese gay media landscape to position the *ikanimo-kei* as the default and hegemonic form of masculinity. Similarly, in the image introducing the "monsters" to app users, depicted in figure 7, the Type that most informants understood as indexing the *ikanimo-kei*—the Sporty Panther—is also prominently located in the center. Despite the fact that 9monsters appears to welcome other Types, it is clear from the centrality of the Sporty Panther that the *ikanimo-kei's* hard masculinity is privileged over others. Thus 9monsters is engaged in the neoliberal logics that produce fantasies of choice at the same time as limiting options for the purpose of capitalist exploitation.[27]

Many young gay who I met in Ni-chōme explained that using 9monsters to find casual sex partners formed part of the *ikanimo-kei* lifestyle, which they understood as normatively desirable. For these reasons, 9monsters' positioning as an *ikanimo-kei* app is unsurprising. Conversely, using Jack'd leads to an individual being positioned by other users as *kawaii-kei*, and using Grindr likewise positions individuals as interested in White foreigners. These complex processes of positioning and Typing strongly impact not only attitudes toward the apps but also whether a user will be deemed an "authentic" and "desirable" individual. Simply put, these processes of normative positioning impact a user's ability to sell his self within the marketplace of desire attached to Ni-chōme, with the regimes of desire that privilege heteronormativity similarly impacting the success of offline interactions. Since the Japanese gay media landscape privileges the hard bodily aesthetics of the *ikanimo-kei* and its attendant consumerist lifestyles, the regimes of desire that circulate throughout this media landscape also privilege the use of 9monsters. The effect of this privileging is that most of the men with whom I spoke viewed as undesirable the use of other apps, which are tied to marginalized identities such as the *kawaii-kei*. In fact, the choice to use Jack'd and Grindr was derided by many individuals who identify as *ikanimo-kei*. One young man, for instance, rather chauvinistically suggested that Jack'd represented a space where Ni-chōme's "losers" (*makegumi*) go to lick their wounds, whereas 9monsters represented a space for "winners" (*kachigumi*). In his conversation with me, this man drew upon the influential social discourse of societal winners and losers that has emerged within precarious Japan in the wake of neoliberalism's rise.[28] The subtext of this man's statement was that the "losers" had somehow failed—perhaps due to their lack of the desirable hard masculinity tied to the figure of the *ikanimo-kei*.

Furthermore, I learned through my conversations with young gay men who regularly use 9monsters that to successfully negotiate an offline encounter via a location-based dating app in Ni-chōme, one is required to ascribe to the Type that is considered normative to the particular app being used. In practical terms, this meant that only users who ascribed to *ikanimo-kei* ideals of hard masculinity would be considered "desirable" users of 9monsters and would thus represent "winners" within the marketplace of desire tied to both this app and Ni-chōme more broadly. It was this construction of apps as possessing Types that ultimately impacted the agency of Junho, Yōichi, and Shōtarō, limiting the freedom they expected such apps to provide.

In thinking through these processes of positioning and their effects on individual agency, I feel it instructive to draw upon Louis Althusser's seminal concept of interpellation. Althusser developed the concept of interpellation within his theorization of the role "ideological state apparatuses" such as the mass media and "repressive state apparatuses" such as the police play in the raising of "class consciousness" among members of the working class within capitalist societies.[29] Althusser argues that when individuals interact with ideological or repressive state apparatuses—the seminal examples he gives are religious institutions and the police force—they are "hailed" by them and thus made aware of their status within the overall social system through this interaction, whether they initially sought out the interaction or not.[30] This in turn raises awareness on behalf of the positioned individual of their abject role within systems of social control, making a society's political economy explicit to the "hailed" subject. Interpellation therefore represents the process by which an individual's subjective identity is produced and subsequently influenced by the ideological systems of control that circulate throughout society. Althusser describes the experience of interpellation as both potentially "violent" and "uncomfortable" for the social subject since it has the potential to disrupt their preexisting understandings of their subjectivity.[31] Indeed, interpellation also has the potential to alienate an individual by raising awareness of their subjugation to dominant forms of societal control.[32]

Use of dating apps, then, represents an example of interpellation within Ni-chōme because a young Japanese gay man's positioning as a particular Type and subsequent rejection by others due to a perceived inability to perform identities deemed desirable makes them aware of how little control over their identity they truly have. It is for this reason that I have described the agency and control superficially provided by location-based dating apps as illusory throughout this chapter. Both rejection and acceptance via online dating are clear examples of when the regimes of desire that circulate throughout the Japanese gay media landscape explicitly act as ideological systems of control over successful socialization in Ni-chōme's gay culture. If one conforms to the bodily and behavior norms of the *ikanimo-kei* through the possession of a hard *gatai* bodily aesthetic and participation in its attendant straight-acting party boy lifestyle, one is easily accepted into the neighborhood's gay bars as a "desirable" man, or "winner." Conversely, if one's identity contravenes heteronormative understandings of appropriate gender performance through the adoption of a *kawaii-kei* identity, for example, then processes of interpellation not only construct one as undesirable, they also explicitly make a subject aware of their transgression of the regimes of desire. Furthermore, since use of an app is read by others as a marker of one's Type, young gay men active in Ni-chōme appear to be doubly interpellated. First, they must be deemed desirable via the norms of the app, and then they must be deemed desirable according to the broader regimes of desire that resuscitate hegemonic masculinity through desires for hardness.

Interpellation limits agency within this context since a young gay man's control over his own desirability is relegated to whether or not he conforms to the expectations of others. Indeed, similar processes occur in Ni-chōme's gay bars, where men who do not "match" a certain bar's normative Type will be refused service and politely asked to leave, as discussed in chapter 1. But for Junho, Yōichi, and Shōtarō, location-based dating apps represented a much more insidious form of this phenomenon, which they variously described as "dangerous" (*abunai*), "poisonous" (*dokudokushii*), or "frustrating" (*kuyashii*). Yōichi, who explained toward the end of my initial fieldwork period in 2013 that he wished to find a romantic partner, suggested that he found the processes of interpellation described above particularly difficult on dating apps since the rejection did not have a clear economic rationale as it does within gay bars. Rather, it was based in explicit, personal deficiencies. In many ways, interpellation made the political economy of Typing and the concomitant hierarchization of desires discussed throughout this book undeniably visible to young gay men. Shōtarō, who tried to mitigate his potentially undesirable lack of a hard *gatai* body by explicitly mentioning in his Grindr and 9monster profiles that he aspired to become an *ikanimo-kei*, often found himself harshly criticized by others even before they met face to face. Explaining that such behaviors strongly impacted his self-esteem, Shōtarō came to believe that such discrimination was particular to Japan and to the system of Typing endemic to Ni-chōme. Whether this is true or not, Shōtarō certainly linked his disappointment over his loss of agency to a narrative of the Japanese gay culture's deficiencies, which eventually motivated him to move to Canada, as discussed in chapter 2.

Strategically manipulating Typing on online dating services thus ultimately limited the agency of young gay men rather than providing them the utopic ability to control their identities as my key interlocutors had initially believed. Akiko Takeyama, in thinking through how neoliberalism compromises Japanese women's abilities to explore their desires through visiting host clubs where intimacy is sold, highlights that contemporary Japanese society is typified by a sense of alienation from sexual desire produced through neoliberal consumption.[33] For both Gabriella Lukács and Akiko Takeyama, neoliberal systems of identity management such as Typing within which desire becomes commoditized are inherently limiting via the logics of the market.[34] That is, the sense of agency that Junho, Yōichi, Haruma, and Shōtarō initially experienced through their use of online dating services in fact forms part of the system of control that seeks to economically exploit individuals in a neoliberal society by creating fantasies of expanded choice. By providing an illusion of choice, apps such as 9monsters are better able to cater to numerous Types of gay men at the same time as disciplining these consumers to conform to specific norms—in this case, the hard masculinity of the *ikanimo-kei* that resuscitates heteronormative logics—so as to eventually consolidate a narrow market. While interpellation may be uncomfortable or violent, it also serves the necessary and vital function of making individuals aware of both their loss of agency and their exploitation under neoliberal systems of control, a point I explore more thoroughly in the conclusion.

For Yōichi in particular, the "shock to the system" that he experienced while searching for romance online led to a complete reevaluation of his life as a *hayatteru ikemen* and eventually led him to completely withdraw from Ni-chōme. I would theorize that, in so doing, Yōichi was able to reclaim the agency that the regimes of desire of the Japanese gay media landscape had obscured through their neoliberal logics. As a beneficiary of the system given his alignment with the hard masculine ideals of the *ikanimo-kei*, Yōichi had been unable to see beyond his privileged position until his eyes were opened in a moment of rupture produced through his attempt to find romance through his use of dating apps. As he developed consciousness of the systems of control within Ni-chōme, Yōichi was finally made aware of how his belief systems had been manipulated and how he had contributed to the development of a homonormative culture in Japan. Read through Sara Ahmed's queer phenomenological theory,[35] Yōichi was orientated away from heteronormativity and thus slanted "sideways." After this great rupture, Yōichi expressed to me in our final interview that he felt overwhelmed with shame and regret, and he set out to drastically change his life. I lost contact with him after this moment, and so I can only hope that he continued to reflect and question the heteronormative regimes of desire that structure knowledge about same-sex attraction in the Japanese gay media landscape and which have produced extremely explicit systems of marginalization in gay dating apps such as Grindr, Jack'd, and 9monsters.

## Conclusion

In this chapter, I have examined how Typing operates as a form of strategic marketing deployed on online dating services such as JP MEN'S CLUB and location-based dating apps as a method to manage self-identity within a marketplace of desire. My exploration of online dating services once again revealed that rather than representing an empowering space within which one can exert agency, these apps promote a valorization of hard masculinity that contours experiences of socialization within Ni-chōme gay bars. In many ways, dating services were some of the most restrictive media with which the young men I met in the neighborhood engaged, and various expectations concerning their use influenced how online daters are perceived by others. Throughout my analysis, I consistently encountered the heteronormativity that dominates the Japanese gay media landscape, demonstrating that the emancipatory potential of online dating services is consistently stymied by ideological regimes of desires.

Indeed, these regimes of desire that circulate throughout Japanese gay media, including via the discourses of desire appearing on gay dating sites such as JP MEN'S CLUB as well as normative understandings of the specific Types associated with a given app, have caused my four principal informants much anxiety. This sense of anxiousness was not limited to these four young men, however. Many of the men with whom I spoke in Ni-chōme voiced similar concerns about loss of control over their desirability in general and personal identity management in particular. The valorization of heteronormative modes of gay experience and the promotion of consumerist, neoliberal understandings of gay identity throughout Japan's gay media landscape clearly demonstrate that homonormative gay cultures critiqued by Lisa Duggan have become ascendant in the Japanese context,[36] with the regimes of desire examined in this book strongly impacting individuals' sense of self. In the conclusion of this book, I evaluate this loss of agency from the perspective of Japan's recent LGBT boom and think through how discourses of hope may mitigate the processes of interpellation that position gay men who "fail" to live up to *ikanimo-kei* ideals as undesirable.

# Conclusion

## Regimes of Desire and Hope in Japan's LGBT Boom

While standing together in Lumière and looking at photographs of Koh Masaki in *Bádi*, Shōtarō introduced me to the *ikanimo-kei* and the idea that Japanese gay media provides alternative understandings of gay desire that challenge the tendency for homosexuality to be understood as perverted and unnatural. During this early stage of my fieldwork in 2013, Shōtarō's discussions with me focused on the notion that the symbol of the *ikanimo-kei* affirms the masculinity of Japanese gay men, allowing them to distance themselves from the *onē kyara* depicted on mainstream Japanese variety shows. Throughout my fieldwork, however, I increasingly encountered views that contrasted with those of Shōtarō, although it became apparent that Shōtarō himself also had a more complicated relationship than he initially expressed with the regimes of desire that circulate throughout the Japanese gay media landscape. Men such as Haruma, for example, indicated that the privileging of the *ikanimo-kei* marginalized those who could not live up to the Type's physical ideals. Indeed, as a socio-semiotic system for understanding desire, Typing ultimately appeared to reduce the agency of the young gay men who gather in Ni-chōme through its conflation of identity with normalizing discourses based in consumption and in the desire for particular heteronormative gendered identities.

It emerged through my fieldwork that these young gay men's consumption of media not only was anchored to but was also influenced by participation in Ni-chōme's gay bar culture. This is important because within this space, Typing represents the dominant method by which knowledge concerning desire is organized. Typing as expressed in Japanese gay media, such as GV, magazines, and manga, and on online dating services plays an important role not only in disseminating the discourses of the Japanese gay media landscape but also in the ongoing and reflexive structuring of Ni-chōme as a space where knowledge about gay desire can be obtained. As became apparent during my discussions with young men in the district, a number of regimes of desire operated to privilege heteronormative modes of masculinity as ultimately desirable within Ni-chōme via the system of Typing. As I have explored throughout this book, these regimes of desire ultimately resuscitated hard masculine fantasies of the past tied to such figures as the salaryman, producing a political economy of desire that denigrated gender performances that challenge the hetero system that continues to dominate Japanese conceptualizations of sexuality.[1]

Within this concluding chapter, I first summarize the main findings of *Regimes of Desire* to lay the groundwork for further theorization of the role of gay media in the lives of young gay men active in Ni-chōme's gay bar culture. Unlike a traditional conclusion, however, my aim here is rather to then draw upon this summary to further theorize how desire operates as a conditioning discourse that both produces and sustains a homonormative, apolitical culture anchored by the symbol of the *ikanimo-kei*. Reflecting upon Lauren Berlant's theory of cruel optimism,[2] I argue for a reading of these regimes of desire as neoliberal constructs designed to incite gay men to consume media without questioning its heteronormative logics. But this is only half the story to be told. When I returned to Japan in 2015 to debrief my principal informants about the outcomes of my initial fieldwork, I found myself within a media landscape in the process of transition. Because of the LGBT boom in Japan's mainstream media that resulted from Japanese reporting on the US Supreme Court's 2015 decision to extend the legality of same-sex marriage across the entire US,[3] I found that the attitudes of Junho, Shōtarō, and Haruma toward their media consumption and its relation to their desires had changed once again. I spent much time discussing these changes with these three young men—unfortunately, I was unable to reconnect with Yōichi—throughout 2015 and a subsequent trip to Japan in 2017. I feel it necessary to end this monograph critically investigating how these three young men's hope for the future operates as an epistemological challenge that destabilizes the power of the heteronormative regimes of desire discussed in this book. In so doing, I seek to lay the groundwork for future explorations of gender identity, sexuality, and desire in the context of Japan's continuing LGBT boom.

*Consuming Gay Media in Tokyo: Some Reflections*

My ethnography revealed that the Japanese gay media landscape was much more complex than I initially believed when I first stepped foot in Ni-chōme with the naive intention to investigate the emancipatory potential of Japanese gay media. As my discussions with various young gay men and my discursive analyses of gay media content revealed, the Japanese gay media landscape was highly homonormative. That is, the neoliberalism inherent to the media landscape promoted apolitical consumption tied to heteronormative regimes of desire that ultimately fail to challenge the status quo. Ni-chōme emerged as central to my ethnographic understanding of the Japanese gay media landscape, with this "gay town" (*gei machi*) representing a marketplace devoted to the buying and selling of gay men's desires. As such, Ni-chōme reflects the neoliberal focus of the Japanese gay media landscape, where desire becomes commodified and subsequently exploited for profit. Indeed, my ethnography revealed that Ni-chōme is dominated by various companies that strategically circulate media to promote a specific gay lifestyle based in discourses of youth, heteronormative masculinity, and constant partying: the *ikanimo-kei*. Ni-chōme, and the media circulating in it, play an important role in situating understandings of identity within patterns of consumer behavior that have been consciously attached to various Types to maximize profits. Consuming media in Ni-chōme ultimately means that individuals come to understand their same-sex attraction within an ideological environment where certain desires are always already constructed as less normative than others, creating a hierarchy of desires intimately tied to heteronormative systems of understanding gender and sexuality. Figure 8 presents a loose schematic of this hierarchy of desires as mapped onto Typing and the privileging of hard masculinity.

In Japan's queer literature, the plethora of Types found in Ni-chōme is often presented as a positive aspect of the district. As many of the young men I met during fieldwork mentioned, they believed that "there is no rubbish to be thrown away in Ni-chōme" (*Ni-chōme ni suteru gomi nashi*). But there were some men I met, including Shōtarō and Haruma, who found their desires marginalized within the neighborhood, even though the space broadly supported the expression of gay desire itself by providing spaces for gay men to socialize. My fieldwork revealed that Ni-chōme represents a site where particular desires are legitimated and others are marginalized. It is therefore problematic to approach Ni-chōme as some

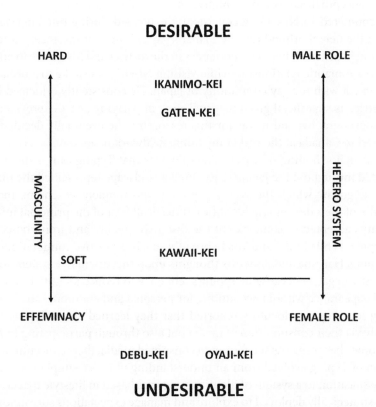

Figure 8. Schematic representing the regimes of desire examined in this book.

sort of gay utopia, as has become commonplace within both popular and academic writing on the district. One common criticism of Ni-chōme that I encountered during my discussions with young gay men was that the district was becoming increasingly focused on the dissemination and consumption of pornography and that this process of "pornographication" led to a valorization of identities based in youth, muscular physicality, and a party boy lifestyle focused on casual sex. The pornographication of Ni-chōme—and of the Japanese gay media landscape more broadly— has led some men to believe that Japan's gay community is eroding, with gay identity becoming increasingly superficial as it is reduced to the pursuit of pleasure. Drawing upon the tendency for experiences in Tokyo to be conceptualized as representative of national culture, the young men I encountered in Ni-chōme consistently expressed during our interviews that the neighborhood reflected Japan's gay culture. For instance, Shōtarō strongly believed that his experiences in the district and his failure to enter into a romantic relationship while visiting Ni-chōme's spoke to a broader problem with the gay community of Japan. He consistently criticized the district as superficial given its privileging of partying and the prevalence of pornography; and it was for this reason that he eventually decided to travel to Canada at the end of my initial fieldwork in 2013.

A major finding of my ethnography was that Typing as it is disseminated throughout the Japanese gay media landscape represented the main paradigm by which the young gay men who frequent Ni-chōme make sense of their desires and identities. Indeed, all four of the principal informants accepted to some extent the discursive reality and importance of Typing. While Junho and Yōichi broadly attached positive connotations to Typing, Haruma and Shōtarō's thoughts upon this discursive system were mostly negative because of Typing's tendency to reduce identity to physical appearance without accounting for personal and emotional attributes. My four key interlocutors reported that they learned about Typing not only via their consumption of media but also through participating in Ni-chōme's bar scene. As the four men consumed media, their conceptualization of Typing evolved from an understanding of it as a simple system of classification to a system of identity categories based in lifestyle that could be strategically deployed to explore and manage expectations surrounding gay desire. For these men, media consumption and Ni-chōme were thus intrinsically linked.

My analysis revealed that Typing is particularly prevalent within GV, where it classifies the models in films based upon physical appearance. Each GV production company focuses upon making films featuring specific Types, which leads consumers to understand that Type as representative of the company overall. By using Typing, GV companies are better able to create a market for themselves, catering to individuals who prefer specific physical characteristics. This use of Typing is an explicit example of the tendency for desire to become commoditized in the Japanese gay media landscape, as GV companies exploit markets based in the desire for particular body types and associated gender performances and identity categories. Furthermore, my quantitative analysis of a corpus of GV DVD covers revealed that only *tai'ikukai-kei* (Gym Type), *kawaii-kei* (Cute Type), *debu-kei* (Chubby Type), *josō-kei* (Cross-Dressing Type), and *gaijin* (Foreigner) films are produced by Japan's largest and most popular GV production companies. By explicitly producing films targeting a limited number of Types, the GV companies are better able to manipulate the market and directly appeal to the largest number of consumers. An unintended consequence of this, however, is that only a few specific Types are rendered desirable in Japan's gay pornographic media. Although five Types were commonly featured in GV, the frequency with which they were featured differs dramatically, with *tai'ikukai-kei* films representing well over half of the films in the corpus.

Conversely, I found that the gay magazine *Bádi* explicitly referred to Typing only in porn reviews and event listings where it acted similarly to Typing on gay tube sites as a method of categorization. Instead, *Bádi* relied upon a discourse of "gay lifestyle" to discuss modes of being gay in Japan, creating a "national" discourse that sold the lifestyles of Ni-chōme as fundamental to living a "happy gay life" in Japan. By drawing upon the discourse of lifestyle, *Bádi* ultimately promoted a particularly consumerist understanding of gay desire and identity founded in heteronormative gender performances that resonates with recent homonormative trends in the global gay publishing industry. It became apparent via interviews with informants, however, that many young gay men read Typing into *Bádi*, conflating the neoliberal lifestyle promoted by the magazine with the *ikanimo-kei*. Of particular interest was the fact that the lifestyle politics depicted in *Bádi* operated as a neoliberal compulsion that conflated gay lifestyle to the bodily aesthetics and gendered performances of the *ikanimo-kei*, implicitly suggesting that living an alternative gay life would represent an impediment to happiness. Although *Bádi* may have ceased publication in 2019, its neoliberal logics likely remain influential in contemporary Japan.

My ethnography also uncovered that the users of online dating services commonly deployed Typing in their posts as a way to talk about their own identities and the identities of their desired partners. The use of Typing was so prevalent on dating sites that, I argue, presenting one's identity via Typing represents a communicative norm on Japanese gay dating services, including both dating sites and location-based dating apps on smartphones. An important related finding was that specific dating sites and apps were understood to have a particular Type because of the normative Type of their user base, and expectations around the ethnic backgrounds and gendered performances of certain apps are incredibly common among the men I met during fieldwork. This in turn marks as undesirable and inauthentic a user of a dating service who fails to live up to the expectations of these normative Types. The prevalence of Typing on dating services is a strong indication of its importance to sociality in the Japanese gay culture more broadly, as it represents a semiotic vocabulary or shorthand that individuals draw upon to make sense of the desires and identities of the gay men with whom they are interacting. This also indicates, however, that to successfully navigate the online dating world requires knowledge of Typing, meaning that those who reject Typing or are unfamiliar with it may be disadvantaged as they lack the capability to utilize the system to successfully appeal to other users of dating services.

## Cruel Optimism in Shinjuku Ni-chōme's Homonormative Culture

The Japanese gay media landscape contains a number of hierarchical regimes of desire that construct certain modes of being gay as more normative than others. My ethnography revealed that more than simply representing a system of knowledge, desire acted as a set of ideologies that contoured understandings of queer experience more broadly. Ultimately, through these regimes of desire, the Japanese gay media landscape upholds heteronormative understandings of sexuality and gender that privilege the hegemonic expression of masculinity as rough and active, representations that circulate in other parts of Japanese society via tropes such as the salaryman. These regimes produce a political economy of desire based on the system of gender/sexual duality that forms part of the hetero system critiqued by Fushimi Noriaki.[4] This political economy, in turn, functions to normalize fantasies of hard masculinity through denigrating softness and its perceived links to effeminacy. A particular Type is thus judged as desirable or undesirable depending upon the gendered performance associated with the Type and just how normatively masculine it is. The Japanese gay media landscape promotes a binary understanding of desirability in which desirability is situated in a masculine gay identity rather than an effeminate gay identity. Nowhere is this more explicit than on the gay dating site JP MEN'S CLUB, where users mark desirable identities by drawing upon a meta-discourse of hunkiness (*sawayaka*) aligned with heteronormative understandings of masculinity.

By consuming media, young gay men such as my key informants come into contact with the regimes of desire that construct the *ikanimo-kei* as most normatively desirable. The men who frequent the bars and clubs of Ni-chōme are highly aware of the normativity of the *ikanimo-kei* as it informs their understandings about their potential desirability in the community and provides them with insight into the norms and expectations of the neighborhood. This was particularly true of the four principal informants in this study, who consciously situated themselves in relation to the *ikanimo-kei* by either accepting (Junho, Yōichi, and Shōtarō) or rejecting (Haruma) its normative appeal. Overall, the hard masculinity of the *ikanimo-kei* was positioned as an explicitly Japanese form of gay masculinity through the consumption of media such as GV and *Bádi*, and this tied into broader ideologies connecting sexuality and ethnicity in Ni-chōme. The figure of the *ikanimo-kei* became valorized within sites set aside as Japanese-only establishments throughout the district, and it is unsurprising that young men who visit Ni-chōme would thus situate the *ikanimo-kei* as a supposed national symbol of Japan's gay culture more broadly. The regimes of desire that circulate throughout the Japanese gay media landscape thus explicitly promote the *ikanimo-kei* as an identity that is synonymous with being a Japanese gay man. This is an idea that a broader ethnographic study beyond the borders of Shinjuku Ni-chōme could usefully explore in the future.

The *ikanimo-kei* is constructed as normatively desirable in Japan's gay media by conflation with the figure of the heterosexual male. This was an idea inculcated in the young gay men with whom I spoke during visits to Ni-chōme through their consumption of GV, in which the figure of the straight man is fetishized. *Bádi*'s focus on promoting a specific gay lifestyle located in consumer behavior also implicitly promotes the *ikanimo-kei* as normatively desirable, as the lifestyle promoted in *Bádi* is equated with the *ikanimo-kei* by the magazine's readers. Through the promotion of the *ikanimo-kei*, Japanese gay media thus reinforces heteronormative understandings of gender roles in Japan. This is particularly true of GV, where the figure of the *nonke* (straight man) is fetishized and normative desirability is equated with heterosexuality and heteronormative masculinity. The gendered performances of the *ikanimo-kei* have become conflated with those of the heteronormative *nonke*, which has also led many of the men with whom I conversed in Ni-chōme to understand the physical appearance and personality of a stereotypical *ikanimo-kei* as possessing "*nonke* characteristics." The marginalization of Types other than the *ikanimo-kei*, especially the *kawaii-kei*, is often justified due to the effeminacy (*onnarashisa*) of these Types. At a time when mainstream media is increasingly constructing desirable heterosexual masculinity as soft, the

Japanese gay media landscape thus continues to valorize hard masculinity and, in so doing, promotes heteronormative conceptualizations of sexuality and gender as normal.

Throughout this book, I have argued that Typing in general and the regimes of desire that privilege the *ikanimo-kei* in particular fundamentally limit the agency of young gay men to creatively explore and manage their desires and identities. While it is certainly true that individuals have agency to select and consume the media that best matches their own conceptualizations of what it means to desire the same sex, these choices are always constrained by the Japanese gay media landscape's neoliberal systems of knowledge production. My ethnography and interviews with Junho, Yōichi, Haruma, and Shōtarō revealed two highly explicit instances where the socio-semiotic system of Typing—which, it must be emphasized, primarily functions as a neoliberal means of segmenting markets for the purposes of economic exploitation[5]—limited young men's agency when exploring their desires and identities. First, encountering Typing within Ni-chōme and in the Japanese gay media landscape influenced the vocabulary that young gay men could draw upon to conceptualize their desires. As discussed throughout the previous chapters, after becoming socialized into spaces that normalize the use of Typing to discuss one's desire for others, young Japanese gay men could no longer conceptualize their desires without drawing upon Typing as a shorthand to organize their thoughts. That is, even when explicitly asked to avoid using Typing to describe their ideal partners, informants reported to me that they could no longer do so. Second, and perhaps more explicitly, when JP MEN'S CLUB introduced compulsory Typing of the Desired Other within post headers in 2013, I noticed a drastic decrease in the length of an average post to the Serious Forum. It was as if the introduction of Typing onto this previously highly descriptive dating site stifled its users' ability to discuss their desires in complex and creative ways, leading to stunted descriptions of potential desired partners.

The privileging of heteronormativity through the production of the *ikanimo-kei* as normative strongly impacts the agency of young men active in Ni-chōme's gay bar culture. Nowhere is this clearer than in the experiences of Haruma and his relationship with his former boyfriend Akito. When recounting how Akito utilized gay media such as *Bádi* magazine to impress upon Haruma—a self-proclaimed herbivorous boy (*sōshoku-kei danshi*) who was heavily invested in his own "cute" persona—the necessity to act in a manly manner, Haruma often drew upon the trope of losing control. Haruma came to view media that valorized the *ikanimo-kei* as poisonous, explaining that the heteronormative nature of the Japanese gay media landscape negatively impacted his self-esteem. Eventually, Haruma rejected Typing and found refuge in a community of young men who embraced the desirability of the *kawaii-kei*, but in so doing, his understandings of gay desire and identity became positioned as niche by the regimes of desire of the Japanese gay media landscape. That is, Haruma's attempts to reassert his agency alienated him from the homonormative culture of Ni-chōme, where softness was not only viewed as undesirable but also as a threat to the stability of Japanese masculinity itself.

It is not just men such as Haruma with explicitly negative experiences of loss of control who have their agency compromised by the heteronormative regimes of desire investigated in this book. Yōichi, whose initial consumption of Japanese gay media played an important role in helping him accept that same-sex attraction did not compromise his identification with normative masculinity, also found himself losing his sense of control toward the end of my initial fieldwork in 2013. As long as he had conformed to the norms of the *ikanimo-kei* through his performance as a *hayatteru ikemen*—that is, possessing a hard *gatai* body and participating in a party boy lifestyle of casual sex and drinking and dancing in clubs— Yōichi experienced a sense of empowerment and agency over his sense of self. But when he decided to begin searching for a romantic relationship, Yōichi found that his previous adherence to the norms of Ni-chōme's gay bar culture began to impede his search for happiness. Indeed, men would often reject him precisely because he conformed to the stereotypical depictions of an identity category that Yōichi's consumption of Japanese gay media had explicitly led him to believe was desirable. Both Haruma and Yōichi chose at various stages of their lives to reject the normative expectations of the Japanese gay media landscape and in so doing found that their agency had become compromised. This demonstrates the ideological influence that these heteronormative regimes of desire truly possess. Not only do these ideological regimes contour knowledge about gay desire and identity, but they also directly impact the lived experiences of young gay men seeking to understand their complex lives.

For these reasons, I argue that the regimes of desire that privilege the *ikanimo-kei* as the symbolic representation of a normatively desirable gay man in Shinjuku Ni-chōme introduce a sense of cruel optimism into the district's gay bar culture. As theorist Lauren Berlant has stated in her study of the function of optimism in neoliberal society, "A relation of cruel optimism exists when something you desire is actually an obstacle to your flourishing."[6] In situations where cruel optimism is in effect, Berlant argues, the typically "animating potency" of one's desires instead functions to close access to the object of those desires.[7] Simply put, cruel optimism represents the maintenance of an attachment to a desired object that may cause harm to the desirer.[8] The figure of the *ikanimo-kei* represents just such a desire in the sense that the need to meet the heteronormative ideals of the Japanese gay media landscape causes harm to those who are unable to attain or maintain such a lifestyle. Because of the heteronormative regimes of desire that circulate throughout them, Japanese gay media do not in fact truly provide an escape from mainstream society's positioning of same-sex attraction as fundamentally perverse or abnormal. By centering desirability within heteronormative gender performances and an attendant lifestyle typified by consumerist behaviors, the emancipatory potential of Japanese gay media has been compromised. This strikes at the heart of Berlant's theory of cruel optimism, which she suggests has emerged in contemporary neoliberal society to subordinate humanity's innate optimism for a better future to a presentist "singularity"— subordinated to the logics of late capitalist markets—that fundamentally denies the existence of a future to increase consumption within the "now."[9] Cruel optimism thus maintains the status quo because it is in the interests of capitalist structures and neoliberal states such as Japan to induce mindless and uncritical consumption.

The cruel optimism of the heteronormative regimes of desire that circulate throughout the Japanese gay media landscape also plays an important role in producing a culture of homonormativity within Ni-chōme. As mentioned at the beginning of this book, Lisa Duggan has persuasively argued that neoliberalism has produced "a privatized, depoliticized gay culture anchored in . . . consumption" that fails to challenge heteronormative understandings of sexuality and gender.[10] As interviews with informants revealed, the *ikanimo-kei* was partly viewed as desirable precisely because of this Type's disavowal of politics and its investment in consumption. In reducing individual agency, heteronormative regimes of desire thus also ultimately limit the ability of young gay men to challenge the status quo and in fact encourage consumers to retreat into fantasies of the past when faced with contemporary social disadvantage. It is for this reason that, during 2013, I encountered numerous voices that positioned Shinjuku Ni-chōme as a bastion for so-called traditional hard masculinity. The district's homonormative culture relied upon presenting change as dangerous since the introduction of alternative visions of masculinity, such as had arguably been occurring within young women's popular culture, disrupted the narratives of consumerist escape at the heart of the district's culture. Yet in 2015, when I reconnected with Junho, Haruma, and Shōtarō, I found that these men had been reinvigorated by Japan's recent LGBT boom and had begun reevaluating their own desires in this new discursive context. While it is my belief that the Japanese gay media landscape still remains dominated by the privileging of heteronormative understandings of desire and identity, I wish to conclude this book by investigating how hope reorganizes knowledge and provides agency for young gay men to challenge the neoliberalism of Japan's gay media landscape.

## Hope in the LGBT Boom

Anthropologist Anne Allison has provocatively argued that contemporary Japan is typified by a sense of precarity. In Japan's neoliberal society, young people in particular feel alienated, overwhelmed by an affective state that Allison terms "the pain of life" (*ikizurasa*).[11] Japan's young people continually find themselves excluded from the affluent lifestyles experienced by previous generations, denied access to the security of lifetime employment since the collapse of the Japanese economic miracle and the subsequent neoliberal restructuring of Japanese corporate life initiated by former Prime Minister Koizumi Jun'ichirō at the beginning of the 21st century.[12] Fundamentally, contemporary Japan represents a "hope deficit society" (*kibō kakusa shakai*) where young people's access to the resource of hope has been compromised by the monopolization of opportunity by the so-called *kachigumi* (social winners).[13] Young gay men, by virtue of their youth and their supposedly nonnormative sexual desires, find themselves doubly precarious in contemporary Japan. They both suffer from "the pain of life" by virtue of their generational economic exclusion from the *kachigumi* as well as ostracism from heteronormative society based in continued discrimination against sexual minorities. It is for these reasons that the cruel optimism of the Japanese gay media landscape is so insidious. By failing to challenge the status quo, the regimes of desire investigated in this book limit the agency of young gay men and potentially compromises their hope by providing them a sense of optimism that harms rather than comforts. Furthermore, those gay men who fail to conform to the normative modes of identity promoted within the Japanese gay media landscape may also find themselves placed precariously within the bars and clubs of Ni-chōme due to the niching of their desires and identities. There is thus the potential for such young men to experience triple precarity.

Upon returning to Japan in 2015 to reconnect with the four principal informants whose subjective experiences form the backbone to the analysis presented in *Regimes of Desire*, I was surprised to find that the sense of pessimism that had pervaded our final discussions in 2013 had somewhat faded when I met with Junho, Haruma, and Shōtarō (who coincidentally happened to be visiting Japan from Canada at the same time I was there). I reconnected with these three young men during a time when Japanese mainstream media was undergoing the LGBT boom briefly discussed in the introduction. This was a heightened time of visibility for Japan's sexual minority communities when both mainstream media and government agencies appeared to be seriously responding to over three decades of Japanese sexual minority community activism. As Japan's mainstream media—spurred by the US Supreme Court decision to legalize same-sex marriage—continued to report on queer rights issues under the conspicuous label of "LGBT" (which became a new buzzword in Japan's press), young men I met in Ni-chōme reported to me that they felt a strong sense of change. These feelings were soon justified as corporate sponsors began flocking to support pride events such as the Tokyo Rainbow Parade in 2016 and local governments across Japan started to introduce ordinances designed to recognize same-sex couples and reduce anti-LGBT discrimination. Furthermore, the Japanese gay media landscape also appeared to be responding to the LGBT boom in limited ways. In December 2015, for instance, I was surprised to see prominent reporting of LGBT politics in *Bádi*'s political articles when I was flipping through a copy of the magazine with Haruma during a visit to the *gei shoppu* Lumière.

Curious to learn more about the impacts of this new LGBT boom, I transformed my initial debriefing interviews with Junho, Haruma, and Shōtarō into opportunities to discuss this new mainstream media moment. During a discussion concerning the origins of the LGBT boom, Junho pointed out that discussion of LGBT issues in Japanese mainstream media seems to have exploded with the awarding of the 2020 Summer Olympic Games to the city of Tokyo. Shōtarō indicated that he believed another stimulus for the LGBT boom was the much-publicized decision by the local government of Tokyo's Shibuya Ward to begin issuing "certificates acknowledging marriage-like relationships" (*kekkon sōtō pātonāshippu shōmeisho*) to registered same-sex couples. Whatever the cause of this boom, LGBT rights had become a significant issue in Japanese politics. Both of Japan's major political parties developed working groups on LGBT issues and drafted antidiscrimination legislation, and LGBT rights played a significant role in debates during the 2016 Tokyo gubernatorial elections. Reflecting upon these political developments during a later discussion in July 2017, Haruma reported that he felt a "new era" of Japanese LGBT activism was sweeping across the nation, spurred in part by young men and women intensely interested in creating a "Japanese form" of queer rights discourse that was "in sync" with global activist concerns, including trans rights. Importantly for Haruma, the uptake of queer rights politics by young gay men at this time also represented a challenge to the Japanese gay media landscape's deliberately apolitical focus on consumption.

Haruma's statement concerning the development of a Japanese form of queer identity politics is particularly important, resonating with beliefs expressed by both Junho and Shōtarō during interviews in 2015. All three of these young gay men passionately argued that the LGBT boom did not simply represent an example of Western rights discourse liberating "backwards" Japanese society. This argument is important since there have been criticisms among Japanese and foreign commentators that the LGBT boom may erase Japan's long history of activism prior to this moment and present a narrative of Japanese sexual minority communities being liberated by Western discourse.[14] Rather, the LGBT boom represented a corrective to the mainstream media's previously problematic representational politics when it came to sexual minorities, although all three men did highlight that cross-dressing *onē kyara* remained prevalent on Japanese television. What was most important to Junho, Haruma, and Shōtarō was the fact that the LGBT boom was shifting the conversation concerning same-sex attraction in interesting new directions both within Japan's gay spaces and beyond. Haruma highlighted that he encountered more young men in Ni-chōme who were open to discussing politics, as did Shōtarō. In July 2017, Junho explained that the broader mainstream visibility of LGBT in Japan had led him to openly march in the parade that forms part of Tokyo Rainbow Pride and to abandon his previous plans to marry a woman to appease his family, although he remained closeted with them. Shōtarō mentioned that his experiences in Canada, including his relationship with a Chinese Canadian man, had reignited his desire to publish a manga concerning his experiences growing up as a gay man in Japan and believed the LGBT boom may facilitate its publication. Throughout our conversations, each of the three men expressed that the LGBT boom had given them "hope" (*kibō*) for a future Japan in which sexual minorities would be accepted within mainstream Japanese society.

Junho, Haruma, and Shōtarō continued to view the Japanese gay media landscape as a problematic discursive space that did not fully gel with their desires and identities. All three made a point of highlighting the fact that they still believed that Japanese gay media—which they all still consumed, although in Junho's case the frequency of consumption had lessened—promoted the *ikanimo-kei* as desirable and that this was problematic. Perhaps most importantly, when I shared my overall argument that the *ikanimo-kei* was founded in heteronormative understandings of gay desire that fundamentally alienate young gay men from their own experiences of same-sex attraction, they all agreed with my interpretation of their previously stated opinions. Yet the initial sense of loss of agency that had emerged during interviews in 2013 had been replaced by the aforementioned hopes for the future. Contrary to economist Genda Yūji's claim that young people have lost access to hope in contemporary Japan,[15] these three young men deployed their hopes to reinject a sense of agency into their lives. That is to say, hope operated as a way for these three men to cope with the pressures of the heteronormative regimes of desire that circulate throughout the Japanese gay media landscape and that construct a neoliberal, homonormative culture within Ni-chōme.

The conversations I had with my principal informants in 2015 during the debriefing stage of my project thus revealed a tension between cruel optimism as a conditioning situation that lessens agency and hope as a resource that reinjects a sense of agency via an explicit focus on the future. The way that Junho, Haruma, and Shōtarō appeared to deploy hope resonated with cultural anthropologist Hirokazu Miyazaki's notion that hope "serves as a radical temporal reorientation of knowledge."[16] For Miyazaki, hope does not represent the subject of knowledge but instead represents a method of conceptualizing and organizing knowledge that is specifically future-oriented.[17] In this sense, hope functions much like desire in that it represents a discursive resource that individuals can draw upon to make sense of the world in which they live. This was certainly the case for Junho, Haruma, and Shōtarō whose sense of empowerment within the context of the LGBT boom gave them the ability to begin challenging the discourses that they had been encountering within the Japanese gay media landscape when I first interviewed them in 2013. As Shōtarō noted during an interview, one of the reasons he left Japan and moved to Canada was because his experiences in Ni-chōme had made him believe that he would have no future in Japan's gay culture. After all, he ruefully admitted, Japanese gay men appeared uninterested in him whenever he sought to arrange dates because the regimes of desire that promote the *ikanimo-kei* were too inflexible. That is, men were unwilling to accept a partner who did not conform to what was "normal." But returning to Japan during the LGBT boom made him feel that the inflexibility of Japan's gay culture was lessening, and he reported hearing more critical voices among the gay men with whom he spoke concerning the *ikanimo-kei*. Haruma, on the other hand, was much blunter, explicitly stating that the "age of the *ikanimo-kei* is now over."

My primary criticism of the heteronormative regimes of desire investigated in this book is that the system of Typing alienates individuals' understandings of their desires from their individual experiences, promoting market-based conceptualizations of gay desire and identity as both normative and natural. This is the central function of neoliberalism, which operates on fantasies of expanded choice when instead one's agency to choose is systematically limited through alienating affects.[18] Miyazaki, drawing upon the theorization of hope developed by German Marxist philosopher Ernst Bloch, argues that hope emerges out of alienation from self-knowledge as a kind of temporal corrective that reemphasizes the future's importance within our understandings of the world.[19] This suggests that the loss of agency promoted by the regimes of desire circulating throughout the Japanese gay media landscape will eventually promote hopefulness among consumers. While such a utopic reading may appear naive, the experiences of Junho, Haruma, and Shōtarō indicate that no matter how alienating the heteronormative logics of the Japanese gay media landscape may be, young gay men in Japan still possess the agency to challenge the notion that certain kinds of gay desire and identity are somehow nonnormative. While it is my belief that the Japanese gay media landscape continues to promote a homonormative conceptualization of gay desire even at the time of writing in 2020, the LGBT boom is providing hope to those men disenfranchised by said ideological regimes. As a consequence, the currency of these regimes of desire are gradually becoming destabilized, and young gay men appear to be finding agency to challenge the precarious situations with which they are faced.

It is important to note that Japan's recent LGBT boom has not been without its critics. There are also some compelling counterarguments proposed by Japanese queer studies scholars and activists that challenge my more reparative reading of this seminal media moment. There have been frequent discussions in the Japanese press concerning the LGBT boom's dark side, including the May 2017 issue of *AERA* titled "The Lies of the LGBT Boom" (*LGBT būmu no uso*) and a special section of the June 2017 issue of *Sekai* titled "The Light and Shadow of the LGBT Boom" (*LGBT būmu no hikari to kage*). In *Sekai*, queer theorist Shimizu Akiko critiques the LGBT boom particularly for forming part of a broader strategy of the ruling Liberal Democratic Party to utilize diversity politics in the service of neoliberal economics.[20] Situating LDP debates over LGBT rights and antidiscrimination as part of a broader history of Japanese governmental efforts to stimulate the economy through discrimination law reform, Shimizu argues that the LGBT boom pays lip service to antidiscrimination in order to create an environment that facilitates economic growth.[21] Analyzing LGBT boom rhetoric, Shimizu reveals that the notion of "diversity" is consistently deployed as a way to entice sexual minority communities to actively participate in Japanese capitalism and hence become "productive members of society." Shimizu further notes that much governmental and corporate discourse seems to be framed within the context of attracting foreign LGBT talent to Japan (particularly, she alleges, from the US).[22] Shimizu ultimately questions the radical queer intervention of the LGBT boom, suggesting that it is both highly instrumentalist and focused less on the actual lived realities of discrimination that Japanese sexual minorities face than on a broader governmental project of reviving the economy by transforming LGBT individuals into heteronormative, tax-paying citizens.[23]

In response to such a critique, it is instructive here to think more concretely about how hope operates as a form of queer praxis that may frustrate the neoliberal imperatives of the LGBT boom. According to the work of queer theorist José Esteban Muñoz, hoping for a future is an inherently queer act that deconstructs the everyday in the production of emancipatory fantasies.[24] Whereas the regimes of desire discussed in the book function to tie individuals to the past to promote the mindless consumerism at the heart of neoliberal identity politics, the hopes that my principal informants expressed within the context of the LGBT boom radically break apart experiences of same-sex attraction from fantasies of the past to open up spaces of imagination that challenge the heteronormative status quo. The cruel optimism of the Japanese gay media landscape, where softness is configured as a threat to the primacy of a hard and hegemonic masculinity tied to fantasies of the Japanese past, thus collapses before Junho,

Haruma, and Shōtarō's hopes engendered by the LGBT boom. Thinking in terms of Sara Ahmed's queer phenomenological theories,[25] these hopes disrupt the heteronormative "smoothing" that sits at the heart of the Japanese gay media landscape and allows for same-sex desiring subjects to disorient themselves from the neoliberal logics that underpin the regimes of desire that privilege hard masculinity. For Junho, Haruma, and Shōtarō, hope was an affect that disrupted homonormative culture and empowered them to reject consumerism by turning their attention to a brighter future. While the logics that drove the LGBT boom may, as Shimizu suggests, be just as neoliberal as the prevailing regimes of desire, the LGBT boom had produced emancipatory affects for my three principal informants, and it is this affective response that I wish to center within my concluding reflections on my fieldwork.

The analysis presented in this book clearly demonstrates that the Japanese gay media landscape is dominated by regimes of desire that promote heteronormative understandings of gender and sexuality as normatively desirable. My ethnographic investigation of the consumption of Japanese gay media by young gay men reveals that these processes of consumption limit agency within the context of Shinjuku Ni-chōme's gay bars and clubs, inculcating a particularly homonormative understanding of gay desire and identity among the young men who gather there. Thinking back to my discussion with Shōtarō in Lumière, where his reflections over a need to perform a straight-acting identity rendered him visibly upset, I can certainly see how media that have traditionally been theorized as emancipatory instead appear to maintain the heteronormative status quo. But the experiences of my principal informants within the context of the recent LGBT boom demonstrate that hope remains strong among young gay men active in Shinjuku Ni-chōme. In the years to come, it will be increasingly important to understand how hope contours understandings of gender and sexuality in Japan, charting its impacts on a new generation of young consumers from a variety of backgrounds. Furthermore, there will be a need to chart how the regimes of desire investigated in this book may evolve as young people in Japan embrace hope as a method to conceptualize more productive futures that are decidedly emancipatory. It is my own hope that the stories of Junho, Yōichi, Haruma, and Shōtarō provide a fertile ground for launching just such an investigation, with these four men's own hopes, dreams, and experiences inspiring others to challenge the heteronormative and homonormative systems of oppression that continue to circulate throughout Japan and the wider world.

# Glossary of Terms

| | |
|---|---|
| akogare | yearning, longing |
| anime | animated films and TV series, often based on manga |
| bishōnen | beautiful male youth with "soft" masculinity |
| BL (bōizu rabu) | abbreviation of Boys Love; homoerotic media primarily produced for and by heterosexual women |
| dōseiai | homosexuality |
| furītā | "freeter" (employed in casual labor) |
| gaijin | foreigner, especially White foreigners |
| gatai | "hard" muscular body gained through gym training |
| gaten | muscular-yet-chubby body deriving from physical labor |
| gei | gay |
| gei boi | cross-dressing performers popular in the 1960s and 1970s |
| geikomi | homoerotic comics produced for and by gay men |
| gei shoppu | stores where gay media is sold in Shinjuku Ni-chōme |
| GV (geibideo) | Japanese gay pornographic videos |
| hatsukoi | first love |
| hatsutaiken | first sexual experience |
| hayatteru ikemen | popular gay men active on social media, like "influencers" |
| homo | identity category for same-sex-desiring men linked to hard masculinity |
| katai | hard |
| kawaii | cuteness |
| koi | carnal love |
| manga | Japanese style comics |
| minzoku | race/ethnicity |
| nanshoku (danshoku) | premodern discourse of male-male homoerotics |
| nonkerashii/ nonkeppoi | straight-acting |
| nonke | straight man, heterosexual (slang) |
| okama | pejorative term for a gay man, like "faggot" in English |
| onē kyara | cross-dressing performer popular in 1990s to today |
| onēkotoba | camp language that parodies women's speech |
| onnarashii | feminine |

| | |
|---|---|
| otaku | obsessive fans, particularly of anime and manga; geeks/nerds |
| otokorashii | masculine |
| oyaji | old man, old geezer |
| ren'ai | romantic love |
| sakariba | entertainment districts central to Japan's consumer culture |
| sawayaka | hunkiness (on gay dating sites), literally "refreshing" |
| seme | active penetrating partner in a BL text |
| shōjo manga | girls' comics |
| sōshoku-kei danshi | "herbivorous boys," a subculture based in soft masculinity |
| uke | passive penetrated partner in a BL text |
| yaoi | term for amateur BL works common in the 1980s and 1990s |
| zainichi (zainichi kankokujin) | Korean resident in Japan |

## Summary of Types

| | |
|---|---|
| -kei | form, style; a Type that describes an identity |
| amaenbō-kei | Spoiled Type, like "sugar baby" |
| debu-kei | Chubby Type |
| gachimuchi-kei | Muscular-but-Chubby Type |
| gaten-kei | Working-Class Type |
| ikanimo-kei | Obviously Gay Type, privileged in Shinjuku Ni-chōme |
| imafū-kei | Trendy Type |
| janīzu-kei | Johnny's Type, named after idols managed by Johnny's and Associates |
| josō-kei | Cross-Dressing Type, pornography containing cross-dressing men |
| kawaii-kei | Cute Type |
| majime-kei | Serious Type |
| nenpai-kei | Elderly Type |
| oyaji-kei | Old Geezer Type |
| rīman-kei | Salaryman Type |
| supōtsuman-kei | Sportsman Type |
| tai'ikukai-kei | Gym Type |
| yancha-kei | Naughty Type (a mischievous younger man) |
| -sen | specialty; Type describing attributes to which one is attracted |
| dare-sen | someone who will sleep with anyone |
| gai-sen | Foreigner Specialty, prefers White men |
| kawaii-sen | Cute Specialty |
| kuma-sen | Bear Specialty, attracted to bulkier, older men (often hairy) |
| okami-sen | Wolf Specialty, attracted to thin, older men (often hairy) |
| sūtsu-sen | Suits Specialty, attracted to salarymen |
| uri-sen | a man who sells sex; sex worker |

# Notes

## Introduction

1. The terminology used in Japan to refer to same-sex desiring men is complex. The subjects in this book tended to utilize the term *gei*, a Japanese version of the English word "gay" that broadly refers to cis-gendered men who desire other men. This term has the widest currency in contemporary Japan, rising in popularity in the 1990s. Throughout this book, I render this term "gay" for ease of reading. See McLelland, *Male Homosexuality in Modern Japan*, 2.

2. See Maree, *Onēkotoba ron*, 15.

3. See, for example, Sunagawa, *Shinjuku Ni-chōme no bunka jinruigaku*; and Yajima, *Dansei dōseiaisha*.

4. As I argue below, Japan's gay culture is dominated by a supposed "hetero system" that privileges heteronormative understandings of sex and gender. See Fushimi, *Seiyoku mondai*.

5. By heteronormativity, I refer to a globally dominant "regulatory order" that constructs heterosexuality as the default "compulsory" sexuality for all social subjects and that subsequently marginalizes same-sex attraction as "unnatural" and "perverse." See Rich, "Compulsory Heterosexuality"; and Warner, "Introduction."

6. See Rofel, *Desiring China*, for an example of how the post-socialist Chinese state deploys neoliberal cosmopolitanism in its marketization of queerness.

7. Puar, *Terrorist Assemblages*.

8. Duggan, *Twilight of Equality?*, 50.

9. Brown, *Undoing the Demos*, 31.

10. Chasin, *Selling Out*.

11. Duggan, *Twilight of Equality?*, 50.

12. See, for example, Mackintosh, *Homosexuality and Manliness*; and McLelland, *Queer Japan*, for book-length treatments of this point.

13. Tōgō, *Jōshiki o koete*.

14. Ōtsuka, *Ni-chōme kara uroko*.

15. Fushimi, *Gei to iu keiken*.

16. Ryū, "*Kieru Shinjuku Ni-chome.*"

17. Itō and Yanase, *Coming Out in Japan*.

18. Tagame, *Gei karuchā no mirai e.*
19. Stein, "Three Models of Sexuality," 1–2.
20. Nakamura Momoko, "*Onnakotoba.*"
21. Butler, *Gender Trouble*, 173.
22. Connell, *Gender*, 55.
23. Warner, "Introduction."
24. Foucault, *History of Sexuality*, 33.
25. Foucault, 167.
26. Foucault, 28.
27. Foucault, 33.
28. McLelland, *Queer Japan.*
29. Frühstück, *Colonizing Sex*, 2.
30. Fushimi, *Seiyoku mondai.*
31. Maree, "Weddings and White Dresses."
32. Mackie, "Dimensions of citizenship," 203, my emphasis.
33. Fushimi, *Seiyoku mondai*, 21.
34. Fushimi, 68.
35. Nakamura Mia, *Kuia sekusoroji*, 19.
36. In his history of Japan's sexual minority communities, McLelland defines pronatalism as a politico-scientific discourse that views sexual behavior only through the lens of procreation. See McLelland, *Queer Japan*, 32.
37. Fushimi, *Seiyoku mondai*, 71–72.
38. Fushimi, 72.
39. Fushimi, 68.
40. Fushimi, 69.
41. Fushimi, 77.
42. Maree, *Onēkotoba ron*, 15–16.
43. Maree, 16.
44. Maree, 3.
45. See, for example, the criticism raised in Lunsing, "Politics of *Okama.*"
46. See Fushimi et al., *Okama wa sabetsu ka.*
47. Fushimi, *Seiyoku mondai*, 68.
48. See Slater and Galbraith, "Re-Narrating Social Class and Masculinity," n.p.
49. Shirahase, "Demography as Destiny," 11.
50. See Dasgupta, *Re-Reading the Salaryman*; and Mathews, "Being a Man in Straitened Japan."
51. Allison, *Precarious Japan.*
52. Allison, 14.
53. Slater and Galbraith, "Re-Narrating Social Class and Masculinity," n.p.
54. Dasgupta, *Re-Reading the Salaryman*, 2.
55. See, for example, Hidaka, *Salaryman Masculinity*; Roberson, "Fight! Ippatsu!"; and Ueno Chizuko, "Kigyō senshitachi."
56. Dasgupta, *Re-Reading the Salaryman*, 46.
57. Ueno Chizuko, "Kigyō senshitachi."
58. See Connell, *Men and the Boys.*
59. Dasgupta, *Re-Reading the Salaryman*, 7.

60. Connell, *Men and the Boys*, 10.
61. See Kaufman, "Men, Feminism, and Men's Contradictory Experiences," 144.
62. See Roberson, "Becoming *Shakaijin.*"
63. Bardsley, "*Oyaji* Gets a Makeover."
64. See Iida, "Beyond the 'Feminization of Masculinity'"; Darling-Wolf, "Male Bonding and Female Pleasure"; Kinsella, "Narratives and Statistics"; and Prough, *Straight from the Heart*.
65. Miller, *Beauty Up*, 127.
66. Miller, *Beauty Up*, 126.
67. Hambleton, "When Women Watch."
68. See Condry, "Love Revolution"; and Galbraith, "'Otaku Research.'"
69. See Cook, "Expectations of Failure."
70. See Deacon, "All the World's a Stage."
71. Slater and Galbraith, "Re-Narrating Social Class and Masculinity," n.p.
72. Dasgupta, *Re-Reading the Salaryman*, 159–60.
73. Condry, "Love Revolution," 265.
74. D'Emilio, "Capitalism and Gay Identity."
75. Vincent, *Two-Timing Modernity*, 4.
76. Watanabe and Iwata, *Love of Samurai*.
77. Watanabe and Iwata, 16.
78. Pflugfelder, *Cartographies of Desire*, 5.
79. Leupp, *Male Colors*, 72–74.
80. Pflugfelder, *Cartographies of Desire*, 146.
81. Furukawa, "Changing Nature of Sexuality."
82. Pflugfelder, *Cartographies of Desire*, 146.
83. See Angles, *Writing the Love of Boys*; and Reichert, *In the Company of Men*.
84. Angles, *Writing the Love of Boys*, 17–18.
85. Robertson, *Takarazuka*, 68.
86. Frühstück, *Colonizing Sex*, 3.
87. Murakami and Ishida, "Sengo Nihon no zasshi media," 521.
88. Frühstück, *Colonizing Sex*, 3.
89. McLelland, *Love, Sex, and Democracy*.
90. McLelland, 71.
91. Ryang, *Love in Modern Japan*, 64.
92. McLelland, *Queer Japan*, 79.
93. McLelland, 2.
94. Maekawa, *Dansei dōseiaisha no shakaishi*, 61.
95. Murakami and Ishida, "Sengo Nihon no zasshi media," 530.
96. McLelland, *Queer Japan*, 111.
97. Mackintosh, *Homosexuality and Manliness*; and Maekawa, *Dansei dōseiaisha no shakaishi*.
98. For in-depth introductions to each of these magazines, see Mackintosh, *Homosexuality and Manliness*, 63–77.
99. This *homo* culture in the US, tied to macho culture, was critiqued for its homogeneity and for producing "clones." See Levine, *Gay Macho*.
100. See Itō, *Bara yo eien ni*.

101. Suganuma, *Contact Moments*, 132–33.
102. Mackintosh, *Homosexuality and Manliness*, 90.
103. Murakami and Ishida, "Sengo Nihon no zasshi media," 539.
104. See Welker, "Telling Her Story."
105. McLelland, *Queer Japan*, 177.
106. Suganuma, *Contact Moments*, 133.
107. McLelland, *Queer Japan*, 198.
108. McLelland, 177.
109. See McLelland, *Male Homosexuality in Modern Japan*.
110. See Taniguchi, "Legal Situation."
111. McLelland, *Queer Japan*, 212–13.
112. Lunsing, *Beyond Common Sense*; McLelland, *Male Homosexuality in Modern Japan*; and Yajima, *Dansei dōseiaisha*.
113. Shimizu, "Daibāshiti kara," 137.
114. Sunagawa, "Tayō na shihai," 100.
115. Sunagawa, 106.
116. Cameron and Kulick, *Language and Sexuality*, 109–10.
117. Deleuze and Guattari, *Thousand Plateaus*.
118. Vance, "Anthropology Rediscovers Sexuality."
119. Ahmed, *Queer Phenomenology*.
120. Butler, *Gender Trouble*, 197.
121. Cameron and Kulick, *Language and Sexuality*, 104.
122. Cameron and Kulick, *Language and Sexuality*, 104.
123. Butler, *Gender Trouble*, 197, original emphasis.
124. See Karatani, "Discursive Space of Modern Japan"; and Miyoshi, *Off Center*.
125. Kelsky, *Women on the Verge*, 21.
126. Cameron and Kulick, *Language and Sexuality*, 103.
127. Cameron and Kulick, 133.
128. See Ahmed, *Queer Phenomenology*.
129. Cameron and Kulick, *Language and Sexuality*, 107.
130. Cameron and Kulick, 114.
131. Cameron and Kulick, 110–11.
132. Brown, *Undoing the Demos*, 28.
133. Ahmed, "Affective Economies," 117, 119.
134. Berlant, *Cruel Optimism*, 24–25.
135. Money Scoop, "*1000-en de koibito ga dekiru?*"
136. For examples, see Maekawa, *Dansei dōseiaisha no shakaishi*; McLelland, *Male Homosexuality in Modern Japan*; and Yajima, *Dansei dōseiaisha*.
137. Hall, "Encoding/Decoding."
138. Halberstam, *Female Masculinity*, 13.
139. Schein, "Homeland Beauty," 205–6.
140. Miller, *Beauty Up*, 15.
141. For an extended discussion of the necessity for reflexivity in contemporary ethnographic practice, see Shah, "Ethnography?"
142. Moriyama, *Gei komyuniti*, 160.
143. Weiss, "Always After," 634.

144. See Gill, *Yokohama Street Life*.
145. Shah, "Ethnography?," 49
146. Shah, 49.
147. Szabó and Troyer, "Inclusive Ethnographies," 309.
148. Szabó and Troyer, 307.


Chapter One

1. Brown, *Undoing the Demos*, 28.
2. Simply put, an intercept interview refers to approaching a potential informant in the field and conducting a brief conversation to clarify one's observations. My intercept interviews often expanded into longer conversations about masculinity, media, and gay desire. For a broader discussion of this ethnographic practice, see Gudelunas, "There's an App for That."
3. Ishida, "Jendā to sekushuariti no shinkūken."
4. McLelland, *Queer Japan*, 77.
5. See Fujime, "Japanese Feminism and Commercialised Sex."
6. Suganuma, "Ways of Speaking about Queer Space in Tokyo," 352.
7. Suganuma, 349.
8. Ōtsuka, *Ni-chōme kara uroko*.
9. For an extended study of the influences of urban development on sexual minority community spaces in North America and Europe, see Abraham, *Metropolitan Lovers*.
10. D'Emilio, "Capitalism and Gay Identity."
11. See Hanhardt, *Safe Space*, 9–15.
12. Hanhardt, 185–89.
13. Chasin, *Selling Out*, 184.
14. Tipton, "Faces of New Tokyo," 186.
15. Takeyama, *Staged Seduction*, 24.
16. Sunagawa, *Shinjuku Ni-chōme no bunka jinruigaku*.
17. Sunagawa, 197.
18. Sunagawa, 300.
19. Suganuma, "Ways of Speaking about Queer Space in Tokyo."
20. Suganuma, 353.
21. Suganuma, 348.
22. Berlant and Warner, "Sex in Public," 563.
23. Ahmed, *Queer Phenomenology*.
24. Bell and Binnie, "Authenticating Queer Space," 18.
25. Suganuma, "Ways of Speaking about Queer Space in Tokyo," 357.
26. Sunagawa, *Shinjuku Ni-chōme no bunka jinruigaku*, 105.
27. Sunagawa, 328.
28. See Isoda, *Shisō toshite no Tōkyō*.
29. See Wallace, "Stepping Up."
30. Lunsing, "Kono sekai."
31. Lunsing, 68.
32. Ryū, "*Kieru Shinjuku Ni-chome*," 181.

33. Ryū, 187.
34. Ryū, 180.
35. For an explication of the Tokyo Metropolitan Government's urban renewal plans for Shinjuku, see Tonuma, *Shinjuku gaku*.
36. Allison, *Precarious Japan*, 8.
37. Abe, "Lesbian Bar Talk in Shinjuku, Tokyo," 210.
38. Lunsing, "Kono sekai," 58.
39. Rather than adopting a translation approach that "domesticates" this phrase to the English expression "gay shop" (a term that has very little currency in English-language usage), I choose to signal the particularly Japanese tendency of creatively deploying "Japan-made English" (*wasei eigo*) throughout this book by rendering this term in transliteration. In so doing, I hope to signal that these stores represent important cultural nodes in Ni-chōme and should be treated as a distinct Japanese cultural formulation despite its purported borrowing from English.
40. Fushimi, *Dōseai Nyūmon*, 54.
41. Fushimi, 103.
42. For examples, see Allison, *Permitted and Prohibited Desires*; and Bornoff, *Pink Samurai*.
43. Abidin, "Influencer Extravaganza," 159.
44. Morimura, *Guiding Your Friends around Ni-chōme*, 110.
45. Moriyama, "'Ni-chōme ni suteru gomi nashi,'" 246.
46. Morimura, *Guiding Your Friends around Ni-chōme*, 86.
47. Morimura, 84.
48. Morimura, 80.
49. Ryū, "*Kieru Shinjuku Ni-chome*."
50. McNair, *Porno? Chic!*, 3.
51. For a discussion of young people's positive views of pornography, focusing on Australia, see McKee, Albury, and Lumby, *Porn Report*.
52. McNair, *Porno? Chic!*, 121.
53. Takeyama, *Staged Seduction*, 23.
54. Takeyama, 27.
55. Toshiya Ueno, "Techno-Orientalism and Media-Tribalism," 96–97.
56. Takeyama, *Staged Seduction*, 38.
57. Sunagawa, *Shinjuku ni-chōme no bunka jinruigaku*.
58. Moriyama, *Gei komyuniti*, 170.
59. See Maekawa, *Dansei dōseiaisha no shakaishi*, 78.
60. Mackintosh, *Homosexuality and Manliness*, 137.
61. Ōtsuka, *Ni-chōme kara uroko*.
62. See Kabiya, "Gei bā no seitai."
63. Clammer, *Contemporary Urban Japan*, 11.
64. Moriyama, *Gei komyuniti*, 160.
65. Chasin, *Selling Out*.
66. Brown, *Undoing the Demos*, 28.
67. Moriyama, *Gei komyuniti*, 44.
68. Ishida, "Jendā to sekushuariti no shinkūken," 84.
69. See Ishida, "Tachi/neko, seme/uke," 385–86.

70. Baudinette, "Ethnosexual Frontiers in Queer Tokyo," 469.

71. Suganuma, *Contact Moments*, 95.

72. Suganuma, *Contact Moments*, 84.

73. Kawai, "Deracialised Race," 28.

74. Kelsky, *Women on the Verge*, 28.

75. For examples of such men and their attitudes, see McLelland, *Male Homosexuality in Modern Japan*, 171–73.

76. Morimura, *Guiding Your Friends around Ni-chōme*, 34, my emphasis.

77. Moriyama, *Gei komyuniti*, 170–71.

78. Moriyama, 170.

79. For an in-depth discussion and critique of this trend, see Padva, "Heavenly Monsters."

80. Kong, *Chinese Male Homosexualities*, 82.

81. See Baudinette, "Cosmopolitan English, Traditional Japanese."

82. Puar, *Terrorist Assemblages*.

83. Duggan, *Twilight of Equality?*, 50.

84. Baudinette, "Constructing Identities on a Japanese Gay Dating Site," 253.

85. Baudinette, "Spatialisation of Desire," 519.

86. Baudinette, 513.

87. For an extended critique of the global homogenization of queer culture, see Bernstein Sycamore, *Why Are Faggots So Afraid of Faggots?*

88. Duggan, *Twilight of Equality?*

89. Moriyama, *Gei komyuniti*, 159.

90. Ahmed, *Queer Phenomenology*.

91. See Baudinette, "Spatialisation of Desire."

Chapter Two

1. To protect the key informants' anonymity, I have assigned pseudonyms.

2. For a discussion of the increasing valorization of overseas experience among young people, see Kawashima, "Japanese Working Holiday Makers."

3. Layder, *Modern Social Theory*, 47.

4. Layder, 49.

5. Layder, 50.

6. Layder, 49.

7. Stake, *Art of the Case Study*.

8. Schein, "Homeland Beauty," 206.

9. Korean residents became able to naturalize and become full Japanese citizens in the late 1960s, and as many as 10,000 Korean residents in Japan choose to naturalize each year. See Chapman, *Zainichi Korean Identity and Ethnicity*, 54–55.

10. For an in-depth ethnography of Japan's hostess bars, see Allison, *Nightwork*.

11. See Allison, *Precarious Japan*.

12. Yōichi's decision to travel throughout Southeast Asia mirrors the experiences of Japanese gay men in the early 1990s who found the region a safe space to explore their sexuality. See Suganuma, *Contact Moments*, 96.

13. Leach, "Gay Japanese Pornstar Masaki Koh Dead Age 29."

14. This name is also a pseudonym.

15. See Baudinette, "Evaluation of Physicality."

16. McLelland and Welker, "Introduction to 'Boys Love' in Japan," 3.

17. See Nishimura, *BL karuchā-ron*, 127. These concepts are also explored briefly in chapter 3.

18. My key interlocutors therefore differ to the men surveyed in previous work by McLelland. See McLelland, *Male Homosexuality in Modern Japan*, 174–76.

19. Ryang, *Love in Modern Japan*, 14.

20. Ryang, 13.

21. McLelland, *Love, Sex, and Democracy*, 15.

22. See Garon, *Molding Japanese Minds*, 100.

23. Suganuma, *Contact Moments*, 142.

24. McLelland, *Male Homosexuality in Modern Japan*; and Yajima, *Dansei dōseiaisha*.

25. Suganuma, *Contact Moments*, 191–92.

26. See Dörnyei, *Research Methods*, 138–39.

27. Jenkins, *Convergence Culture*, 2.

28. Galbraith and Karlin, *Media Convergence in Japan*, 2–3.

29. McLelland and Welker, "Introduction to 'Boys Love' in Japan," 3.

30. McLelland, *Male Homosexuality in Modern Japan*, 150.

Chapter Three

1. Miller, *Beauty Up*, 152.

2. Miller, 127.

3. Ibid.

4. Miller, 130.

5. Miller, 126.

6. Fushimi, *Seiyoku mondai*.

7. Duggan, *Twilight of Equality?*, 50.

8. Bernstein Sycamore, *Why Are Faggots So Afraid of Faggots?*

9. Andreasson and Johansson, "New Fitness Geography."

10. Miller, *Beauty Up*, 152–53.

11. Dasgupta, *Re-Reading the Salaryman*, 44.

12. Slater and Galbraith, "Re-Narrating Social Class and Masculinity," unpaginated.

13. Within young women's popular culture, a trend emerged where men's faces were categorized according to various condiments. A salty face was one of the faces understood as cute (*kawaii*).

14. See, for example, Dale, "Cute Studies"; and Pujar, "Korean Cuties."

15. See Ōta, "Janīzu no sengoshi."

16. Miller, *Beauty Up*, 130.

17. Yonezawa, interviewed by Prough, *Straight from the Heart*, 110.

18. Prough, 117–18.

19. Prough, 121.

20. Miller, *Beauty Up*, 126.

21. See Galbraith, "'Otaku Research.'"

22. See Furuya, *Wakamono wa hontō ukeika*.

23. McLelland, *Queer Japan*, 111.

24. For an extended historical discussion of these magazines, see Mackintosh, *Homosexuality and Manliness*.

25. Mackintosh, 163.

26. I borrow this classification of Mishima from Vincent, *Two-Timing Modernity*, 175.

27. Vincent, 176.

28. Mishima, "Bungaku ni okeru kōha."

29. Angles, *Writing the Love of Boys*, 17–18.

30. Mishima, "Bungaku ni okeru kōha." For Mishima's critique of the decadence of "Western" romance, see Mishima, *Shin ren'ai kōza*.

31. Lorcin, "Imperial Nostalgia; Colonial Nostalgia," 97.

32. Mishima, *Sun and Steel*, 17.

33. Mishima, 18–19.

34. Fushimi, *Gei to iu keiken*, 355.

35. Mishima, *Sun and Steel*, 41.

36. Mishima, 42.

37. Bernstein Sycamore, *Why Are Faggots So Afraid of Faggots?*

38. McLelland and Welker, "Introduction to 'Boys Love' in Japan," 3.

39. See Lunsing, "Yaoi Ronso"; and Tagame, "Gei erotikku āto no shinzui."

40. See Baudinette, "Evaluation of Physicality."

41. Baudinette, 115.

42. McLelland, *Male Homosexuality in Modern Japan*, 69.

43. Mackintosh, *Homosexuality and Manliness*, 18.

44. Ishida, "Representational Appropriation," 221.

45. Ishida, 221–22.

46. Tagame, "Gei erotikku āto no shinzui," 116.

47. See Baudinette, "Evaluation of Physicality," 118.

48. See Lunsing, "*Yaoi ronsō*."

49. See Satō, "Shōjo manga to homofobia."

50. See Tagame, "Gei erotikku āto no shinzui."

51. Fujimoto, *Watashi no ibasho wa doko ni aru no?*; and Mizuma, *In'yu to shite no shōnen'ai*.

52. Ishida, "Representational Appropriation," 217.


Chapter Four

1. McKee, Albury, and Lumby, *Porn Report*, 84–85.

2. See Jacobs, "Internationalizing Porn Studies."

3. McNair, *Porno? Chic!*, 1.

4. Wong and Yau, *Japanese Adult Video Industry*.

5. Jacobs, "Internationalizing Porn Studies," 115.

6. See Mercer, "Homosexual Prototypes."

7. Jacobs, "Internationalizing Porn Studies," 115.
8. Duggan, *Twilight of Equality?*; and Puar, *Terrorist Assemblages*.
9. See Nguyen, *View From the Bottom*.
10. Fushimi, *Gei to iu keiken*, 169.
11. Kawamoto, *Poruno zasshi no Shōwa-shi*, 18.
12. These statistics are derived from estimates published in Inoue, *AV Sangyō*.
13. See Richie, *Lateral View*, 156.
14. Sharp, *Behind the Pink Curtain*, 300.
15. Sharp, 301.
16. Wong and Yau, *Japanese Adult Video Industry*, 48.
17. McLelland, *Male Homosexuality in Modern Japan*, 141.
18. McLelland, 154.
19. See Mercer, "Homosexual Prototypes."
20. McLelland, "Sex, Censorship and Media Regulation," 410.
21. This practice in Japanese porn's cinematography represents a disruption of the hard-core porn narrative that typifies Western films, as elucidated by Williams, *Hard Core*.
22. Wong and Yau, *Japanese Adult Video Industry*, 43.
23. This practice is also common in AV. See Suzuki, *AV Joyū no shakaigaku*.
24. See Berg, "'A Scene Is Just a Marketing Tool.'"
25. Club CK, http://www.coat.co.jp/
26. Ahmed, *Queer Phenomenology*.
27. I note that there was some minor variation in naming practices across the corpus, with some companies using *asurīto-kei* instead of *tai'ikukai-kei* or *janīzu-kei* instead of *kawaii-kei*. Conversations with the men I met during fieldwork revealed that the differences in naming practice were superficial, and it is for this reason I have chosen to group works via the five most commonly used Types.
28. Fushimi, *Seiyoku mondai*, 71–72.
29. See Escoffier, "Gay-for-Pay."
30. This is the case because passive structures and the modal verb *shimau*, which denotes finality and completion, are typically utilized in Japanese to either express unwillingness or a sense of completion with negative outcomes. See Shibatani, *Languages of Japan*.
31. See Williams, *Hard Core*.
32. See Hambleton, "When Women Watch."
33. Mackintosh, *Homosexuality and Manliness*, 170–78.

Chapter Five

1. See Zenkoku Zasshi Kyōkai, *2017-nen shuppan ichiba*.
2. Miller, "There's More Than *Manga*," 320.
3. Miller, 321.
4. Miller, 322.
5. Clammer, *Contemporary Urban Japan*, 118.
6. Ivy, "Formations of Mass Culture," 254.

7. Lukács, *Scripted Affects*, 121.
8. Clammer, *Contemporary Urban Japan*, 112–13.
9. Monden, *Japanese Fashion Cultures*; and Hambleton, "Women and Sexual Desire."
10. Moriyama, *Gei komyuniti*, 146–71.
11. Abe, "Community of Manners."
12. Clammer, *Contemporary Urban Japan*, 115.
13. Clammer, 115.
14. Moeran, "Elegance and Substance Travel East," 234.
15. McLelland, *Male Homosexuality in Modern Japan*, 61.
16. Abe, "Community of Manners," 200.
17. Abe, 201.
18. Baudinette, "Evaluation of Physicality," 121.
19. Hall, "Encoding/Decoding."
20. *Bádi*, March 2012, 42, my emphasis.
21. Miller, *Beauty Up*, 129.
22. Miller, 2.
23. See Monden, *Japanese Fashion Cultures*, 45–76.
24. Lukács, *Scripted Affects*, 7.
25. Lukács, 42.
26. Brown, *Undoing the Demos*, 28.
27. Lukács, *Scripted Affects*, 43.
28. See Padva, "Heavenly Monsters."
29. Duggan, *Twilight of Equality?*, 50.
30. Moriyama, *Gei komyuniti*, 160.
31. McCracken, *Decoding Women's Magazines*, 169.
32. Corrigan, *Sociology of Consumption*, 87.
33. Lukács, *Scripted Affects*, 43.
34. See Charlesbois, "Herbivore Masculinity"
35. Fushimi, *Seiyoku mondai*.
36. Duggan, *Twilight of Equality?*, 50.
37. See Baudinette, "Spatialisation of Desire."
38. See Baudinette, "Cosmopolitan English, Traditional Japanese."
39. Ahmed, "Affective Economies."
40. Lukács, *Scripted Affects*, 43.
41. Lukács, 8.
42. McLelland, *Male Homosexuality in Modern Japan*; and Yajima, *Dansei dōseiaisha*.
43. Sunagawa, "Tayō na shihai."
44. Fushimi, *Seiyoku mondai*, 71–72.

## Chapter Six

1. Whitty, "Art of Selling One's 'Self.'"
2. Whitty, 64.
3. Whitty, 68.

4. For example, see Bogetić, "Normal Straight Gays"; and Milani, "Are 'Queers' Really 'Queer'?"

5. The name JP MEN'S CLUB is a pseudonym for this service. I have chosen to anonymize this data and hide the URL in accordance with advice given by the human research ethics committees at the institutions that hosted me while I conducted my fieldwork. Although JP MEN'S CLUB is a publicly accessible website and the posts made to the dating service are visible without registration, users post with a reasonable expectation for privacy, and anonymizing the website is an important method of protecting this privacy. See Baudinette, "Constructing Identities on a Japanese Gay Dating Site," 239–40.

6. Baudinette, 245–46.

7. Previously published in Baudinette, 245.

8. Milani, "Are 'Queers' Really 'Queer'?"

9. For a comparative history of English and Japanese gay slang, see Long, "Formation Processes of Some Japanese Gay Argot Terms."

10. Baudinette, "Constructing Identities on a Japanese Gay Dating Site," 247.

11. Baudinette, 249.

12. Baudinette, 249.

13. Baudinette, 250.

14. Baudinette, 250.

15. Baudinette, 250.

16. Baudinette, 256–57.

17. Previously published in Baudinette, 257.

18. Baudinette, 255.

19. Bernstein Sycamore, *Why Are Faggots So Afraid of Faggots?*

20. Duggan, *Twilight of Equality?*, 50.

21. Clammer, *Contemporary Urban Japan*, 10–12.

22. Baudinette, "Ethnosexual Frontiers in Queer Tokyo," 474.

23. Baudinette, 473.

24. Baudinette, 478.

25. Baudinette, 475.

26. This may possibly be due to the supposed invisibility of Asian foreigners in Nichōme. See Baudinette, "Ethnosexual Frontiers in Queer Tokyo," 473.

27. Brown, *Undoing the Demos*, 28.

28. See Allison, *Precarious Japan*.

29. Althusser, "Ideology and Ideological State Apparatuses."

30. Althusser, 162.

31. Althusser, 174.

32. Althusser, 174.

33. Takeyama, *Staged Seduction*.

34. Lukács, *Scripted Affects*; and Takeyama, *Staged Seduction*.

35. Ahmed, *Queer Phenomenology*.

36. Duggan, *Twilight of Equality?*, 50.

## Conclusion

1. Fushimi, *Seiyoku mondai.*
2. Berlant, *Cruel Optimism.*
3. Sunagawa, "Tayō na shihai," 100.
4. Fushimi, *Seiyoku mondai.*
5. Brown, *Undoing the Demos*, 28.
6. Berlant, *Cruel Optimism*, 1.
7. Berlant, 25.
8. Berlant, 24.
9. Berlant, 15.
10. Duggan, *Twilight of Equality?*, 50.
11. Allison, *Precarious Japan*, 15.
12. Allison, 31.
13. See Genda, *Kibōgaku.*
14. See Shimizu, "Daibāshiti kara"; and Maree, "Writing Sexual Identity."
15. Genda, *Kibōgaku.*
16. Miyazaki, *Method of Hope*, 5.
17. Miyazaki, 11.
18. Brown, *Undoing the Demos*, 28.
19. Miyazaki, *Method of Hope*, 19.
20. Shimizu, "Daibāshiti kara," 137.
21. Shimizu, 138.
22. Shimizu, 138–39.
23. Shimizu, 140.
24. Muñoz, *Cruising Utopia*, 1–3.
25. Ahmed, *Queer Phenomenology.*

# References

Abe, Hideko. "A Community of Manners: Advice Columns in Lesbian and Gay Magazines in Japan." In *Manners and Mischief: Gender, Power, and Etiquette in Japan*, ed. Jan Bardsley and Laura Miller, 196–218. Berkeley: University of California Press, 2011.

Abe, Hideko. "Lesbian Bar Talk in Shinjuku, Tokyo." In *Japanese Language, Gender, and Ideology: Cultural Models and Real People*, ed. Janet Shibamoto Smith and Shigeko Okamoto, 205–21. Oxford: Oxford University Press, 2004.

Abidin, Crystal. "Influencer Extravaganza: A Decade of Commercial 'Lifestyle' Micro-celebrities in Singapore." In *Routledge Companion to Digital Ethnography*, ed. Larissa Hjorth, Heather Horst, Genevieve Bell, and Anne Galloway, 158–68. London: Routledge, 2017.

Abraham, Julie. *Metropolitan Lovers: The Homosexuality of Cities*. Minneapolis: University of Minnesota Press, 2009.

Ahmed, Sara. "Affective Economies." *Social Text* 22.2 (2004): 117–39.

Ahmed, Sara. *Queer Phenomenology: Orientations, Objects, Others*. Durham, NC: Duke University Press, 2006.

Allison, Anne. *Nightwork: Sexuality, Pleasure, and Corporate Masculinity in a Tokyo Hostess Club*. Chicago: University of Chicago Press, 1994.

Allison, Anne. *Permitted and Prohibited Desires: Mothers, Comics, and Censorship in Japan*. Berkeley: University of California Press, 2000.

Allison, Anne. *Precarious Japan*. Durham, NC: Duke University Press, 2013.

Althusser, Louis. "Ideology and Ideological State Apparatuses." In *Lenin and Philosophy and Other Essays*, ed. Louis Althusser, 127–86. New York: Monthly Review Press, 1971.

Andreasson, Jesper, and Thomas Johansson. "The New Fitness Geography: The Globalization of Japanese Gym and Fitness Culture." *Leisure Studies* 36.3 (2017): 383–94.

Angles, Jeffrey. *Writing the Love of Boys: Origins of Bishōnen Culture in Modernist Japanese Literature*. Minneapolis: University of Minnesota Press, 2011.

Bardsley, Jan. "The *Oyaji* Gets a Makeover: Guides for Japanese Salarymen in the New Millennium." In *Manners and Mischief: Gender, Power, and Etiquette in Japan*, ed. Jan Bardsley and Laura Miller, 114–35. Berkeley: University of California Press, 2011.

Baudinette, Thomas. "An Evaluation of Physicality in the *Bara* Manga of *Bádi* Magazine." In *Manga Vision: Cultural and Communicative Perspectives*, ed. Sarah Pasfield-Neofitou and Cathy Sell, 107–24. Melbourne: Monash University Press, 2016.

Baudinette, Thomas. "Constructing Identities on a Japanese Gay Dating Site: Hunkiness, Cuteness, and the Desire for Heteronormative Masculinity." *Journal of Language and Sexuality* 6.2 (2017): 232–61.

Baudinette, Thomas. "Cosmopolitan English, Traditional Japanese: Reading Language Desire into the Signage of Tokyo's Gay District." *Linguistic Landscape* 4.3 (2018): 238–56.

Baudinette, Thomas. "Ethnosexual Frontiers in Queer Tokyo: The Production of Racialised Desire in Japan." *Japan Forum* 28.4 (2016): 465–85.

Baudinette, Thomas. "The Spatialisation of Desire in a Japanese Gay District through Signage." *ACME* 28.3 (2017): 500–527. http://acme-journal.org/index.php/acme/article/view/1357

Bell, David, and Jon Binnie. "Authenticating Queer Space: Citizenship, Urbanism and Governance." *Urban Studies* 41.9 (2004): 1807–20.

Berg, Heather. "'A Scene Is Just a Marketing Tool': Alternative Income Streams in Porn's Gig Economy." *Porn Studies* 3.2 (2016): 160–74.

Berlant, Lauren. *Cruel Optimism*. Durham, NC: Duke University Press, 2011.

Berlant, Lauren, and Michael Warner. "Sex in Public." *Critical Inquiry* 2.2 (1998): 547–66.

Bernstein Sycamore, Mattilda. *Why Are Faggots So Afraid of Faggots? Flaming Challenges to Masculinity, Objectification, and the Desire to Conform*. Oakland, CA: AK Press, 2012.

Bogetić, Ksenija. "Normal Straight Gays: Lexical Collocations and Ideologies of Masculinity in Personal Ads of Serbian Gay Teenagers." *Gender and Language* 7.3 (2013): 333–67.

Bornoff, Nicholas. *Pink Samurai: The Pursuit and Politics of Sex in Japan*. London: Grafton, 1991.

Brown, Wendy. *Undoing the Demos: Neoliberalism's Stealth Revolution*. Brooklyn: Zone Books, 2015.

Butler, Judith. *Gender Trouble: Feminism and the Subversion of Identity*, 2nd ed. New York: Routledge, 1999.

Cameron, Deborah, and Don Kulick. *Language and Sexuality*. Cambridge: Cambridge University Press, 2003.

Chapman, David. *Zainichi Korean Identity and Ethnicity*. London: Routledge, 2008.

Charlebois, Justin. "Herbivore Masculinity as an Oppositional Form of Masculinity." *Culture, Society and Masculinities* 5.1 (2013): 89–104.

Chasin, Alexandra. *Selling Out: The Gay and Lesbian Movement Goes to Market*. New York: St Martin's Press, 2000.

Clammer, John. *Contemporary Urban Japan: A Sociology of Consumption*. Malden, MA: Blackwell, 1997.

Condry, Ian. "Love Revolution: Anime, Masculinity, and the Future." In *Recreating Japanese Men*, ed. Sabine Frühstück and Anne Walthall, 262–83. Berkeley: University of California Press, 2011.

Connell, R. W. *Gender*. Cambridge, UK: Polity, 2002.

Connell, R. W. *The Men and the Boys*. St. Leonards, Australia: Allen and Unwin, 2000.

Cook, Emma. "Expectations of Failure: Maturity and Masculinity for Freeters in Contemporary Japan." *Social Science Journal Japan* 16.1 (2013): 29–43.

Corrigan, Peter. *The Sociology of Consumption: An Introduction*. Thousand Oaks, CA: Sage, 1997.

Dale, Joshua Paul. "Cute Studies: An Emerging Field." *East Asian Journal of Popular Culture* 2.1 (2016): 5–13.

Darling-Wolf, Fabienne. "Male Bonding and Female Pleasure: Refining Masculinity in Japanese Popular Cultural Texts." *Popular Communication* 1.2 (2003): 73–88.

Dasgupta, Romit. *Re-Reading the Salaryman in Japan: Crafting Masculinities.* London: Routledge, 2013.

Deacon, Chris. "All the World's a Stage: Herbivore Boys and the Performance of Masculinity in Contemporary Japan." In *Manga Girl Seeks Herbivore Boy: Studying Japanese Gender at Cambridge*, ed. Brigitte Steger and Angelika Koch, 129–76. Zurich: LIT Verlag, 2013.

Deleuze, Gilles and Félix Guattari, *A Thousand Plateaus: Schizophrenia and Capitalism.* Trans. Brian Massumi. Minneapolis: University of Minnesota Press, 1987.

D'Emilio, John. "Capitalism and Gay Identity." In *The Lesbian and Gay Studies Reader*, ed. Henry Abelove, Michèle Aina Barale, and David Halperin, 467–76. New York: Routledge, 1993.

Dörnyei, Zoltán. *Research Methods in Applied Linguistics.* Oxford: Oxford University Press, 2007.

Duggan, Lisa. *The Twilight of Equality? Neoliberalism, Cultural Politics and the Attack on Democracy.* Boston: Beacon Press, 2003.

Escoffier, Jeffrey. "Gay-for-Pay: Straight Men and the Making of Gay Pornography." *Qualitative Sociology* 26.4 (2003): 531–55.

Foucault, Michel. *The History of Sexuality, Volume 1: An Introduction.* Trans. Robert Hurley. New York: Vintage, 1978.

Frühstück, Sabine. *Colonizing Sex: Sexology and Social Control in Modern Japan.* Berkeley: University of California Press, 2003.

Fujime, Yuki. "Japanese Feminism and Commercialised Sex: The Union of Militarism and Prohibitionism." *Social Science Journal Japan* 9.1 (2006): 33–50.

Fujimoto Yukari. *Watashi no ibasho wa doko ni aru no? Shōjo manga ga utsutsu kokoro no katachi* [Where is the place that I belong? The shape of the heart as reflected in girls' comics]. Tokyo: Gakuyō Shobō, 1998.

Furukawa, Makoto. "The Changing Nature of Sexuality: The Three Codes Framing Homosexuality in Modern Japan." *U.S.-Japan Women's Journal English Supplement* 7 (1994): 98–127.

Furuya Tsunehira. *Wakamono wa hontō ni ukeika shite iru no ka?* [Are young people really tending to the right?]. Tokyo: Asupekuto, 2014.

Fushimi Noriaki. *Dōseiai nyūmon* [Introduction to homosexuality]. Tokyo: Potto Shuppan, 2003.

Fushimi Noriaki. *Gei to iu keiken: Zōhoban* [The experience called being gay: Extended version]. Tokyo, Potto Shuppan, 2004.

Fushimi Noriaki. *Seiyoku mondai: Hito wa sabetsu o nukusu tame dake ni ikiru no de wa nai* [The problem of sexual desire: People do not just live in order to remove discrimination]. Tokyo: Potto Shuppan, 2007.

Fushimi Noriaki, Oikawa Kenji, Noguchi Katsuzo, Matsuzawa Kureichi, Kurokawa Nobuyuki, and Yamanaki Toshiko, eds. *Okama wa sabetsu ka? "Shūkan kin'yōbi" no sabetsu hyōgen jiken* [Is okama discriminatory? The "Weekly Friday" discriminatory expression incident]. Tokyo: Potto Shuppan, 2002.

Galbraith, Patrick. "'Otaku Research' and Anxiety about Failed Men." In *Debating Otaku in Contemporary Japan: Historical Perspectives and New Horizons*, ed. Patrick Galbraith, Thiam Huat Kam, and Björn-Ole Kamm, 21–34. London: Bloomsbury, 2015.

Galbraith, Patrick, and Jason Karlin, eds. *Media Convergence in Japan*. Tokyo: Kinema Club, 2016.

Garon, Sheldon. *Molding Japanese Minds: The State in Everyday Life*. Princeton, NJ: Princeton University Press, 1997.

Genda Yūji, ed. *Kibōgaku* [Hope studies]. Tokyo: Chuō Kōron Shinsha, 2006.

Gill, Tom. *Yokohama Street Life: The Precarious Career of a Japanese Day Laborer*. Lanham, MD: Lexington Books, 2015.

Gudelunas, David. "There's an App for That: The Uses and Gratifications of Online Social Networks for Gay Men." *Sexuality and Culture* 16 (2012): 347–65.

Halberstam, Jack. *Female Masculinity*. Durham, NC: Duke University Press, 1998.

Hall, Stuart. "Encoding/Decoding." In *Culture, Media, Language: Working Papers in Cultural Studies, 1972–79*, ed. Centre for Contemporary Cultural Studies, 128–38. London: Hutchinson, 1980.

Hambleton, Alexandra. "When Women Watch: The Subversive Potential of Female-Friendly Pornography in Japan." *Porn Studies* 3.4 (2016): 427–42.

Hambleton, Alexandra. "Women and Sexual Desire in the Japanese Popular Media." In *Women and Media in Asia*, ed. Youna Kim, 115–29. Houndsmill, UK: Palgrave, 2012.

Hanhardt, Christina B. *Safe Space: Gay Neighborhood History and the Politics of Violence*. Durham, NC: Duke University Press, 2013.

Hidaka, Tomoko. *Salaryman Masculinity: Continuity and Change in Hegemonic Masculinity in Japan*. Leiden: Brill, 2010.

Iida, Yumiko. "Beyond the 'Feminization of Masculinity': Transforming Patriarchy with the 'Feminine' in Contemporary Japanese Youth Culture." *Inter-Asian Cultural Studies* 6.1 (2005): 56–74.

Inoue Setsuko. *AV Sangyō: Itchōen shijō no mekanizumu* [The AV industry: Mechanisms of a one billion yen marketplace]. Tokyo: Shinhyōron, 2002.

Ishida Hitoshi. "Jendā to sekushuariti no shinkūken: Shinjuku Ni-chōme ni okeru shōteki sōgo kōi jissen" [Gender and sexuality's categorical vacuum: The commercial interaction practices in Shinjuku Ni-chōme's gay bars]. *Chuō daigaku bungakubu kiyō* 14 (2004): 81–98.

Ishida, Hitoshi. "Representational Appropriation and the Autonomy of Desire in *Yaoi/BL*." Trans. Katsuhiko Suganuma. In *Boys Love Manga and Beyond: History, Culture, and Community in Japan*, ed. Mark McLelland, Kazumi Nagaike, Katsuhiko Suganuma, and James Welker, 210–32. Jackson: University Press of Mississippi, 2015.

Ishida, Hitoshi. "Tachi/neko, seme/uke" [Top/bottom, attacker/receiver]. In *Seiteki na kotoba* [Sexual language], ed. Shōichi Inoue, Hikaru Saitō, Tomomi Shibuya, and Junko Mitsuhashi, 384–90. Tokyo: Kōdansha Gendai shinsho, 2010.

Isoda Kōichi. *Shisō toshite no Tōkyō: Kindai bungaku shiron nōto* [Tokyo as idea: Notes for a historical treatise on modern literature]. Tokyo: Kokubunsha, 1989.

Itō Bungaku. *Bara yo eien ni: Barazoku henshūchō 35-nen no tatakai* [Roses for eternity: The 35-year battle of Barazoku's editor-in-chief]. Tokyo: Kyūtensha, 2006.

Ito, Satoru, and Yanase, Ryuta. *Coming Out in Japan*. Trans. Francis Conlan. Melbourne: Trans Pacific Press, 2001.

Ivy, Marilyn. "Formations of Mass Culture." In *Postwar Japan as History*, ed. Andrew Gordon, 239–58. Berkeley: University of California Press, 1993.

Jacobs, Katrien. "Internationalising Porn Studies." *Porn Studies* 1.1–2 (2014): 113–19.

Jenkins, Henry. *Convergence Culture: Where Old and New Media Collide*. New York: New York University Press, 2006.

Kabiya Kazuhiko. "Gei bā no seitai" [The lifestyles of the gay bars]. *Amatoria* (July 1955): 38–46.

Karatani, Kojin. "The Discursive Space of Modern Japan." In *Japan in the World*, ed. Masao Miyoshi and Harry Harootunian, 288–315. Durham, NC: Duke University Press, 1993.

Kaufman, Michael. "Men, Feminism, and Men's Contradictory Experiences of Power." In *Theorizing Masculinities*, ed. Harry Brod and Michael Kaufman, 142–63. Thousand Oaks, CA: Sage, 1994.

Kawai, Yuko. "Deracialised Race, Obscured Racism: Japaneseness, Western and Japanese Concepts of Race, and Modalities of Racism." *Japanese Studies* 35.1 (2015): 23–47.

Kawamoto Kōji. *Poruno zasshi no Shōwa-shi* [A history of porn magazines in the Showa era]. Tokyo: Chikuma Shinsho, 2011.

Kawashima, Kumiko. "Japanese Working Holiday Makers in Australia and Their Relationship to the Labour Market in Japan: Before and After." *Asian Studies Review* 34.3 (2010): 267–86.

Kelsky, Karen. *Women on the Verge: Japanese Women, Western Dreams*. Durham, NC: Duke University Press, 2001.

Kinsella, Sharon. "Narratives and Statistics: How Compensated Dating (Enjo Kousai) Was Sold." In *A Sociology of Japanese Youth: From Returnees to NEETs*, ed. Roger Goodman, Yuki Imoto, and Tuukka Toivonen, 54–80. London: Routledge, 2012.

Kong, Travis S. K. *Chinese Male Homosexualities: Memba, Tongzhi, and Golden Boy*. London: Routledge, 2011.

Layder, Derek. *Modern Social Theory: Key Debates and New Directions*. London: University College London Press, 1997.

Leach, Anna. "Gay Japanese Pornstar Masaki Koh Dead Age 29." *Gay Star News*, May 22, 2013, http://www.gaystarnews.com/article/gay-japanese-pornstar-masaki-koh-dead-age-29220513

Leupp, Gary. *Male Colors: The Construction of Homosexuality in Tokugawa Japan*. Berkeley: University of California Press, 1995.

Levine, Martin. *Gay Macho: The Life and Death of the Homosexual Clone*. New York: New York University Press, 1998.

Long, Daniel. "Formation Processes of Some Japanese Gay Argot Terms." *American Speech* 71.2 (1996): 215–24.

Lorcin, Patricia. "Imperial Nostalgia; Colonial Nostalgia: Differences of Theory, Similarities of Practice?" *Historical Reflections/Réflexions Historiques* 39.3 (2013): 97–111.

Lukács, Gabriella. *Scripted Affects, Branded Selves: Television, Subjectivity, and Capitalism in 1990s Japan*. Durham, NC: Duke University Press, 2010.

Lunsing, Wim. *Beyond Common Sense: Sexuality and Gender in Contemporary Japan*. London: Keegan Paul, 2001.

Lunsing, Wim. "*Kono Sekai* (the Japanese Gay Scene): Communities or Just Playing

Around?" *Japan at Play: The Ludic and the Logic of Power*, ed. Joy Hendry and Massimo Riveri, 57–71. London: Routledge, 2002.

Lunsing, Wim. "The Politics of *Okama* and *Onabe*: Uses and Abuses of Terminology Regarding Homosexuality and Transgender." In *Genders, Transgenders, and Sexualities in Japan*, ed. Mark McLelland and Romit Dasgupta, 81–96. London: Routledge, 2005.

Lunsing, Wim. "*Yaoi Ronsō*: Discussing Depictions of Male Homosexuality in Japanese Girls' Comics, Gay Comics, and Gay Pornography." *Intersections* 12 (2006). http://intersections.anu.edu.au/issue12/lunsing.html

Mackie, Vera. "The Dimensions of Citizenship in Modern Japan: Gender, Class, Ethnicity, and Sexuality." In *Citizenship and Democracy in a Global Era*, ed. Andrew Vandenburg, 245–57. London: Macmillan, 2000.

Mackintosh, Jonathan. *Homosexuality and Manliness in Postwar Japan*. London: Routledge, 2010.

Maekawa Naoya. *Dansei dōseiaisha no shakaishi: Aidentiti no juyō, kurōzetto e no kaihō* [A social history of male homosexuality: Reception of identity and liberation from the closet]. Tokyo: Sakuhinsha, 2017.

Maree, Claire. *Onēkotoba ron* [On the language of queens]. Tokyo: Seidōsha, 2013.

Maree, Claire. "Weddings and White Dresses: Media and Sexual Citizenship in Japan." *Sexualities* 20.1–2 (2017): 212–33.

Maree, Claire. "Writing Sexual Identity onto the Small Screen: *Seiteki Shōsūsha* (Sexual Minorities) in Japan." In *Routledge Handbook of Japanese Media*, ed. Fabienne Darling-Wolf, 200–212. London and New York: Routledge, 2018.

Mathews, Gordon. "Being a Man in Straitened Japan: The View from Twenty Years Later." In *Capturing Contemporary Japan*, ed. Satsuki Kawano, Glenda S. Roberts, and Susan Orpett Long, 60–80. Honolulu: University of Hawai'i Press, 2014.

McCracken, Ellen. *Decoding Women's Magazines: From Mademoiselle to Ms*. New York: Palgrave Macmillan, 1993.

McKee, Alan, Kath Albury, and Catharine Lumby. *The Porn Report*. Carlton, Australia: Melbourne University Press, 2008.

McLelland, Mark. *Love, Sex, and Democracy in Japan During the American Occupation*. New York: Palgrave Macmillan, 2014.

McLelland, Mark. *Male Homosexuality in Modern Japan: Cultural Myths and Social Realities*. London: Routledge, 2000.

McLelland, Mark. *Queer Japan from the Pacific Age to the Internet Age*. Lanham, MD: Rowman and Littlefield, 2015.

McLelland, Mark. "Sex, Censorship, and Media Regulation in Japan: A Historical Overview." In *Routledge Handbook of Sexualities in East Asia*, ed. Mark McLelland and Vera Mackie, 402–13. Oxon, UK: Routledge, 2014.

McLelland, Mark, and James Welker. "An Introduction to 'Boys Love' in Japan." In *Boys Love Manga and Beyond: History, Culture, and Community in Japan*, ed. Mark McLelland, Kazumi Nagaike, Katsuhiko Suganuma, and James Welker, 1–20. Jackson: University Press of Mississippi, 2015.

McNair, Brian. *Porno? Chic! How Pornography Changed the World and Made It a Better Place*. London: Routledge, 2013.

Mercer, John. "Homosexual Prototypes: Repetition and the Construction of the Generic in the Iconography of Gay Pornography." *Paragraph* 25.1–2 (2003): 280–90.

Milani, Tommaso. "Are 'Queers' Really 'Queer'? Language, Identity and Same-Sex Desire in a South African Online Community." *Discourse and Society* 24.5 (2013): 615–33.

Miller, Laura. *Beauty Up: Exploring Contemporary Japanese Body Aesthetics*. Berkeley: University of California Press, 2006.

Miller, Laura. "There's More Than Manga: Popular Nonfiction Books and Magazines." In *A Companion to the Anthropology of Japan*, ed. Jennifer Robertson, 314–26. Malden, MA: Blackwell, 2005.

Mishima, Yukio. "Bungaku ni okeru kōha: Nihon bungaku no danseiteki genten" [The hard faction within literature: The masculine bases for Japanese literature]. In *Mishima Yukio hyōron zenshū 1* [Complete critical works of Mishima Yukio 1], 1015–17. Tokyo: Shinchōsha, 1989.

Mishima, Yukio. *Shin ren'ai kōza: Mishima Yukio no essei 2* [New lectures about love: Mishima Yukio's essays 2]. Tokyo: Chikuma Shobō. 1995.

Mishima, Yukio. *Sun and Steel: Art, Action, and Ritual Death*. Trans. John Bestor. London: Secker and Warburg, 1971.

Miyazaki, Hirokazu. *The Method of Hope: Anthropology, Philosophy, and Fijian Knowledge*. Stanford, CA: Stanford University Press, 2004.

Miyoshi, Masao. *Off Center: Power and Culture Relations Between Japan and the United States*. Cambridge, MA: Harvard University Press, 1996.

Mizuma Midory. *In'yu toshite no shōnen'ai: Josei no shōnen'ai shikō to iu genshō* [Boys love as metaphor: The phenomenon of women's inclination for boys love]. Osaka: Sōgensha, 2005.

Moeran, Brian. "Elegance and Substance Travel East: 'Vogue' Nippon." *Fashion Theory* 10.1–2 (2006): 225–58.

Monden, Masafumi. *Japanese Fashion Cultures: Dress and Gender in Contemporary Japan*. London: Bloomsbury, 2014.

Money Scoop, "*1000-en de koibito ga dekiru? Gei no pātī* [You can get a lover for 1000 yen? Gay parties]." *Fuji Television*, April 13, 2015, http://www.fujitv.co.jp/moneyscoop/015.html

Morimura, Akio. *Guiding Your Friends around Shinjuku Ni-chōme in English*. Tokyo: Potto Shuppan, 2008.

Moriyama Noritaka. *Gei komyuniti no shakaigaku* [A sociology of the gay community]. Tokyo: Keiso Shobō, 2012.

Moriyama Noritaka. "Ni-chōme ni suteru gomi nashi to hito wa iu keredo" [Although people say that no rubbish is thrown away in Ni-chōme]. *Yurīka* 9 (2014): 246–53.

Muñoz, José Esteban. *Cruising Utopia: The Then and Now of Queer Futurity*. New York: New York University Press, 2009.

Murakami Takanori and Ishida Hitoshi. "Sengo Nihon no zasshi media ni okeru 'otoko o ai suru otoko' to 'joseika shita otoko' no hyōshō-shi" [A representational history of 'men who love men' and 'feminized women' in postwar Japanese magazine media]. In *Sengo Nihon josō dōseiai kenkyū* [Research on postwar Japanese cross-dressing men and homosexuality], ed. Masami Yajima, 519–47. Hachiōji: Chuō Daigaku Shuppanbu, 2006.

Nakamura Mia. *Kuia sekusorojī: Sei no omoikomi o tokihogusu* [Queer sexology: Unravelling misconceptions concerning sex]. Tokyo: Inpakuto Shuppankai, 2008.

Nakamura Momoko. *"Onnakotoba" wa tsukurareru* [Women's language is constructed]. Tokyo: Hitsuji Shobō, 2007.

Nguyen, Tan Hoang. *A View from the Bottom: Asian American Masculinity and Sexual Representation*. Durham, NC: Duke University Press, 2014.

Nishimura Mari. *BL karuchā-ron: Bōizu rabu ga wakaru hon* [A cultural study of BL: A book for understanding BL]. Tokyo: Seikyūsha, 2015.

Ōta Shōichi. *"Janīzu no sengoshi: Janī Kitagawa wa nani o nokoshita no ka?"* [A postwar history of Johnny's: Just what has Johnny Kitagawa left behind?]. *Yurīka* 51.18 (2019): 29–39.

Ōtsuka Takashi. *Ni-chōme kara uroko* [Tales from Ni-chōme]. Tokyo: Shōeisha, 1995.

Padva, Gilad. "Heavenly Monsters: The Politics of the Male Body in the Naked Issue of *Attitude* Magazine." *International Journal of Sexuality and Gender Studies* 7.4 (2002): 281–92.

Pflugfelder, Gregory. *Cartographies of Desire: Male-Male Sexuality in Japanese Discourse, 1600–1950*. Berkeley: University of California Press, 1999.

Prough, Jennifer. *Straight from the Heart: Gender, Intimacy, and the Cultural Production of Shōjo Manga*. Honolulu: University of Hawai'i Press, 2011.

Puar, Jasbir. *Terrorist Assemblages: Homonationalism in Queer Times*. Durham, NC: Duke University Press, 2007.

Pujar, Aljosa. "Korean Cuties: Understanding Performed Winsomeness (Aegyo) in South Korea." *The Asia Pacific Journal of Anthropology* 19.4 (2018): 333–49.

Reichert, Jim. *In the Company of Men: Representations of Male-Male Sexuality in Meiji Literature*. Stanford, CA: Stanford University Press, 2006.

Rich, Adrienne. "Compulsory Heterosexuality and Lesbian Existence." *Signs* 5.4 (1980): 631–60.

Richie, Donald. *A Lateral View: Essays on Culture and Style in Contemporary Japan*. Berkeley, CA: Stone Bridge Press, 1987.

Roberson, James. "Becoming *Shakaijin*: Working-Class Reproduction in Japan." *Ethnology* 34.4 (1995): 527–49.

Roberson, James. "Fight! Ippatsu! 'Genki' Energy Drinks and the Making of Masculine Ideology in Japan." *Men and Masculinities* 7.4 (2005): 365–84.

Robertson, Jennifer. *Takarazuka: Sexual Politics and Popular Culture in Modern Japan*. Berkeley: University of California Press, 1988.

Rofel, Lisa. *Desiring China: Experiments in Neoliberalism, Sexuality, and Public Culture*. Durham, NC: Duke University Press, 2007.

Ryang, Sonia. *Love in Modern Japan: Its Estrangement from Self, Sex, and Society*. London: Routledge, 2006.

Ryū Susumu. *"Kieru Shinjuku Ni-chōme": Itan bunka no Hanazono no meimyaku o tatsu no wa dare da?* ["Disappearing Shinjuku Ni-chōme": Just who is severing the threads to the garden of heresy?]. Tokyo: Sairyūsha, 2009.

Satō Masaki. "Shōjo manga to homofobia" [Girls' comics and homophobia]. In *Kuia Sutadīzu 96* [Queer studies 96], ed. Kuia Sutadīzu Henshū Iinkai, 161–69. Tokyo: Nanatsumori Shokan, 1996.

Schein, Louisa. "Homeland Beauty: Transnational Longing and Hmong American Video." In *Media, Erotics, and Transnational Asia*, ed. Purnima Mankekar and Louisa Schein, 203–32. Durham, NC: Duke University Press, 2013.

Shah, Alpa. "Ethnography? Participant Observation, a Potentially Revolutionary Praxis." *HAU: Journal of Ethnographic Theory* 7.1 (2017): 45–59.

Sharp, Jasper. *Behind the Pink Curtain: The Complete History of Japanese Sex Cinema*. Guildford, UK: FAB Press, 2008.

Shibatani, Masayoshi. *The Languages of Japan*. Cambridge: Cambridge University Press, 1990.

Shimizu Akiko. "Daibāshiti kara kenri hōsho e: Toranpu ikō no beikoku to 'LGBT būmu' no Nihon" [From diversity to safeguarding rights: America after Trump and Japan's "LGBT boom"]. *Sekai* (May 2019): 134–43.

Shirahase, Sawako. "Demography as Destiny: Falling Birthrates and the Allure of a Blended Society." In *Japan: The Precarious Future*, ed. Frank Baldwin and Anne Allison, 11–35. New York: New York University Press, 2015.

Slater, David and Patrick Galbraith. "Re-Narrating Social Class and Masculinity in Neoliberal Japan: An Examination of the Media Coverage of the 'Akihabara Incident' of 2008." *Electronic Journal of Contemporary Japanese Studies* (2011). https://japanesestudies.org.uk/articles/2011/SlaterGalbraith.html

Stake, Richard E. *The Art of the Case Study*. Thousand Oaks, CA: Sage, 1995.

Stein, Arlene. "Three Models of Sexuality: Drives, Identities, and Practices." *Sociological Theory* 7.1 (1989): 1–13.

Suganuma, Katsuhiko. *Contact Moments: The Politics of Intercultural Desire in Japanese Male-Queer Cultures*. Hong Kong: University of Hong Kong Press, 2012.

Suganuma, Katsuhiko. "Ways of Speaking about Queer Space in Tokyo: Disorientated Knowledge and Counter-Public Space." *Japanese Studies* 31.3 (2011): 345–58.

Sunagawa Hideki. *Shinjuku Ni-chōme no bunka jinruigaku: Gei komyuniti kara toshi o manazasu* [A cultural anthropological study of Shinjuku Ni-chōme: Looking at the city from the perspective of the gay community]. Tokyo: Tarōjirō Editāzu, 2015.

Sunagawa Hideki. "Tayō na shihai, taiyō na teikō" [Diverse domination, diverse resistance]. *Gendai shisō* 43.16 (2015): 100–106.

Suzuki Suzumi, *AV joyū no shakaigaku: Naze kanojotachi wa jōzetsu ni mizukara o kataru no ka* [A sociology of female AV performers: Why do these women speak about themselves so much?]. Tokyo: Seidōsha, 2013.

Szabó, Peter, and Robert A Troyer. "Inclusive Ethnographies: Beyond the Binaries of Observer and Observed in Linguistic Landscape Studies." *Linguistic Landscape* 3.3 (2017): 306–26.

Tagame Gengoroh. "Gei erotikku āto no shinzui o egaku" [Drawing the essence of gay erotic art]. *Bijutsu Techō* 66.1016 (2015): 114–19.

Tagame Gengoroh. *Gei karuchā no mirai e* [Towards a gay future]. Tokyo: Ele-king, 2017.

Takeyama, Akiko. *Staged Seduction: Selling Dreams in a Tokyo Host Club*. Stanford, CA: Stanford University Press, 2016.

Taniguchi, Hiroyuki. "The Legal Situation Facing Sexual Minorities in Japan." *Intersections* 12 (2006). http://intersections.anu.edu.au/issue12/taniguchi.html

Tipton, Elise. "Faces of New Tokyo: Entertainment Districts and Everyday Life During the War Years." *Japanese Studies* 33.2 (2013): 185–200.

Tōgō Ken. *Jōshiki o koete: Okama no michi 70-nen* [Overcoming common sense: Walking the *okama* road for 70 years]. Tokyo, Potto Shuppan, 2002.

Tonuma, Eichi. *Shinjuku gaku: Shinjuku no rekishi to miraizu o teigi suru* [Shinjuku studies: Defining the future plans and history of Shinjuku]. Tokyo: Kinokuniya Shoten, 2013.

Ueno Chizuko. *"Kigyō senchitachi"* [The corporate warriors]. In *Danseigaku: Nihon no feminizumu bessatsu* [Men's studies: Special issue on feminism], ed. Inoue Teruko, Ueno Chizuko, and Ehara Yumiko, 215–16. Tokyo: Iwanami Shoten, 1995.

Ueno, Toshiya. "Techno-Orientalism and Media-Tribalism: Japanese Animation and Rave Culture." *Third Text* 13.47 (1999): 95–106.

Vance, Carole. "Anthropology Rediscovers Sexuality: A Theoretical Comment." *Sociological and Scientific Medicine* 33 (1991): 875–84.

Vincent, Keith. *Two-Timing Modernity: Homosocial Narrative in Modern Japanese Fiction.* Cambridge, MA: Harvard University Press, 2012.

Wallace, Jane. "Stepping Up: 'Urban' and 'Queer' Cultural Capital in LGBT and Queer Communities in Kansai, Japan." *Sexualities* 23.4 (2020): 666–82.

Warner, Michael. "Introduction: Fear of a Queer Planet." *Social Text* 29 (1991): 3–17.

Watanabe, Tsuneo, and Iwata, Jun'ichi. *The Love of Samurai: A Thousand Years of Japanese Homosexuality.* Trans. D. R. Roberts. London: GMP, 1989.

Weiss, Margot. "Always After: Desiring Queerness, Desiring Anthropology." *Cultural Anthropology* 31.4 (2016): 627–38.

Welker, James. "Telling Her Story: Narrating a Japanese Lesbian Community." *Journal of Lesbian Studies* 14.4 (2010): 359–80.

Whitty, Monica. "The Art of Selling One's 'Self' On an Online Dating Site: The BAR Approach." In *Online M@tchmaker*, ed. Monica Whitty, Andrea J. Baker, and James Inman, 57–69. New York: Palgrave Macmillan, 2007.

Williams, Linda. *Hard Core: Power, Pleasure, and the 'Frenzy of the Visible.'* London: Pandora Press, 1990.

Wong, Heung-Wah, and Hoi-Yan Yau. *The Japanese Adult Video Industry.* Oxon, UK: Routledge, 2018.

Yajima Masami. *Dansei dōseiaisha no raifu hisutorī* [Male homosexual life histories]. Tokyo: Gakubunsha, 1997.

Zenkoku Shuppan Kyōkai. *2017-nen shuppan shijō* [The 2017 publishing market]. Tokyo: Zenkoku Shuppan Kyōkai Shuppanbu, 2018.

# Index